Can We Measure What Matters Most?

Can We Measure What Matters Most?

Why Educational Accountability Metrics Lower Student Learning and Demoralize Teachers

J. M. Beach

ROWMAN & LITTLEFIELD
Lanham • Boulder • New York • London

Published by Rowman & Littlefield
An imprint of The Rowman & Littlefield Publishing Group, Inc.
4501 Forbes Boulevard, Suite 200, Lanham, Maryland 20706
www.rowman.com
6 Tinworth Street, London, SE11 5AL, United Kingdom

Copyright © 2021 by J. M. Beach

All rights reserved. No part of this book may be reproduced in any form or by any electronic or mechanical means, including information storage and retrieval systems, without written permission from the publisher, except by a reviewer who may quote passages in a review.

British Library Cataloguing in Publication Information Available

Library of Congress Cataloging-in-Publication Data
Name: Beach, J. M. (Josh M.) author.
Title: Can we measure what matters most?: why educational accountability metrics lower student learning and demoralize teachers / J. M. Beach.
Description: Lanham: The Rowman & Littlefield Publishing Group, [2021] | Includes bibliographical references and index. | Summary: "This book examines the idea of educational accountability, which has become a new secular gospel"—Provided by publisher.
Identifiers: LCCN 2021013123 (print) | LCCN 2021013124 (ebook) | ISBN 9781475862270 (cloth) | ISBN 9781475862287 (paperback) | ISBN 9781475862294 (epub)
Subjects: LCSH: Educational accountability. | Educational change. | Education and state.
Classification: LCC LB2806.22.B43 2021 (print) | LCC LB2806.22 (ebook) | DDC 379.1/58—dc23
LC record available at https://lccn.loc.gov/2021013123
LC ebook record available at https://lccn.loc.gov/2021013124

For A. J., may your natural curiosity, love of learning, and exploration never cease.

And for David Labaree, a scholar without parallel, who inspired my path to teaching when I was an undergraduate, and who was a guiding light for this project. Thank you for your support of both books.

"If you can't measure it, you can't manage it"—Robert S. Kaplan and David Norton, *The Balanced Scorecard*

"It is wrong to suppose that if you can't measure it, you can't manage it—a costly myth."—W. Edwards Deming, *The New Economics*

"Not everything that is important is measurable, and much that is measurable is unimportant."—Jerry Z. Muller, *The Tyranny of Metrics*

"Measuring the wrong thing is often worse than measuring nothing, because you get what you measure."—Jeffrey Pfeffer, *Leadership BS*

"We must measure what matters. The starting point has to be deciding what matters most."—Daniel Koretz, *The Testing Charade: Pretending to Make Schools Better*

Praise for *Can We Measure What Matters Most?*

"J. M. Beach provides a devastatingly effective analysis of the accountability metrics that have wrought so much havoc in the American system of schooling. The accountability pandemic is now a global phenomenon, pushed by governments around the world. As Beach shows, the problems with this system are legion. He makes the case for why accountability metrics are the problem, not the solution."—David F. Labaree, Professor Emeritus, Graduate School of Education, Standard University. He is author of *How to Succeed in School without Really Learning*, *Someone Has to Fail*, and *A Perfect Mess*

"J. M. Beach offers a searing polemic against quantification and top-down management in education. Skillfully navigating a broad range of topics, he reminds us of the importance of authentic learning, and shows how we might once more elevate that aim. While Beach is a skeptic of what passes for school reform these days, he ultimately offers a hopeful view of what educators, young people, and communities can accomplish together."—Jack Schneider, Assistant Professor of Education, University of Massachusetts at Lowell, Co-Editor of History of Education Quarterly, and Director of Research at Massachusetts Consortium for Innovative Education Assessment. He is author of *Beyond Test Scores*, *Excellence for All*, and *A Wolf at the Schoolhouse Door*

"Beach has done an amazing job of blending the wisdom of many of the world's most thoughtful educators with his own ideas about what makes for better schooling. Both volumes deal with issues of assessment and accountability, and the desperate need for more humane systems of using these tools and ideas. These highly readable and well referenced books both inform and stimulate."—David C. Berliner, Regents' Professor

Emeritus, Arizona State University. He is author of *50 Myths and Lies that Threaten America's Public Schools*, *Collateral Damage*, and *The Manufactured Crisis*

"In his two new books, Beach delivers a two-part assault on the logic of using measurement-based accountability regiments to reform educational systems. In Part 1, *Can We Measure*, Beach expertly excoriates the accountability movement that has dominated our K–12 public schooling system for decades showing how it has dismantled student learning and teacher morale. Although the chorus of accountability critics has grown louder and stronger over time, Beach's interdisciplinary approach involving the lessons from history, philosophy, management, measurement, learning theories, motivation, and higher education makes a uniquely powerful contribution to the school reform debate."—Sharon L. Nichols, Professor of Educational Psychology, University of Texas at San Antonio, and author of *Collateral Damage: How High-Stakes Testing Corrupts America's Schools* and *Educational Policies and Youth in the 21st Century*

Contents

Foreword		xi
Preface: We Aren't Measuring What Matters Most		xv
Introduction: Investigating the Myths of Measurement and the Management of Schools		xix
1	A Different Kind of Reform: The Neoliberal Gospel of Education	1
2	Getting Our Money's Worth: A Short History of Accountability Movement in the U.S.	13
3	What Do Grades Measure? Investigating Grades as an Accountability Metric	43
4	Education as a Social Practice: The Foundations of Teaching and Learning	61
5	Nurture and Nature: The Complex Ecology of Student Learning	85
6	A Managerial Coup d'État	109
Conclusion: Can We De-School Our Schools?		131
Epilogue: Learning to Learn—Revising the Liberal Arts		147
References		149
Preview: *The Myths of Measurement and Meritocracy*		171
Index		173
About the Author		181

Foreword

Accountability Metrics Misread the Nature of Education

David Labaree, Professor Emeritus, Graduate School of Education, Stanford University

In this book, J. M. Beach provides a devastatingly effective analysis of the accountability metrics that have wrought so much havoc in the American system of schooling. The accountability movement started at the state level in the U.S. in the 1970s under the label of curriculum standards, ramped up as a national issue in 1983 with the publication of the report A Nation at Risk, and made its way into federal law in 2002 with the passage of the No Child Left Behind Act. This sweeping reform process set out a radical agenda for schools, which dictated that the prime criterion for success for students, teachers, and school systems was scores on tests that measured student understanding of core curriculum subjects.

The accountability pandemic is now a global phenomenon, pushed by governments around the world and enforced by the tests written by OECD's Programme for International Student Assessment (PISA). These scores are averaged out for each country and the countries are then ranked by score, creating an international measure of educational fame and shame. Heaven help the government in power when the latest scores show the country has fallen in the rankings. PISA rules.

As Beach shows, the problems with this system are legion. But it's worth noting that the urge for accountability is not unreasonable. Education should be accountable. It's a public institution that needs to be effective at meeting the goals society sets for it, and such determinations can't just be left to the preferences of teachers or parents or students or administrators. In addition, it's not ok that many students don't succeed in school and that their social origins are key determinants of their success or failure. Schooling whose outcomes simply reproduce its inputs is not good schooling. These equity concerns are visible in the names of the two key US laws governing accountability: No Child Left Behind and its 2013 successor, Every Student Succeeds Act.

The problems with accountability lie in the way it is implemented. The accountability movement in the U.S. and in the world of school reform has relied on a method that defines school success through a small number of metrics—scores in tests that measure comprehension of the formal curriculum.

One problem is that even if these measures capture core aims of schooling—which, as I'll suggest, they don't—they would still become distorted by the effort to achieve them. These outcomes—test scores—become the primary target for everyone's educational efforts (students, teachers, administrators, policymakers). This is a glaring case of what has come to be known as Goodheart's law, named for the British economist who developed it: "Any observed statistical regularity will tend to collapse once pressure is placed upon it for control purposes."

In regular language this means that when you have a valid measure of some social phenomenon, it loses its validity when it becomes a target of policy, because it motivates actors to attain this metric by any means possible. Instead of teaching the curriculum, you teach to the test, so you end up raising scores instead of improving learning.

A more basic problem is that this accountability system, when applied to education, radically narrows the aims for schooling to a few outcomes that are readily measurable but not very important. It turns our attention to one-shot scores on tests of a tiny number of academic subjects—language, math, and science—at the expense of the larger goals that explain why we have invested so much time and money into erecting school systems. We want schools to serve a political goal, creating competent citizens who can function in a democracy. We want them to serve an economic goal, creating productive workers who can fuel economic growth. And we want them to serve a social goal, allowing individuals to prove their merit in the pursuit of social opportunity. It's not obvious how test scores capture or promote any of these goals.

Accountability metrics misread the nature of the educational system and in the process end up creating dysfunctions that are no less damaging for being inadvertent. Start with the fact that schooling is a complex social process that requires the cooperation of a huge number of actors in a large number of institutional settings, including 50 million students and 3 million teachers in 100,000 schools.

It's a system that depends on the motivated compliance of the key actors, teachers and students. Teachers can't make students learn. They need to find ways to motivate students to learn what they're teaching, and this isn't easy since students didn't arrive in the classroom begging to be taught. Instead, they're compelled to attend by truancy laws and by the credentialing requirements for entry into the workforce. These are not problems that face other professionals, such as lawyers and doctors, who work with clients and patients who ask for their help. Students don't contract with teachers to teach them reading and algebra. Teaching is forced on them, and it only succeeds if they choose to play along and learn the curriculum.

As a result, teaching and learning in schools is a messy and inefficient process that doesn't necessarily work as planned. Grounded on the indirect process of motivating the student, it doesn't operate on the kind of mechanical rules that apply to factory production. There is no one right way to teach effectively. Instead, teaching involves an ongoing relationship with individual students. It requires teachers to figure out how to draw on their own personal and professional resources in order to get through to students who come in with different levels of skill, knowledge, and motivation.

The whole massive and complex educational system comes down to the student-teacher relationship in three million classrooms across the country. A top-down mandate to raise test scores only makes it harder on teachers to do their jobs. Instead of intense pressure from above, they need the support, resources, and autonomy they need in order to make the pedagogical relationship work, classroom by classroom and student by student. Beach recognizes this core issue and makes the case for why accountability metrics are the problem, not the solution.

Preface

We Aren't Measuring What Matters Most

What do students learn in school? In the 21st century, this question has become a political dilemma for countries all across the globe. It is a deceptively simple question, but there has never been an easy answer.

The problem of measuring student learning appears to express an educational problem: What and how much do students learn? And yet, when you investigate the educational accountability movement, especially in the United States where it began, you realize that the preoccupation with student learning is not about education. Calls for accountability have always been more focused on politics and economics (Labaree, 1997b).

The accountability movement in schools, which started in the United States in the early 20th century, and spread across the world a century later, is not about education. It is about furthering a neoliberal political agenda, which has sought the economic transformation of all institutions and the state. Economic efficiency and organizational accountability have been two of the central political agendas of neoliberal reformers (Senge [1990] 2006, xii). One of the main political slogans of neoliberalism has been, "If you can't measure it, you can't manage it" (Kaplan and Norton 1996, 21).

I wrote this book, and a second companion volume on accountability in higher education, because I believe that public intellectuals, academics, policy makers, school administrators, and teachers need to ask critical questions about what has been done over the past century in the monumental, expensive, and futile effort to keep schools "accountable."

Over the course of the 20th century, the traditional faith in the sacred value of schooling, which was broadly shared by all classes and cultures for thousands of years, was slowly dissolved. Now there is a new orthodoxy. We have given up traditional ideals about inculcating the young and replaced them with neoliberal accountability programs focused on standardized tests and ritualized schooling (Schneider 2017; Ravitch 2010).

Biological anthropologist Terrence W. Deacon (1997) once noted, "Some of the greatest discoveries in many fields have been made by people outside the inner circle of true experts." He argued, "The experts are often too acquainted with a problem to see it in a novel way" (49).

Likewise, the communications theorist Marshall McLuhan quipped that "we don't know who discovered water, but it wasn't the fish" (qtd. in Edmondson 2012, 194). I am not a tenured specialist perched high in a research university using conventional wisdom to write an academic book on educational reform. I am more of a "wandering intellectual," as the educational psychologist Jerome Bruner (1983) once described his own idiosyncratic methodology (8).

I will be going against the narrow focus of most other books on the topic of educational accountability. While specialized academic disciplines are very useful, they are also very limited and highly inaccurate when trying to understand complex social practices, like education and schooling. Educational reforms have been fractionally studied in hundreds of disciplines and subdisciplines to the point of obscurity. We need better clarity. And for that, we need to see the bigger picture.

Like many of the scholars I most admire, such as Jerome Bruner (1983), Raymond Callahan (1962), David Tyack (1974), Lawrence Cremin (1990), Diane Ravitch (2010), W. Norton Grubb and Marvin Lazerson (1988, 2004), and David Labaree (2010), I have tried to get away from the limited perspective of siloed academic disciplines (Tett, 2015). I want to look at the big, complex, messy, sometimes contradictory, and always contested subject of modern schooling and the accountability movement in order to look deep at structural issues (Senge [1990] 2006, 40).

My scope and research methodology have been inspired by big-picture philosophers and social scientists, like those scholars mentioned above, as well as Isaiah Berlin, John Gray, Charles Taylor, and Anthony Giddens. Thus, instead of offering narrow analysis from one particular disciplinary angle, I have tried to present the social practices of teaching, learning, schooling, and the assessment of schooling in a broad, interdisciplinary perspective.

Stylistically, I have tried to avoid academic conventions and jargon. I have tried to write like the journalist and public intellectual Walter Lippmann. I've tried to translate very complex ideas into plain language so as to reach beyond my primary audience of professional academics, graduate students, school administrators, and working teachers.

In this effort, I have adopted the prose of the journalist and the historian, more than the academic social scientist. Thus, I use a lot more introductions, generalizations, and direct quotes than one would find in most specialized academic books. In particular, like historians and journalists, I have used a lot of quotations to give my prose the feeling of a conversation between diverse participants who each identify a piece of the larger puzzle. I have also tried not to assume any specialized knowledge on the part of my reader, although I do still use some technical terminology, which I try to fully explain.

Rather than bland, academic prose, I do at times deliver a sharp, critical tone, especially in the conclusion of this book, where my subjective judgment becomes more fully pronounced. In that respect, I have taken the Italian virologist Roberto Burioni, the management professor Jeffrey Pfeffer, education professor Daniel Koretz, and the educational sociologist and historian David F. Labaree as stylistic mentors.

Roberto Burioni recently became famous in Italy for denouncing opponents of vaccines with a blunt, no-nonsense aesthetic, declaring: "The Earth is round, gasoline is flammable, and vaccines are safe and effective. All the rest are dangerous lies" (qtd. in Starr 2020, 16). Burioni argued that "science needs to find a new voice—not the language of scientific congresses, but a language that's understandable, passionate, and convincing" (19). The pathologist Guido Silvestri has argued that Burioni is "the one scientist who stood up and said, 'This is bullshit'" (qtd. in Starr 2020, 19).

Likewise, management professor Jeffery Pfeffer (2015) has also not been afraid to explain the facts and call "bullshit" where it's warranted. He wrote a book called *Leadership BS* to decry all the invalid, "sugar-laced," "toxic potions" being passed off as effective "cures" in the business management industry (x). Finally, professors of education Daniel Koretz (2017) and David F. Labaree (2010), who I cite throughout this book, have both employed sharp, critical, and no-nonsense analysis to education reforms in order to deflate popular platitudes.

I am in debt to these wise researchers and their monumental scholarship. I have tried emulate the substance and tone of their work in my book in order to promote critical, scientific thinking and attack widespread myths and popular false beliefs.

The topic of this book is deeply personal. While I have studied the research on school reform and the accountability movement for over a decade, I wrote this book from the lens of a teacher and a student. I have been a student in one way or another for most of my life, and I have been an educator for over twenty years, teaching in three countries (the U.S., South Korea, and China).

As an instructor, I have taught a diverse range of students from preschool to university to training professional teachers. As a teacher, I have also been the object of many types of accountability measurements. I have personally suffered the unfair consequences of meaningless metrics. And from what I have seen, I am deeply skeptical about what schools, and the reformers of schools, can actually accomplish using accountability measurements.

But while I am skeptical of school reform, I continue to believe in the transformative power of education because I have seen its effect on my own life, on the life of my son, and on the lives of many of my students. For accountability measurements to work, whether it be in schools or any other organization or business, we have to measure what actually matters rather than just measuring what is easiest or cheapest or most politically expedient.

Thus, as professor of education Daniel Koretz (2017) has argued, "The starting point has to be deciding what matters most" (220). I hope this book raises some deep questions about what should matter most when it comes to education and schooling, and what we should and should not be measuring if we want our schools, and the lives of students, to improve.

Introduction

Investigating the Myths of Measurement and the Management of Schools

Rather than believing in the traditional value of education, in the 21st century, most schools now have to prove their worth with quantitative data, while also being cost effective organizations, just like businesses (Friedman [1962] 2002; Drucker 1969; Muller 2018). Organizational accountability schemes have been advertised as fact-based, results-oriented assessments of institutional goals and organizational performance. But under the veneer of scientific legitimacy and economic efficiency lie irrational assumptions based on unexamined political myths. The purpose of this book is to critically examine some of those myths.

This book will be examining the very notion of organizational accountability. The idea of keeping public institutions accountable, especially schools, has become a new "secular gospel," which has been documented and deconstructed by several insightful scholars over the past couple decades, especially by Diane Ravitch (2010), Jerry Z. Muller (2018), and Daniel Koretz (2017). These critics have pointed out, "There is an often-unexamined faith that amassing data and sharing it widely . . . will result in improvements of some sort" (Muller 2018, 47; see also Taleb 2012, 307; Schneider 2017, 62).

In the 19th century, educational reform in the U.S. was focused on lofty, messianic missions to promote democracy, knowledge, equality, public spirit, self-discipline, and self-sacrifice. Naïve in many ways, but based on ideals of the greater good. In the 21st century, according to Diane Ravitch (2010), educational reform has devolved into a technocratic "measurement strategy" that has "no underlying educational vision at all" (16). Test-based accountability, according to Daniel Koretz (2017) has "become an end in itself . . .

unmoored from clear thinking about what should be measured, how it should be measured, or how testing can fit into a rational plan for evaluating and improving our schools" (5).

Schools are now drowning in accountability data (Schneider 2017, 62). Most of this data is trivial. And a lot of it compromised by invalid methodology. But few policy makers or school administrators have bothered to ask if their accountability programs actually work. Do accountability policies or accountability data actually make schools any better at what they do? Or is this just a myth?

Schools in the U.S. have been subjected to wave after wave of accountability reforms over the past century. But almost every initiative has been ineffective, so the notion that accountability measurements improve schools seems to be a myth (Elmore and McLaughlin 1988; Tyack and Cuban 1995; Payne 2008; Cuban 2013; Labaree 2012; Koretz 2017). Part of the problem is that reformers have often relied on "bad measures of school quality," which has usually misidentified both the actual problems and the needed solutions (Schneider 2017, 4).

This is tragically ironic given that educational researchers have known about core best practices for almost 50 years (Argyris 1993, 30).

Because of this record of failure, historian and sociologist David F. Labaree (1992) quipped that reforming schools has been "steady work" for enterprising crusaders (130). The central problems of schooling never seem to get solved. New reform proposals seem to pop up every year. However, most schools never actually get reformed, especially the most challenged schools that serve the neediest students. For about half a century, educational researchers have documented and warned that schools have been "producing the very consequences of ineffective schooling that they decry" (Argyris 1993, 29).

But even when problems are properly identified, and there are a lot of problems with American schools, it's hard work to actually fix these issues. Educational historians David Tyack and Larry Cuban (1995) somberly noted in their history of school reform, "To bring about improvement at the heart of education—classroom instruction . . . has proven to be the most difficult kind of reform" (134). Few initiatives have actually changed the deep, institutional "grammar" (5) of schooling. This failure has led to many academic books on school reforms with subtitles like "change without reform" (Cuban 2013), "the persistence of failure" (Payne 2008), or "pretending to make schools better" (Koretz 2017).

David Labaree (2012) actually recommended that school reformers should become more pessimistic as a sarcastic solution. He argued that would-be reformers should assume from the start "that you might just be wrong and that the reform might actually make things worse" (159). Many school crusaders haven't taken his recommendation, but it's good advice.

Alongside a belief in measurements, accountability reforms also believe that teachers are responsible for student learning. This is a widespread assumption, dating back to the late 19th century. Many people believe that teachers produce student learning, much like a factory worker produces a car. But this is a myth.

This dangerous belief has put all teachers into a bind, especially adjunct lecturers in higher education who get paid poverty-level wages with no job security. Teachers feel pressured to behave as if they controlled the educational processes. They don't. So rather than teach and educate, teachers often bend over backward to please students and parents because students are now seen as customers who have the right to complain if they do not get exactly what they want.

Teachers also feel pressured to appease school administrators who care only about the bottom line of measurable results. Accountability policies are often reduced to nothing more than giving customers what they want. And what do students want? Most simply want to play school and earn a magic piece of paper as quickly as possible so they can leave school and get a job.

Administrative pressure to produce results often pushes teachers to sacrifice professional standards in order to follow dictatorial administrative orders and pander to consumers. In order to keep a job and get promoted, which entails minimizing consumer complaints and following the orders of administrators, teachers must often lower standards and inflate effectiveness metrics, such as attendance, grades, student survey comments, or graduation rates (Koretz 2017; Deming 1994; Aguayo 1990).

High-stakes accountability measurements create professional and moral costs for teachers. As professor of education Doris A. Santoro (2018) has documented, many teachers feel "demoralized" because they cannot live up to the professional "values that motivate and sustain their work" as educators (3, 43).

High stakes accountability measurements not only sap morale, but they also damage organizational productivity. Statistician and management professor W. Edwards Deming (1994, 30) derisively called the use of accountability measurements "management by fear" (qtd. in Walton 1986, 90; Aguayo 1990, 27). He believed that the practice of management by objectives was "tyrann[ical]" because it creates an unproductive "prison" for employees (Deming 1994, xv; Walton 1986, 90; Aguayo 1990).

Top-down measurements forced on employees by upper-management have an "insidious side effect," according to Deming (Walton 1986, 91). Managers rely on frivolous numbers that do not measure the most important, core purposes of an organization. Instead, managers usually focus on metrics that can be easily and cheaply counted, or easily falsified, with "no consideration of their quality" (Walton 1986, 91; Deming 1994; Aguayo 1990). For decades up to the 1980s, Deming argued that accountability measurements were "the single most destructive force in American management today" (qtd. in Aguayo 1990, 11).

Accountability metrics don't make organizations perform better. Instead, as Deming (1994) documented, management by objectives destroys organizational effectiveness. Accountability policies perversely reduce the quality of goods and services, drive up costs, and destroy employee morale (Aguayo 1990; Deming 1994, 30).

In the case of schools, accountability measurements actually lower student learning, as well as harm students and faculty in many other ways. Even the relatively straightforward measurement of graduation rates can still create dangerous, unintended consequences (Kimbrough 2020). In fact, all accountability measurements come with costs and produce unintended consequences, but most policy makers and school administrators refuse to acknowledge these effects (Labaree 2011). This book will examine some of these pertinent problems, especially those borne by teachers and students.

Another myth this book will investigate is the belief that school administrators are a competent class of corporate managers who can expertly use management theory and accountability policies to successfully reform schools. All over the world, most people believe that a special class of managers are needed to formally measure and assess the quality of employees and organizational production (Grove 2015; Doerr 2018; Stewart 2009).

In the case of schools, educational administrators are supposed to be able to evaluate teachers and students, as well as manage a host of other organizational tasks (Tyack 1974; Birnbaum 2000; see also Grove 2015; Doerr 2018; Stewart 2009). Reformers have assumed that school administrators are competent organizational leaders and that these managers have access to valid accountability tools that somehow provide direct evidence of the quality of educational production. Furthermore, reformers have assumed that school administrators know now how to use the accountability tools at their disposal.

But what if the most widely used management theories and assessment tools don't work? What if educational accountability tools, especially standardized tests, don't actually measure what they're supposed to? What if accountability data isn't valid, or worse, what if it's meaningless? What if administrators don't know how to use accountability tools or correctly analyze the problematic data these tools produce? What if we can't measure, let alone accurately assess, what matters most with teaching or student learning (Deming 1994; Labaree 2011)? And what if most educational administrators, like the leaders of most businesses, are improperly trained, incompetent, and ineffective managers (Pfeffer 2015)?

As historian and sociologist David F. Labaree (2011) perceptively argued, policy makers, school administrators, and educational researchers have a "strong incentive to focus on what they can measure statistically rather than on what is important" (625). And what can be measured by accountability metrics, especially by standardized tests, is not only trivial, but as professor of education Daniel Koretz (2017) argued, a "corruption of the ideals" of education (6).

Even worse, many school administrators don't understand the important concept of validity so they don't understand the limitations of the accountability measurements that are being used to evaluate schools, especially standardized tests. Koretz (2017) warned that "many of the people with their hands on the levers in education don't understand what tests are and what they can and can't do," which has led to "inappropriate uses of testing" and "distortions of educational practice," as well as outright fraud (11).

This raises another serious problem: the management of schools. Almost all schools are managed by professional administrators, not teachers. Many, if not most, of these bureaucrats have never been educators. School administrators follow orthodox management policies and popular organizational practices drawn from the fields of economics and business management, which supposedly make organizations more efficient and productive (Doerr 2018; Stewart 2009; Pfeffer 2015).

This is another myth this book will examine. Do business management theories and practices actually make organizations more effective? Sadly, professors of management have empirically proven that most management practices are ineffective, if not counterproductive (Pfeffer 2015).

There has been a concerted effort since the late 19th century to make schools operate more like businesses, especially in terms of human resource management and the discrete measurement and control of productivity (Callahan 1962; Tyack 1974; Tyack and Hansot 1982; Grubb and Lazerson 2004; Bok 2009; Washburn 2005; Birnbaum 2000; Sperber 2000). Business organizations have become the ultimate measure of institutional effectiveness.

But professors of business management have pointed out for several decades that most corporate managers don't know what they're doing. Most businesses don't work very well and most businesses aren't efficient or productive (Pfeffer 2015). In fact, management professor W. Edwards Deming went so far as to argue that "we will never transform the prevailing system of management without transforming our prevailing system of education. They are the same system" (qtd. in Senge [1990] 2006, xiii).

It is ironic that school administrators have been admonished to behave more like the managers of businesses because scholars have shown that most corporate managers don't know exactly why a particular business or organization is successful, or not, due to the "messy," "casual ambiguity" of interfirm, intrafirm, and environmental factors that produce organizational success (King 2007, 156). In fact, most professors of management don't even know the actual ingredients of successful businesses (Pfeffer 2015).

Take, for example, professor of management Jeffrey Pfeffer (2015), who argues that business professors and management gurus have had little "positive impact" because most the most popular business beliefs and practices are "problematic" and "invalid;" thus, management practices have mostly resulted in "failure" (4–5). If businesses managers can't identify or practice the ingredients for organizational success, then why should we expect school administrators to be able to accomplish this task?

But perhaps more importantly, we need to be asking if public schools should be managed like for-profit businesses and judged by the same criteria? How is a business-model of economic efficiency supposed to increase the competing and perhaps mutually exclusive ends of schooling, especially public schooling in democracies, which have many diverse goals, such as human development, student learning, personal satisfaction, social mobility, and economic growth (Labaree 1997b)?

A half-century ago, sociologist Philip Selznick insightfully argued that efficiency "as an operating ideal presumes that goals are settled and that the main resources and methods for achieving them are available" (Selznick [1957] 1984, 135). But most schools have never had clear and stable goals or satisfactory resources, especially those schools serving the neediest students with the least resources in the most economically troubled places.

And what if schooling is naturally expensive and can't be efficient? What if accountability programs cost too much in order to be effective? And perhaps most importantly, what if accountability metrics actually harm students by incentivizing the cynical practice of playing school over authentic learning (Labaree 1997a)?

Most people believe that students learn in schools because student learning is supposedly the primary institutional purpose of schools. Most people also believe that schooling helps students succeed in life, especially the most disadvantaged. But what if students don't learn much in schools? What if schools were never designed to produce student learning? What if schools don't help most students, either personally or economically? What if schools aren't meritocratic institutions? What if schooling actually exacerbates inequality and makes the lives of the disadvantaged even worse?

So, if students and teachers are just playing school, and if accountability metrics are only measuring the empty ritual of playing school, then how are accountability measurements going to make schools more efficient or effective? Is it even possible to make schools effective, or are these institutions naturally ineffective because of their traditional, symbolic function?

As the recent *Review of Research in Education* volume, "Changing Teaching Practice in P–20 Educational Settings," states, "We need multidisciplinary approaches applied in a wide range of settings to generate findings that illuminate the common and the contingent elements involved" in educating students from preschool to college (Tocci, Ryan, and Pigott 2019, viii). Thus, in order to study the complex questions presented in this book, this book has extensively surveyed a range of academic disciplines in order to present complex, interdisciplinary answers based on the latest scientific research.

The foundation of this book rests on the social sciences, which includes the fields of education, psychology, sociology, anthropology, economics, philosophy, public policy, and political science. Specifically, this book looks at research on education and schooling historically, both in terms of the history of specific cultures, in particular the United States of America, and also biologically, in terms of genetic and cultural evolution. Thus, this book draws from the history of schooling and the anthropology of education, as well as primatology, biology, sociobiology, and evolutionary psychology.

This book also looks into the field of business management to investigate the nature of schools as an institution. This book looks at the technology of corporate leadership in organizations in order to see how beliefs about corporate managers have influenced the administration of schools.

This book will offer some inconvenient truths about teaching, student learning, accountability initiatives, the sociology of schooling, and how educational practices and institutions are connected to politics and the economy. This book will focus primarily on the United States, one of the first countries to develop both public schooling and accountability programs, but it will also touch upon developments in Europe and Asia as well in order to bring greater historical and cultural perspective to the topic of schooling.

This book seeks not just to expose the irrationality of popular accountability myths, but also to explore the scientific concept of validity and the problematic nature of technical metrics used for institutional evaluation. This book seeks to investigate whether accountability programs based on quantitative data can ever be successful at reforming institutions and reshaping human behavior.

Chapter 1

A Different Kind of Reform
The Neoliberal Gospel of Education

For most of human history, schools were sacred, "faith based" institutions (Grubb and Lazerson 1988, 58; Keeling and Hersh 2012, 27; Labaree 2010). All human cultures have tended to sacralize their social institutions. Churches and schools have been two of the most revered. These two institutions have historically been intertwined because they were largely in control of constituting, legitimizing, and reproducing the moral and political order of a culture through the formal processes of enculturation (Tomasello 2016, 104–5; Ryan 1995, 184).

Because of this sacred political purpose, schools have never had to prove themselves to anyone. "The point about traditions," sociologist Anthony Giddens (1994) once argued, "is that you don't really have to justify them: They contain their own truth, a ritual truth, asserted as correct by the believer" (6).

For most of human history, schools have been sacred institutions upholding sacred traditions. Schools have been endorsed and celebrated by elites. This was because schools have always helped to create the prestige and maintain the authority of the ruling class, while also legitimating the *status quo*. Thus, schools have never had to justify their existence by validating any higher purpose beyond their own traditional functions of social and cultural reproduction.

For thousands of years, administrators, teachers, and the public at large have simply had faith that educational institutions did what they were supposed to do, as long as they were staffed with the *right* sort of people with the *proper* credentials. The philosopher John Dewey, as a young, naïve man, expressed this traditional faith when he boldly asserted, "The teacher always is the prophet of the true God and ushers in the true kingdom of God" (qtd. in Ryan 1995, 133). Of course, the *right* type of person with the *right* credentials (and serving the *right* God) have varied considerably over the centuries and between cultures. All cultures have sacralized their schools in their own ways.

And what are schools supposed to do? You already know the answer. It has now become the same for most cultures. We don't even have to think about it because it is simply common sense (Peurach, et al. 2019, 39). Sociologists John Meyer and Brian Rowan (1978) have called this widely held belief the "schooling rule" (219). It goes like this: A school is a special, officially certified place with teachers in classrooms who deliver curriculums to students through a ritualized process called teaching, which naturally results in student learning (Peurach, et al. 2019, 39).

Learning in schools is measured through oral examinations, written tests, or performances. The teacher evaluates the student and assigns some type of measurement, which many people call a "grade." Then after a set period of time, a number of classes, or the passing of exams, the school awards a symbolic token that validates the character of the student. Often this token takes the form of an officially certified piece of paper. But in some cultures, successful schooling is also certified with titles, clothing, and/or regalia.

The symbolic tokens of schooling don't validate a student's learning so much as verify the student's proper socialization into the formal culture. Academic credentials have always officially signaled that a student demonstrated what was supposed to be demonstrated. The student followed all of the formal requirements and rules in order to become an officially certified, *educated* person in *our* culture (Labaree 2010, 116–117). An academic credential is a mark of distinction (Labaree 2010, 74–75; Labaree 2017, 56, 93). For most of human history, up until the 20th century, relatively few people went to a school, and even fewer graduated.

While all schools in almost every culture have been considered sacred, some brave critics have dared to question the common-sense belief that schools work the way that people believe they are supposed to, or that schooling is self-evidently justified by its very existence. For as long as there have been schools, there have been critics of schooling, albeit the critics have always been a small, courageous minority (Cremin 1990, 3). In most cultures, it has been dangerous to question sacred institutions. Schools in particular have always carefully guarded their aura of solemnity and mystique. Critics have often been denigrated as dangerous radicals, or treated much worse.

One of the earliest educational critics on record was the Greek philosopher Socrates, whose views were recorded and elaborated by his famous student, Plato. In the fourth century B.C.E., Socrates daringly attacked the oral tradition of Greek mythic poetry, the main educational institution of ancient Athens (Havelock 1963, 43). Socrates argued that unscrupulous poets had perverted traditional myths, spreading falsehoods about the gods, which thereby corrupted Athenian youth.

It should come as no surprise that the people of Athens did not appreciate Socrates' ideas. Socrates was put to death for his impertinent critique of Athenian schooling, although he was offered banishment first, which he refused. As Socrates' example illustrates, a critique of schooling often involves a critique of the broader culture, including politics and religion, which is likely to offend most citizens, especially mainstream traditionalists.

Since Socrates there have been many notable educational critics who have made similar arguments against schooling. About two thousand years later, in the late 15th century, the Dutch philosopher and linguist Desiderius Erasmus took aim at European universities run by the Roman Catholic Church. Erasmus argued that higher learning had degenerated, in the words of a modern scholar, into "self-perpetuating oligarchies of obscurantists and suck-ups" ("Citizen of" 2020, para. 7). Erasmus thought his teachers were "quasi theologians" whose "brains are the most addled, tongues the most uncultured, wits the dullest, teachings the thorniest, characters the least attractive, lives the most hypocritical, talk the most slanderous, and hearts the blackest on Earth" (para. 7).

Likewise, in the early 17th century, the English philosopher and statesman Francis Bacon argued that English colleges spun nothing but "cobwebs of learning admirable for the fineness of thread and work," but such "ostentatious" learning had "no substance" (qtd. in Hunter and Nedelisky 2018, 32). Bacon argued that schooling was not worthwhile because it did not "profit" the student or society in any practical way (qtd. in Hunter and Nedelisky 2018, 32).

A couple decades later, the English poet and polemicist John Milton (2006) criticized the institutionalized liberal arts curriculum at Christ's College, Cambridge in England, one of the leading educational institutions of medieval and early modern Europe. Like Bacon, he complained about the "futile and barren controversies and wordy disputes," which served only to "stupefy and benumb the mind" (694). The philosopher John Dewey repeated this same criticism in the early 20th century in the U.S., arguing that students had always been treated as "buckets for the reception of lectures" and as mindless "mills to grind out the due daily grist of a prepared text-book for recitation" (qtd. in Ryan 1995, 63).

These critics were all arguing that schooling was a sham. After two thousand years the institutionalized practice of "learning" in Western schools degenerated into little more than an empty scholastic ceremony driven by tradition and the authority of the church (Hobbins 2009).

As the 18th century philosopher Paul-Henri Thiry, the Baron d'Holbach explained, traditional learning through formal schooling taught students to "despise realities," to "meditate on chimeras," to "neglect experience," and to "indulge" in useless "systems and conjectures" (qtd. in Hunter and Nedelisky 2018, 37). He went on to lament that formal schooling "dares not cultivate [a student's] reason" (37). Instead, d'Holbach argued, schooling was focused on conformity to tradition through the memorization of empty myths and the demonstration of empty rituals.

The 19th century English journalist and scholar Walter Bagehot concurred. Like d'Holbach, Bagehot was a vociferous critic of European schooling. He quipped that most schools turned education into a "narcotic rather than a stimulant" ("The Greatest" 2019, 68), stupefying students by sending them into an intellectual sleep, rather than electrifying the mind to produce useful knowledge. Educational historian Lawrence A. Cremin (1990) once pointed out that educational critiques, like these, are "as old as the world itself" (7; see also Ravitch 2000, 15).

Cremin (1990) also pointed out that critiques of schooling, especially in Western cultures, have all followed the same basic formula. First, critics usually lamented that students were "learning less of what a particular commentator or group of commentators believe they ought to be learning" (7). Second, there was usually a reference to an *ought*, a supreme value. This reference led to "an idealized conception of education and the educated person" (7), which somehow had been desecrated. And finally, critics usually ended with an admonishment to return to the virtue of the past, albeit an idealized and idiosyncratically defined past.

Up until the late 19th century, critics of schooling, like Socrates, Bacon, Milton, d'Holbach, Bagehot, and Dewey, all focused on the curriculum, especially the politics of literacy and moral education, which have been the primary purpose of formal schooling in all cultures (Hirsch Jr. 1988; Elson 1964; Kaestle 1983; Hunter 2000; Sandel 1996, 165). Schools have always indoctrinated students with normative ideals, teaching them to "conform" to the "right way of doing things" in a particular culture (Tomasello 2016, 86, 97).

Thus, critics have often focused their normative attack on some deficiency with the culture-at-large, arguing in effect that we have been doing things the *wrong way* in our schools and in our society, so now we need to start doing things the *right way*. Needless to say, such criticisms met with fierce opposition from traditionalists, as arguments over schooling have always reflected larger social and political conflicts over the broader culture, a type of conflict sociologist James Davison Hunter (1991) has called a *culture war*. Schools have often been the epicenters of culture wars, and remain so today.

THE NEOLIBERAL GOSPEL OF EDUCATION

By the early 20th century, many critics began to break away from this conventional, moral critique of schooling in order to focus on a more immediate and tangible issue: economics. Given a scarcity of resources in a conflict-prone world, many early 20th century educational critics began to ask, who would pay for the new, prolonged, and expensive systems of schooling that were being developed for modern, liberal, welfare states? They also asked, how much was education actually worth to individuals and to society as a whole?

For most of human history, schooling had been reserved for small numbers of elite young men, but since the late 19th and early 20th centuries, first across Europe and the United States, and then the rest of the world, schooling slowly became a publicly funded good available to almost everyone, even to the economically marginalized and the traditionally excluded classes, which included women and ethnic minorities (Glenn 2011; Ravitch 2000; Lucas 1994).

As schooling expanded, it became a very expensive institution, largely funded by public taxes and levies, rather than voluntary donations or fees. Educational institutions served increasingly large numbers of students through an increasingly diverse array of organizations, with increasingly expansive missions, which eventually in the 20th century encompassed a complex "system" of schools, from pre-school through higher education (Tyack and Hansot 1982; Labaree 2010; Labaree 2017).

Given the magnitude of costs to create, coordinate, and administer public school systems, the fields of economics, finance, and business management began to shape not only the vocabulary of education, but also the underlying logic that was used to justify schooling (Callahan 1962; Tyack and Hansot 1982, 107; Grubb and Lazerson 1988, 53; Sandel 2012; Smith, 2003). Over the past century there seems to have been one fundamental question driving most school reforms, and it wasn't the traditional preoccupation with morality and the good society. Instead, reformers have been asking: What is the "most cost-effective way to deploy your resources" (Grove 2015, 10; Doerr 2018; Callahan 1962)?

By the end of the 20th century, public schooling in the U.S. had transformed from a moral and cultural institution into an economic enterprise, and this economic transformation has spread across the world. While this transformation started in the late 19th and early 20th centuries, it became undeniable by the 1970s, a time of war, economic recessions, cultural protests, and political malaise.

Rather than being justified in terms of morality, enlightenment, personal growth, patriotism, or any other lofty principle, schooling was defended more and more as an economic enterprise that produced valuable labor market credentials, which in turn produced personal wealth and national economic development (Grubb and Lazerson 2004; Wolf 2002; Markovits 2019). And it wasn't just schools. Other public institutions, like hospitals, community programs, and government welfare services were making the same economic transformation and being judged by the same economic criteria.

Philosopher Michael J. Sandel (2012) has argued that the United States transformed into a "market society" by the late 20th century, by which he meant all of our social institutions have now been converted into economic enterprises that are justified primarily with economic criteria instead of social or moral principles. We

> live at a time when almost everything can be bought and sold. Over the past three decades, markets—and market values—have come to govern our lives as never before. . . . Today, the logic of buying and selling no longer applies to material goods alone but increasingly governs the whole of life. . . . We have drifted from *having* a market economy to *being* a market society . . . a way of life in which market values see into every aspect of human endeavor. (5, 10–11; see also Harvey 2005, 3, 165; Gray 1995, 153; Murphy 2017)

Many have celebrated this economic transformation. There certainly have been many benefits for consumers, especially the wealthy who can afford to buy almost anything they want.

But not everyone has been happy with this economic transformation. Some critics, like the early 20th century economist Thorstein Veblen, called the market revolution of civil society "the triumph of imbecile institutions over life and culture" (qtd. in Breit and Ransom 1998, 31). More recently the philosopher and political scientist John Gray (1995) called the market society "economic imperialism" (153; see also Breit and Ransom 1998, 21; Sunstein 1997, 71; Murphy 2017, 29).

Economists, financiers, and entrepreneurs have displaced traditional sources of moral authority to become the principal judges for every public problem. Every important issue seems to be judged primarily with economic criteria. Every institution now has to operate like a profit seeking business. And the value of almost everything, no matter how sacred, can now be reduced to money.

How did we all come to live in a market society? To answer this question, we need to understand a larger political movement called liberalism, which slowly became the foundational political ideology of Western Europe and the U.S. over the past four hundred years, and then the rest of the world over the past century.

While there has never been a "singular liberalism" (Kloppenberg 1998, 8; see also Holmes 1995, 1; Gray 1989; Fawcett 2014), it is possible to analyze what philosophers and political scientists have called "the liberal idea" (Holmes 1995, 13; Fawcett 2014), which can be broken down into three distinct periods: classical liberalism, progressive liberalism, and the now dominant ideology of neoliberalism.

The early "classical" phase of liberalism lasted from the 17th century into the late 19th century. This political movement focused on three pillars: individual freedom, which was often linked to democracy, although not always, as well as free-market economics and limiting the power of the state. Many traditional liberals, like Adam Smith, David Hume, and John Stewart Mill, were also interested in broad, humanistic issues, like science and defining the just society and discovering the right way to live (Holmes 1995; Kloppenberg 1998; Cohen 2002; Fawcett 2014).

But the political ideology of traditional liberalism was mostly concerned with constitutional politics, which meant a focus on the power of the state and the rule of law as just institutions to protect the rights of citizens. Classical liberalism, as journalist and historian Edmund Fawcett (2014) explained, was above all a "practice of politics," which focused on controlling the political power of the state to mediate political conflicts, promote individual freedom, and protect private property (25; see also Dawley 1991; Cohen 2002).

The second phase of liberalism formed in the late 19th century and ended after WWII. It was called "progressivism," or the "new liberalism" (Ryan 1995, 26; Kloppenberg 1998; Dawley 1991). Progressives reacted to two diametrically opposed political forces that were transforming the globe.

First, they battled traditional conservatism and the social, political, and economic inequalities created by aristocratic elites. These inequalities were sometimes supported and justified by classical liberals, so there was often an ideological battle over the very idea of liberalism. Progressives also battled the rise of revolutionary socialism, which caused widespread revolts against entrenched inequality that resulted in the violent overthrow of French, Russian, and Chinese monarchies, causing widespread fear of revolutionary violence across the world.

Progressive liberals wanted to promote more political democracy, individual and social freedom, economic equality, the rule of law, and the scientific management of society. Progressives were also capitalists who wanted to protect and expand private property and free markets. Progressives envisioned an ideal "market economy constrained by a democratic process in which citizens are represented as equals" (Sandel 1996, 51), but they also wanted an economy informed by science and governed by experts.

Progressive liberals were critical of traditional elites, but most never wanted radical social, political, or economic equality. Progressives wanted to "save the capitalist system, even if that meant saving it from the capitalist themselves" (Dawley 1991, 414). Toward this goal, progressives lobbied for state control over strategic industries, regulating market activity, and plugging the gap where markets failed, like providing free schooling, public pensions, or healthcare.

Thus, instead of a traditional monarchy or state socialism, progressives promoted capitalism, managerialism, and constitutional democracy. At the same time, progressives created a vast array of welfare programs to protect the poor and disadvantaged from the excesses of the free market.

The "welfare state," as sociologist Anthony Giddens (1994) explained, was a "class comprised" to create a middle-path between the political extremes of aristocratic conservatism and socialism (70). Journalist Walter Lippmann argued that progressives wanted to keep the free market economy in "working equilibrium" to meet the needs of everyone, which meant that experts were needed to "correct the abuses and overcome the disorders of capitalism" (qtd. in Goodwin 2014, 138).

By the 1930s, social scientists, led by Nobel Prize-winning economist Simon Kuznets, created the "first quantitative measure of national macroeconomic output" (Murphy 2017, 17, 20–21). At the same time, economists and central bankers were taking a more active role in both measuring and directing society and the state. The general public was becoming aware, for the first time in human history, of an entity called the "economy," which became a "palpable atmosphere that structured daily life" (Murphy 2017, 17, 20–21).

A decade later, economists would calculate the Gross National Product (GNP) of the United States for the first time. And for the rest of the 20th century, economists would try to measure the inputs and outputs of every organization and institution (22).

During the Cold War, in reaction to expansionist state socialism in the Soviet Union and China, and growing welfare states in the U.S. and Europe, a new form of liberalism emerged, which some have called "new liberalism," "regenerated liberalism," "neoliberalism," "market liberalism," or even the "New Right" (Goodwin 2014, 226, 245; Gray 1995, 141; Gray 1989; Giddens 1994, 23).

The roots of this new political philosophy grew out of older progressive values, but with a radical shift. Neoliberalism was created by intellectuals and academics, like Walter Lippmann and Friedrich Hayek, who were concerned with freedom, the rights of individuals, especially property rights, and free-market economics. Neoliberals believed that human liberty was the most important value of all, so the primary purpose of all governments and the rule of law was to guarantee and protect liberty.

Neoliberals reformulated and expanded many classical liberal ideals, explicitly rejecting the tendency toward centralized planning by elites, which was embraced by both communist state socialism and the progressive welfare state. Neoliberals saw state planning and regulations as a threat to human freedom. It didn't matter if the state was democratic, communist, or fascist. All governments were necessary evils (Lowi 1969, 29; Sandel 1996; Gray 1995; Giddens 1994).

Walter Lippman's *The Good Society*, published in 1937, was one of the most important early statements of neoliberal thought (Goodwin 2014, 233, 245). Lippmann straddled the gap between progressivism and neoliberalism, moving from the former as a young man into the latter as he grew older. While progressive liberalism sought to correct dangerous free-market failures with government policies, neoliberalism sought to correct equally dangerous, if not more dangerous, government failures with free-market policies.

The ideological foundation of neoliberalism was built on modern economic theory, as it was created primarily by academic economists, first at the University of Vienna in the early 20th century (Sigmund 2017), and then at the University of Chicago after World War II (Ebenstein 2015). Hence the quip by economist John Maynard Keynes that all politicians in the 20th century were "usually the slaves of some defunct economist" (qtd. in Goodwin 2014, 236).

Neoliberal economists not only celebrated and extended the classical liberal ideals of free markets and economic development, but they also fashioned these ideals into a broader market ideology that sought to transform all social institutions, as well as the state, into economic entities.

Unlike classical liberals, neoliberals have always been more focused on free-market economics and the rights of individuals, especially on property rights. They have also been critical of the traditional power of governments and even the very idea of government (Harvey 2005; Fawcett 2014, 368–90; Giddens 1994, 34). While classical liberals believed in customary institutions and traditional moral constraints, neoliberals focused more on individual freedom with fewer legal or moral controls. Neoliberals have often defined the individual as fully independent, "unencumbered by aims and attachments it does not choose for itself" and "unbound by moral ties antecedent to choice" (Sandel 1996, 12).

This focus on radical individualism and personal choice has led to a neoliberal politics of "withdrawal," "privatization," and "de-deregulation" (Harvey 2005, ch. 3; Giddens 1994, 35). Neoliberals have tried to limit the control of authoritarian states over institutions, social practices, and the lives of individuals. For neoliberals, as sociologist Anthony Giddens (1994) explained, "The message to governments from the competitive economy is: keep out!" (35).

The anthropologist David Harvey (2005) explained neoliberalism as "a theory of political and economic practices that proposes that human well-being can best be advanced by liberating individual entrepreneurial freedoms and skills within an institutional framework characterized by strong private property rights, free markets, and free trade" (2).

For most neoliberals, the role of the state is largely limited to creating and sustaining the rule of law, which constitutes and serves as the referee for the free market, in which individuals are free to do as they please as they compete with each other for wealth and the pursuit of happiness. While neoliberalism is focused on freedom, as are all forms of liberalism, it is more premised on free-market meritocracy, rather than on the principles of equality, justice, democracy, or traditional morality favored by earlier liberals.

Neoliberals believe in a natural aristocracy of talent, as Thomas Jefferson once phrased it, which emerges through schooling and entrepreneurialism, rather than aristocratic lineage or inherited wealth. In 1938 Walter Lippman explained how neoliberals wanted everyone "to have an equal start and an equal chance under the rules of the game, and then to let the natural and real inequalities of men assert themselves" (qtd. in Goodwin 2014, 183). Neoliberals believe that the people with the most talent who work the hardest, competing in the free market, justly get the highest rewards, while the losers have nobody to blame but themselves. Thus, neoliberals usually accept, if not justify and celebrate, social and economic inequality.

Classical liberalism took for granted that competing human beliefs and social practices, including an inequitable distribution of political and economic power, needed to be controlled and regulated by the state. Neoliberalism, on the other hand, is much more radical (Giddens 1994). Neoliberals believe that everyone is born free to compete equally in the marketplace, which should be relatively unrestricted by rules and regulations.

Everyone should be able to do almost anything they want, as long as the market for that good or practice exists. Many neoliberals come close to being anarchists. These activists believe that free markets, if they are left to work by themselves, will solve or eliminate most social problems, which would leave little for the state to do (Giddens 1994, 34).

Most neoliberals believe that government programs and regulations create unfair or inefficient market distortions that end up doing more harm than good. Thus, not only do neoliberals want to end most government regulation of the market and the lives of individuals, but they also, as Harvey (2005) explained, want to bring "all human action into the domain of the market" (3). This focus on free market ideology has resulted in "the commodification of everything" (165), including schooling, healthcare, and even religion.

Ironically, while neoliberals believe in the principle of freedom for markets and for consumers, they do not extend this principle to most workers who sell themselves as wage-slaves in discriminatory labor markets and then toil as powerless peons in hierarchically managed organizations. Neoliberals have been largely unconcerned about older structural inequalities in society and within organizations based on race, gender, and class, which continue to restrict many people from achieving success and happiness.

Neoliberals believe that traditional inequalities are relics of the past that have been eliminated by the meritocratic marketplace, which enables anyone to succeed if they are willing to work hard enough in school and in the labor market. At the level of the firm, neoliberals believe that all organizations, public and private, should be tightly controlled by credentialed experts using scientific management techniques.

In their glorification of the market and technology, neoliberals have deified corporate managers as meritocratic elites who rightly govern the whole of society because they have efficient technocratic practices and esoteric management principles; thus, managers make a lot more money at their jobs than anyone else.

Neoliberals have come close to being revolutionaries because they have wanted to completely transform the whole of society and the state by recreating all institutions with market principles. As Harvey (2005) explained, "if markets do not exist (in areas such as land, water, education, health care, social security, or environmental pollution) then they must be created, by state action if necessary" (2).

In terms of educational reform over the past century, neoliberal reformers have transformed schools into business-like organizations, which are now justified on market principles. Schools are now seen as economic organizations instead of moral or cultural institutions. All across the world, the neoliberal model of schooling has become a new "secular faith" (Wolf 2002, x). Economist W. Norton Grubb and historian Marvin Lazerson (2004) derisively called it, "The Educational Gospel" (vii; see also Birnbaum 2000, xii; Sandel 2012; Wolf 2002).

Rather than *educating* students, neoliberal schools are credential factories that process students and produce human capital, a private good which enables personal wealth. Schools also contributing to national economic growth, via the hidden hand of the market (Labaree 1997b; Birnbaum 2000, 91; Markovits 2019; Grubb and Lazerson 2004; Wolf 2002). Rather than immature and developing human beings, students are now considered consumers who buy educational products and services, which are investments that will pay dividends in the labor market.

School administrators have become highly-paid, corporate managers who evaluate the efficiency of their educational factories, control their workforce, and raise performance-based capital. Teachers have been reduced to low-paid service providers who seek to please their customers. And as employees, teachers are supposed to follow the orders of their supervisors, who are supposedly experts at keeping schools productive and economically efficient.

As business-like organizations, schools are now expected to satisfy customers and stakeholders by demonstrating their effectiveness with measurable outcomes. Rather than rely on antiquated beliefs that schools do what they're supposed to do, modern school managers believe that they must measure the quantity and quality of the products their educational factories produce so as to justify their precarious budgets, which are increasingly predicated upon performance-based funding (Schneider 2017; Dougherty et al. 2016).

Thus, school administrators now follow the popular advice of business professor Andy Grove (2015), who famously declared, "a measurement—any measurement—is better than none" (17). Since the 20th century, demonstrating the effectiveness of schools with accountability measurements has become the conventional wisdom all across the globe.

Chapter 2

Getting Our Money's Worth

A Short History of the Accountability Movement in the U.S.

In the 1960s Milton Friedman (1962/2002), the Nobel Prize winning economist and neoliberal philosopher, shocked many Americans when he criticized public schooling as a waste of tax dollars. Friedman lamented that Americans were "getting so little per dollar spent" on education because public schools were not being held accountable for measurable results (105). Friedman argued that public schools were an inefficient investment, implying that tax dollars would be better spent elsewhere, like on private schools that had to compete for resources and customers in the free market.

A couple of years later, business professor and neoliberal philosopher Peter F. Drucker (1969) echoed Friedman's concerns, saying "The growing resistance to the cost of education indicates that the public is beginning to be concerned with what it gets for its money. . . . We clearly are not at all convinced that we are getting our money's worth for what we spend on it" (312).

While Friedman and Drucker caused a lot of shock and dismay with their criticisms about the inefficiency of public schooling, they were actually reiterating an old and established mantra that had become conventional wisdom by the middle of the 20th century. Let's look at the origins of this belief.

ACCOUNTABILITY AS ECONOMIC EFFICIENCY

Economic criticisms of schooling became popular with progressive reformers and policy makers by the late 19th and early 20th centuries. As complex systems of schooling were being created because student enrollments were expanding, progressive reformers in America began to criticize public schools as a waste of money. Professor of education William C. Bagley was one of the most influential of these early accountability critics. In 1907 he formalized a new equation to evaluate the economic efficiency of schools, which he set forth in his widely read textbook, *Classroom Management*.

Bagley declared that school administrators needed to become a new class of managerial experts so they could administer schools scientifically (Tyack 1974). He argued that school administrators should not be focused on educating students based on traditional principles or practices. Instead, the school administrator's primary duty was to determine how to "return the largest dividend upon the material investment of time, energy, and money" (qtd. in Callahan 1962, 7).

Bagley was part of a new movement of educational reformers who criticized schools on economic grounds, rather than educational or moral principles. Historian Lawrence Cremin (1961) called these early 20th century liberal reformers, the "administrative progressives" (see also Kliebard 2004, ch. 4; Labaree 2005). These accountability reformers were consumed with social and economic efficiency, and they helped create the intellectual foundations for the neoliberal transformation of schooling.

But it wasn't just schools. These progressive reformers were part of an international movement that wanted to permanently solve all types of social problems by reconstructing society with science, technology, and business practices. They wanted to place expert managers at the top of every organization to make all firms, public and private, rationally organized, productive, and economically efficient.

Progressives believed that scientists, engineers, and managers were a new class of experts who could "generate unquestionable truths," which would enable them to "master" society through purposeful planning based on liberal principles, especially economic principles (Berlin 2000b, 133–34; Giddens 1994, 95; Goodwin 2014, 18; Kliebard 2004, ch. 4). Walter Lippmann, who was one of these early progressive reformers, argued in his widely influential book *Drift and Mastery*, published in 1914, that a new class of experts would boldly refashion all social, political, and economic institutions, and they would bring about lasting peace and prosperity to the world (Goodwin 2014).

But in order to change the world, these progressives first had to reform all existing institutions to make them tightly managed, rationally organized, and economically efficient. To that end, most progressives looked to private business as the model *par excellence* of productivity and efficiency. This mold was then forced on every other type of organization.

Schools were one of the first public institutions to be targeted for transformation. In 1905, at the National Education Association annual meeting, George H. Martin, secretary of the State Board of Education in Massachusetts, argued that in comparison with businesses, schools were "unscientific, crude, and wasteful" (qtd. in Callahan 1962, 6). Progressive reformers were transfixed with the principle of economic *efficiency*, especially in the Northeastern and Midwest parts of the country, where most public schools and institutions of higher education in the U.S. were concentrated.

These educational reformers wanted to create "a capitalistic system" of schooling that would be "run by capital and capitalistic methods" so as to transform American into a "capitalistic society" (Adams [1918] 1961, 344). And in this mission, many progressive crusaders were dressed for the part. In 1914, the journalist Walter Lippman described a room full of leading academics who "looked more like highly trained business men, and if we had been told that this was a convention of steel manufacturers or of general insurance agents, we might easily have believed" (qtd. in Goodwin 2014, 43).

In the early 20th century, William C. Bagley (1912) explained that economic "efficiency seems to be a word to conjure with in these days" (ch. 3, part 1). He used his platform as a university professor to "promote the efficiency of the teaching force" in an effort to transform schools into business-like institutions (ch. 3, part 1). Bagley (1912) wanted "the conditions of efficiency" to be "fulfilled as far as possible" in all types of schools (ch. 3, part 1).

Toward that end, Bagley engineered what would become the basic template for accountability reforms in not only K–12 schools, but also institutions of higher education. Bagley believed that educational accountability boiled down to teachers being "held responsible" for specific student learning outcomes, which would make schools more economically efficient.

Bagley believed that teachers needed to be controlled and "restricted" so that schools could generate measurable markers of student success. The primary duty of administrators was to make sure that teachers delivered a "definite course of study," preselected by scientific experts, which would achieve "explicit and definite" results (ch. 3, part 2; see also Kliebard 2004, ch. 4). Thus, if teachers used "the methods that are most economical and efficient," and if they "test[ed] the efficiency of their own efforts," then teachers could "improve efficiency," not only in their own classroom, but also for the entire school (Bagley 1912, ch. 3, part 3).

In 1913, Frank Spaulding, the superintendent of Newton, Massachusetts, condensed Bagley's new policy of educational efficiency into a simple equation: "A maximum of service at a minimum of cost in every school and in every subject" (qtd. in Callahan 1962, 74). As educational historian Raymond E. Callahan (1962) documented in his influential book on the subject, schooling gradually transformed from a sacred, cultural institution into "a determination of dollar value" (73; see also Birnbaum 2000).

Schools became judged "not on educational, but on financial grounds" (Callahan 1962, 73), and the social value of education became "subordinated to business considerations" (246). As Henry Adams ([1918] 1961) remarked in his famous autobiography, for schooling to "count as success" in early 20th century America, it needed to be "counted as money," it needed to be "equivalent to money," or it "counted for nothing" (348).

As schooling transformed into an economic enterprise, more and more people believed that it needed to be measured and evaluated by expert managers in order to ensure that it produced a sufficient *Return on Investment* (Kaplan and Norton, 1996, 22) so it could be "counted as money," as Adams perceptively pointed out. But the principles of economics could only go so far as an accountability framework for evaluating schools.

Gradually, accountability reformers realized that they needed "a noneconomic equivalent to the profitability yardstick," as business professor Peter F. Drucker (1969, 195) eventually pointed out in the 1960s. The problem was, according to Drucker (1969), "with the exception of business, we don't know how to measure results in most organizations" (196). Thus, over the course of the 20th century, progressive and neoliberal reformers enlisted the help of a new class of scientists called psychologists who would create different types of accountability "yardsticks" for K–12 schools and institutions of higher education.

MEASURING AND CONTROLLING THE INPUTS AND OUTPUTS OF SCHOOLING

Utilizing the new ideology of scientific administration and economic efficacy, early 20th century liberal crusaders wanted to use the precision of science and engineering to reform every public institution, which meant organizing and rationalizing all social practices into discrete and measurable units (Callahan 1962; Tyack 1974; Stewart 2009). As businessmen have liked to say for the past century, "If you can't measure it, you can't manage it" (Kaplan and Norton, 1996, 21).

Industrialists had used this ideology of management and measurement to rationalized the mass production of consumer products into an efficient and replicable process that created highly profitable new types of businesses, like automobiles, toasters, and televisions (Cohen 2003). This methodology was also extended to other areas, like the mass production of industrialized foods (Pollan 2008, 62) and health care (Starr 2017). Likewise, administrative progressives in education wanted to create "the one best system" in order to industrialize and mass produce education (Tyack 1974, 13; Callahan 1962).

While accountability reformers wanted to transform the social practice of schooling into an economic enterprise with clearly defined inputs and outputs, there was a problem. Educating a student wasn't exactly the same as mass producing cars or canned peas. Thus, accountability reformers had to create a new paradigm for understanding the practice of schooling.

So, they asked a series of questions: What purpose did the modern school serve? What were students supposed to be doing in schools? And how could this activity be measured, evaluated, and made economically efficient? If schools were factories, what exactly did they produce? What was the end product? The field of modern psychology came up with the answers.

The academic study of psychology was developing into a scientific enterprise by the late 19th and early 20th centuries (Hunt 1993). Enterprising psychologists in the U.S., Germany, and Russia rebelled against the theoretical system building of traditional philosophers. These researchers wanted to transform the field of psychology into an empirical science, like physics or anatomy. Empirical psychologists wanted to strip human mental processes down into the most objective and measurable terms, which meant replacing speculative ideals and subjective mental phenomena with objective, physiological behavior (Rumbaugh and Washburn 2003; Olson and Hergenhahn 2009; Domjan 2010).

An innovative group of psychologists, which included Edward L. Thorndike, Ivan Petrovich Pavlov, John B. Watson, and B. F. Skinner, joined together to create a new field of science that came to be called *behavioral* psychology. These psychologists established what they believed were objective laws of learning. The most important law of learning was "conditioning," which was a process that manipulated the basic stimulus-response relationship found in all biological beings, from humans to monkeys to mice (Rumbaugh and Washburn 2003, ch. 17; Olson and Hergenhahn 2009; Domjan 2010).

Traditional educational practices, such as moral instruction or higher order thinking, were "dismissed as mentalistic or epiphenomenal" phenomenon that could not be scientifically studied so these topics were ignored (Rumbaugh and Washburn 2003, 271). Behavioralists believed that humans, like animals, merely reacted to their environment based on biologically programmed rules. Therefore, this simple fact would become the basis of all learning in modern schools.

Building upon the influential principles of behaviorist psychology, progressive reformers and school administrators began to revise the purpose of schooling away from the traditional emphasis on moral formation. These scientists and administrators believed that student "intelligence" (Kliebard 2004, 92) was much more important for success in life than the traditional and immeasurable ideal of "character" (Jacoby and Glauberman 1995; Stanovich 2009; Hunter 2000).

Thus, accountability reformers gradually redefined the end-product of schooling as student *learning*. Each discrete unit of new learning either revealed or enhanced a student's "intelligence," depending on one's definition of intelligence, which was either a permanent or malleable biological ability.

Building upon traditional testing practices (Reese 2013), psychologists and school administrators believed that the new educational product of student learning could be objectively measured by scientifically designed standardized tests, which would enable impartial evaluations that could be conveyed with uniform, numerical grades (Hutt and Schneider 2018). This discovery enabled school administrators to realize their mandate as modern managers who could make schools more economically efficient: Schools needed to produce the highest test scores per student with the least amount of cost.

However, not everyone was convinced that student learning could be easily quantified. And to make matters worse, what could be quantified was not necessarily useful to educators or beneficial to students. Standardized tests were widely used because they were economically efficient, not because they were effective measurements of student learning, nor because they helped students learn better (Schneider 2017, 17). Standardized tests were also cheap, easy to mass produce, and easy to administer to large groups of students who needed to be sorted and ranked.

As David F. Labaree (1984) put it, schools were "under intense pressure to develop a system of instruction which was fiscally, socially, and pedagogically efficient," so standardized tests and standardized grades were widely implemented as the most expedient solution to the problem of mass schooling (68; see also Schneider and Hutt 2013).

Most early 20th century progressive reformers believed that science would unlock all the secrets of human nature, which would enable expert managers to rationally organize and efficiently administrate civil society and the state, which included public schools and institutions of higher education. At the time, psychologists believed that there were "laws underlying individual differences," which could be objectively measured by scientists utilizing new educational methods (Strong 1922, 193), which included standardized tests, numerical grades, and the statistical analysis of student grades (Labaree 2011; Schneider and Hutt 2013).

In 1908 at the University of Missouri, psychologist Max Meyer published a widely read and cited article in the prestigious journal *Science*. He argued that there was a natural distribution of intelligence and academic achievement in different human populations. He believed that human intelligence could be precisely measured by standardized tests and accurately labeled with numerical grades, which could then be statistically analyzed to produce a "normal" bell-shaped distribution (Foster 1911, 388; Rogoff 2003, 229).

By comparing the statistical distributions of different populations, Meyer believed that a discerning scientist could identify which individuals or groups were above or below the mean, which could then be used to judge which individuals or groups could be successful in schools, in the military, or at specific kinds of jobs.

In one textbook, *Introduction to the Use of Standardized Tests*, which was published in 1922, the author explained how student test scores could be "represented by a simple graph, say with one line showing the given pupil's attainment in these tests and another line the attainment of the average American child of this age or grade who has taken these tests, then the pupil has his strong and weak points set before him in a manner that is perfectly definite and objective" (Geyer 1922, 8).

Most early 20th century educational psychologists and school administrators came to believe that standardized tests were objective accountability measurements (Schneider and Hutt 2013). However, there were many critics of this new methodology who attacked standardized testing as it was being developed (Labaree 2011). In one early 20th century textbook on educational psychology, Edward Kellogg Strong (1922) admitted that there was "no standard of perfection" to ground standardized tests or the application of numerical grades (204).

Thus, the statistical analysis of student grades, and Meyer's beloved bell curves, were often compromised by biased data. While Strong (1922) argued that "definite standards" and "precise methods" were being developed by scientists, he admitted that most teachers evaluated students "not according to some ideal standard of perfection, but in comparison with our fellows, particularly our competitors" (204). Thus, Strong acknowledged, accountability measurements were based more on normative judgments and social comparisons rather than objective measures of academic performance.

Many teachers also criticized this new testing regime. They knew that memorizing discrete bits of knowledge to get high marks on standardized tests not only trivialized student learning and reduced student motivation, but these test results could also be rigged by teaching to the test.

In 1927 one teacher revealed that it was "quite possible to drill for an examination and to pass a large number of pupils with high ratings without giving any breadth of outlook or grasp of underlying principles" (qtd. in Schneider 2017, 26). In 1938 one critical report noted that standardized tests focused "exclusively on the acquisition and retention of information" that was "relatively unimportant" to both students' immediate life and their future career goals (qtd. in Schneider 2017, 26).

By the 1950s, scholars were warning that many teachers were finding ways to game the system by "teach[ing] for the tests," which reduced standardized testing to an empty, political ritual, instead of a valid accountability measure (Schneider 2017, 30). But testing became big business and was "highly profitable" (31). No criticisms could turn this tide.

By the 1920s there were about 250 commercially manufactured standardized tests that were being used in schools, and by 1937 IBM had created the first automatic test-scoring machine, which eliminated the need for teachers to actually grade and correct tests (32, 27). Standardized testing had become big business.

Critics like Strong warned that despite the rhetoric of science surrounding accountability measurements, these tools were not accurate measures of either student ability or the efficiency of schools, although Strong had faith that these measurements would one day become more objective. As a critic pointed out in 1911, standardized numerical assessments of students were becoming "everywhere awarded on the naïve assumption" that they were grounded on a "scientific basis" (Foster 1911, 388).

However, the practice of assessing a student's academic ability and expressing that ability with a numerical grade never had any "exact meaning" (388), either for the person conducting the assessment or for the student being assessed. This problem became especially transparent with the discovery of I.Q. And while many scholars, like Meyer, were focused on the supposed objectivity of statistical distributions, some scientists, school administrators, and policy makers believed that the bell curve distribution supported a normative framework as well, which placed a student in one of three moral categories: superior, average, or inferior.

THE MORAL DIMENSION OF I.Q. AND THE BELL CURVE

In the early 20th century, the educational psychologists Alfred Binet and Lewis Terman discovered a new mental capacity, which they called "g." This term stood for "general intelligence." It was also commonly known as "I.Q.," or the intelligence quotient, which referred to the number produced by a special standardized test created to measure this ability (Kliebard 2004, 92; McMahon 2013, ch. 5; Richardson 1999; Mukherjee 2016, 344).

Psychologists believed that I.Q. corresponded with a natural aptitude that was located in a specific part of the brain, which was universal to all humans. Psychologists also believed that standardized tests accurately measured this innate intellectual capability (Mitchell 2018, 159; Richardson 1999, 34).

Ironically, after a hundred years of studying the faculty of "intelligence," psychologists have never been able to agree on what I.Q. is or what it's supposed to measure. In one recent survey of psychologists in the U.S., there were 25 different attributes that were supposedly connected with I.Q. However, more than a third of these attributes were cited by less than 10% of the surveyed psychologists, with only three attributes cited by 25% or more of respondents (Richardson 1999, 46).

For almost a century, when it came to measuring "intelligence," the academic experts have never known exactly what they were supposed to be measuring. All they knew was that "intelligence" could be expressed as an I.Q. score, which was highly correlated with academic success on standardized tests in Western schools (Ceci 1991; Mukherjee 2016, 345–49; Rogoff 1990, 43, 47).

Over the last century, psychologists have exhaustively studied the phenomenon of intelligence and discovered that there is "no single way to define, let alone measure" this complex human capability (Rumbaugh and Washburn 2003, 12; see for example Gardner 1993). Psychologist Ken Richardson (1999) went so far as to argue that the concept of intelligence is a "phantom biological" faculty (84, 200).

Many other psychologists have agreed with Richardson (Gardner 1993). Critics have pointed out that the concept of intelligence is at best, a vague theoretical construct, and at worst, a pernicious lie used to haphazardly discriminate against minority groups (Rumbaugh and Washburn 2003, 12; Eberhardt 2020, 142). Some critical scientists have called the concept pure "fiction," especially the highly contested validity of an I.Q. score (Richardson 1999, 84).

Despite a lack of empirical justification, the early 20th century concept of intelligence squared nicely with traditional political beliefs about rulers and the ruled. For millennia in almost every culture, there was a widespread belief that a superior minority was destined to rule over the inferior majority. In most cultures this natural inequality was part of a divinely ordered, hierarchical chain of being that governed the universe. Many cultures deified their privileged minority in religious terms, either as divinely inspired poets or prophets, or as divinely anointed aristocrats and monarchs (McMahon 2013, 56, 65).

By the 18th century, with the rise of British empiricism, early modern science, and republican democracy, this hierarchical belief was secularized and naturalized in terms of the superiority of "geniuses" (80), who were exemplary people who had unique, natural talents. The new concept of "intelligence," discovered in the early 20th century, complimented these traditional beliefs in natural hierarchies.

By the 19th century, romantic philosophers and poets refashioned the traditional notion of hereditary superiority and divine inspiration (130) and made it popular again, especially in Germany. These neotraditionalists influenced the birth of modern psychology, which emerged from 19th century German philosophy and philology departments, and it also led to various racial ideologies, including Anglo-Saxonism and Nazism (McMahon 2013;

Fredrickson 1981; Fredrickson 2002; Horsman 1981). Thus, many early 20th century philosophers and psychologists were using the pseudoscience surrounding the concept of "intelligence" to reinforce traditional racial castes and political aristocracies (McMahon 2013; Fredrickson 1981; Fredrickson 2002; Horsman 1981).

It was during this time that many scientists argued that they had found proof for the hereditary superiority of certain groups of people, and they codified various "scientifically" justified social hierarchies. In *An Account of the Regular Gradation in Man*, published in 1799, the British surgeon Charles White declared that "Nature exhibits to our view an immense chain of beings, endued with various degrees of intelligence and active powers suited to the stations in the general system" (qtd. in Eberhardt 2020, 135).

White men of "genius" and "illustrious men" were at the top of this chain of beings, while the mass of "mediocre," "vulgar," and "average men" were in the middle. At the bottom of the scale were the irredeemably inferior "idiots," "imbeciles," and "morons," which included a wide-range of people, such as women, children, rebellious teenagers, social "deviants," and political radicals (McMahon 2013, 157, 161, 174, 178, 182; see also Mukherjee 2016, 79).

This natural hierarchy was also extended to nations and human cultures, with "white," Western European nations at the top of the hierarchy, who were destined to rule the world, and everyone else was at the bottom, notably the "Mongols" and the "Negros," races who were destined to be ruled by white Europeans because these groups were believed to be naturally inferior (Fredrickson 1981; Fredrickson 2002; Horsman 1981; Eberhardt 2020, 135–137).

As historian Darrin M. McMahon (2013) explained, "By substituting natural for supernatural causes, [modern psychologists] granted the imprimatur of science to what remained, fundamentally, a myth regarding the right and capacity of higher beings to rule the world" (188).

Traditionally, schools were elite institutions that helped legitimate and maintain social and political hierarchies, which included economic elites and privileged racial groups. But with the development of modern, mass schooling, especially in democratizing nations like the U.S. that were expanding suffrage and other political rights to larger amounts of people, the traditional hierarchical purpose of schooling had to be revised to accommodate liberal political beliefs and new student populations who had traditionally been excluded from education.

Thus, by the early 20th century, modern schools came up with a new purpose to accommodate both traditional elites and new populations of marginalized students. Schools would allow almost everyone into the same building, although this took until the later 20th century for racialized minorities. But once inside schools, students would then be sorted and tracked based upon their abilities and other predetermined characteristics (Oakes 1985; Lucas 1999, 2–3; Kalogrides and Loeb 2013). Thereby, schools could become both meritocratic and exclusionary institutions.

On the one hand, modern 20th century schools were supposed to nurture the lofty intellectual capacity of the gifted few who were destined for higher education and highly paid professions. On the other hand, modern schools had to accommodate increasing numbers of marginalized and oppressed groups of people, like women, ethnic minorities, the working class and poor, and students with disabilities. To address this paradox, schools were transformed from elite institutions into processing centers.

Schools needed to assess, label, and manage different groups of students, placing them on separate "tracks" leading to separate outcomes (Oakes 1988). Elite students were college bound; mediocre students were trained for the semiskilled labor; and the incorrigible were destined to drop out of school, many of whom it was expected would wind up incarcerated or institutionalized. Standardized examinations, like I.Q. tests and the SAT, became a convenient way to accomplish this new mission of classifying, ranking, and tracking.

The sociologist of education David Snedden (1920), an influential administrative progressive, focused most of his career on popularizing separate "tracks" in schools for different types of students who would be trained for different types of jobs in the labor market (Kliebard 2004, ch. 5). Snedden (1920) explained that the purpose of schooling was to "fit an individual to pursue effectively a recognized profitable employment" based upon their socioeconomic status and personal characteristics (535). He noted that "men vary greatly in their respective abilities" and "vocational capacity" (4, 7) so they needed to be processed differently by schools.

Snedden (1920) believed that "only persons of exceptional native endowment" (537) would benefit from advanced levels of schooling, which at the time meant high school and for the select few, college. The majority of students had "physical or other unfitness" for professional fields so they needed to be prepared to leave school early for semiskilled work or manual labor (537).

Some early 20th century scientists in the U.S. had more sinister motives for tracking students in schools. Psychologist Lewis Terman wanted to "select more intelligent humans for eugenic breeding" in order to create a master race, just like the Nazis in Germany (Mukherjee 2016, 344, 78–132).

Economist Thomas Nixon Carver, who was also a trustee of the Massachusetts State School for the Feeble-Minded, wanted to keep the low-intelligence students from "reproducing themselves" (qtd. in Goodwin 2014, 10). Carver argued, "economically incompetent people tend to multiply almost at the same rate. That tends to increase the supply of the unemployable as well as those with a low grade of skill. The presence of large numbers of such people, however, is a constant menace to the laborers who are just above that level" (10).

Ken Richardson (1999) has documented how American scientists often used I.Q. tests as a political tool to not only sort people, but also to discriminate against particular social classes and racialized minorities (21, 33; see also Eberhardt 2020, 142). Tellingly, when white American psychologists used I.Q. tests on immigrants in the early 20th century, this supposedly "objective," scientific test revealed that around 80% of immigrants were "feeble-minded," while not surprisingly, most rich, white Americans scored quite high (Richardson 1999, 33; Eberhardt 2020, 142).

CREATING ACCOUNTABILITY AGENCIES TO ESTABLISH STANDARDS IN SCHOOLS

For centuries in Europe, churches had control over the school curriculum, school staff, and school finances. But by the 19th century, newly formed national governments took control over schooling, and expanded this institution systematically to accommodate more students and more subjects, mostly in an effort to support new nationalist identities and programs, like the unification of smaller political units, such the unification of Germany (Glenn 2011).

In the United States, from the colonial period up until the middle of the 20th century, state and local governments were primarily responsible for funding K–12 schools, and for certifying the quality of school staff and curriculums. Higher education in the U.S. had always been a mixture of public and private funding, with most colleges up until the late 19th century controlled by a combination of faculty, churches, and local trustees (Lucas 1994; Thelin 2004).

By the 20th century, national, state, and local governments in the U.S. and Europe became more financially responsible for more social services for more groups of people, including schooling and higher education, as well as monitoring and certifying the quality of these services (Dawley 1991; Gamble 2016). However, after a century of government largess, by the end of the 20th century, due to strained governmental finances, which were caused by large welfare state expenditures, slowing GDP, economic recessions, and tax revolts, consumers started to pay more for their education, especially higher education, while governments paid less (Gamble 2016; St. John and Parsons, 2004; Golderick-Rab 2016).

Plus, many people, like the economist Milton Friedman (1962/2002, 105), came to believe that individuals should bear the costs for their own schooling, especially with higher education. Reversing traditional assumptions, many people came to believe that education was more of a private, luxury good, rather than a public good that should be free to all (Labaree 1997b).

Before the 20th century, the costs of schooling had never been an urgent political issue, predominantly because schooling was exclusively for the privileged. Schools had traditionally served small numbers of elite young men. For most of human history, schooling was a sacred form of official socialization restricted to a privileged few (Milner 1994), especially higher education (Chaffee 1995; Lucas 1994; Seth 2002).

In the late 19th century, the U.S. had the most open educational system in the world, but most people still left school after a few years of primary education, if they attended school at all. At this time, only around 5 percent of students in the U.S. enrolled in high school, and a small fraction of those high school graduates made it to college (Reese 1995).

Up until the 1950s, as law professor Daniel Markovits (2019) pointed out, "elite universities overwhelmingly awarded places based on breeding rather than merit" (6), and the same could be said for most elite K–12 schools. England didn't provide free secondary education for all students until after 1944 (Robinson 2001, 77). Gradually, by the mid- to late twentieth century, nearly all students in the U.S. and Europe went to high school and most graduated with a diploma.

Increasingly, a majority of these high school graduates began to enter college by the 1960s and '70s. Scholars have called this time the era of "mass" public schooling because more students than ever before in human history made it through primary and secondary schooling and into higher education (Peurach, et al. 2019, 34, 38).

In response, governments in the U.S. and Europe opened up and expanded their systems of higher education to meet the growing demand of increasing numbers of high school graduates. With the passage of the GI Bill in the United States after WWII, around 1.5 million decommissioned veterans were directed into higher education, primarily to keep this large, unskilled population from overwhelming the labor market (Thelin 2004).

Then, due to the various Civil Rights movements in the U.S. in the 1960s and '70s, all social groups, including the most impoverished and socially excluded, demanded access to college (Douglass 2007; Thelin 2004). The expansion of higher education included not only accepting large numbers of new student populations, but also the building of new campuses, hiring more faculty, and awarding more financial aid to lower-class students who could not pay for tuition.

Such an expansion required huge capital expenditures that were initially funded by state and federal taxes in the first half of the 20th century. By the end of the century, with the "massification" of higher education, the expenses were too great for most governments to afford, so students bore more and more of the financial responsibility through tuition, fees, and student loans (St. John and Parsons, 2004).

But "the assurance of universal access" to public schooling and higher education "did not bring with it the assurance of quality or equality in students' educational experiences and outcomes," according to many historians and professors of education (Peurach et al. 2019, 35; see also Brint and Karabel 1989; Grubb and Lazerson 2004; Beach 2011a). By the late 1960s, as Peter Drucker (1969) explained, people began to complain that government social programs "cost a great deal but do not achieve much," causing a widespread "disenchantment" with schooling and other public services (212–13).

Naturally, lawmakers and officials wanted some accountability over the vast sums of money being poured into schooling and higher education. Taxpayers wanted oversight, if not reduced costs.

Thus, by the 1970s, there was a push to "greatly improve the efficiency of government," which included reforming schools from kindergarten through college by making them more accountable for their productivity and economic efficiency (Drucker 1969, 231; Wildavsky 1979). However, these new accountability programs were not actually new, as progressive reformers had been unsuccessfully working on these issues since the early 20th century, as we already discussed.

In continental Europe, national governments had controlled all forms of education since the 19th century, but in England and the U.S., educational institutions were largely self-governed or locally governed, although state institutions, like normal schools, agricultural colleges, or state universities, had more government oversight.

In the U.S. up until the late 20th century, institutions of higher education had a "helter-skelter" patchwork of standards and entrance exams (Ravitch 2000, 41). About half of all colleges had low or no admissions standards (Ravitch 2000). Most students got into established colleges based on their social breeding and wealth. Many schools were nothing more than degree mills, where students could enroll and graduate if they simply paid tuition (Markovits 2019).

Schools in the U.S. had been designed as "access-oriented" institutions that sorted students by socioeconomic resources, but there was no "instructionally focused" system at any level of schooling that produced verifiable educational results (Peurach et al. 2019, 38). Policy makers assumed, "If governments supplied schools with more and better teachers and books, students would learn more and better" (Peurach et al. 2019, 35; see also Drucker

1969), but up until the middle of the 20th century, few public or private agencies ever bothered to check to see if student learning was actually happening.

Take for example the schooling of doctors in the United States. There were 42 medical schools in 1850. By 1870, there were 75 schools. There were 100 medical schools by 1880, 133 by 1890, and 160 by the turn of the 20th century (Starr 2017, 42, 112). While there was widespread growth of medical schools, there was no quality control over the medical school curriculum or over how much (or how little) medical students actually learned (Starr 2017).

Typically, students earned a medical degree after only two years of school, but the school year usually lasted only three or four months, so students did not receive much instruction (43). To make matters worse, most medical schools did not require either a high school diploma or a bachelor's degree. Many medical schools required only a single course in "natural and experimental philosophy" as the only prerequisite (43).

Essentially, most medical schools in the U.S. up until the early 20th century were diploma mills that earned money through student fees. If you could pay, you were admitted, and you were all but guaranteed to graduate. Students often paid their tuition directly to professors, who were practicing doctors moonlighting as part-time teachers to make extra money or increase their social status.

Sociologist Paul Starr (2017) explained how "American colleges were intellectual backwaters whose poorly paid professors had little claim to original thought or research" (112–113). Charles Eliot, the late 19th century President of Harvard College, lamented "The ignorance and general incompetency of the average graduate of American Medical Schools, at the time when he receives the degree which turns him loose upon the community, is something horrible to contemplate" (qtd. in Starr 2017, 113).

The lack of quality control in medical schools caused serious problems. The increase in schools, rising student enrollments, and low standards caused widespread degree "inflation," which caused the social and economic devaluation of the medical profession (Starr 2017, 43–44). Literally anyone could become a doctor, although most so-called doctors had no understanding of the treatment of most diseases or injuries. Degree inflation resulted in the "diffusion and degradation" of the traditional elite status of doctors (43–44), as America became "oversupplied with badly trained practitioners" (120).

By the end of the 19th century, the American Medical Association tried to "raise and standardize the requirements" for medical degrees (Starr 2017, 90), but as a voluntary association it was largely powerless to do so until the early 20th century. The medical profession acquired its elite status only after the institutionalization of the research university, the standardization of college degrees, the professionalization of academic disciplines and skilled professions, and the development of state examination boards (104).

By 1915, medical schools were raising their standards by requiring higher prerequisites, like a bachelor's degree, and demanding more rigorous coursework and apprenticeships in hospitals (Starr 2017, 120). This naturally, reduced the number of medical schools, medical students, and credentialed doctors. Many medical schools went out of business because they could not attract enough qualified, fee-paying students.

Gradually, accountability agencies in the U.S. were established for all types of schools, not just medical schools. This work was done by local governments, state boards of education, and professional associations. The College Entrance Examination Board, the first official accountability agency for higher education in the U.S., was established in 1900 (Ravitch 2000, 157). College administrators and faculty wanted more standardization of the curriculum and higher standards for college programs, but they also wanted to retain as much power as they could over the accountability process.

The College Board created "general intelligence examinations" (Ravitch 2000, 157), which were used to select qualified applicants to enter college and help ensure higher standards for the college curriculum. The College Board's most important product was the Scholastic Aptitude Test (SAT), which was initiated in 1926 (157). This test became a rite of passage for all American youth for the next century, even though it has always had questionable validity in terms of what it was supposedly measuring and how accurately it could predict success in college.

An even more important source of standards in U.S. higher education developed after WWII with the GI Bill. The government wanted to develop more formal accreditation agencies to help monitor educational quality, especially as new students and new government money expanded the higher education system in the U.S. after the war. While the North Central Association of Colleges and Universities initiated the first formal accreditation program for higher education in 1915, it wasn't until the 1950s that most institutions of higher education were fully monitored by professional accreditation agencies (Freidson 1986, 74).

Historian Rakesh Khurana (2007) explained how these new agencies were a negotiated "political compromise between Congress, which sought accountability for the use of government resources, and educators, who sought to limit the government's interference in higher education" (213). While these agencies provided an independent assessment of educational quality, they were subservient to the very institutions that they were supposed to oversee because universities supplied the staff, the standards, and the assessment methodology.

For over half a century, many educational officials have regarded the college accreditation process as "the single most reliable indicator of institutional quality in higher education" (qtd. in Khurana 2007, 230). Accredited educational institutions were given an official seal of approval that was indirectly connected to the authority of state and federal governments, which in effect gave consumers a guarantee that the product they were buying was legitimate.

However, due to the waves of unprepared students entering higher education, especially by the 1960s and '70s, there was a "downward pressure" (Khurana 2007, 230) on standards, despite the efforts of accountability reformers and accreditation agencies, as administrators and faculty tried to accommodate these new student populations.

Since the 1970s, most high school graduates have not been fully prepared for success in higher education (Brint and Karabel 1989; Douglass 2007), primarily due to a long history of racial and economic inequality, which has resulted in segregated and unequal schooling, and due to a decrease of academic standards in high schools since the 1960s (Ravitch 2000). This downward pressure on standards was especially severe in community colleges, the lowest tier of the higher education system (Beach 2011a; McGrath and Spear 1991; Eaton 1994).

By the late 20th century, schooling in the U.S. was plagued by contradictory policy goals. After schools were largely desegregated by the 1960s and '70s, with the help of mandatory integration policies, there were several policy contradictions. There was a flood of new students, many of which had either been denied schooling or had endured second-rate schooling in segregated schools. How were schools going to set and enforce high educational standards and maintain some level of social exclusivity, while at the same time enabling all students to gain skills so they could enter the labor market (Labaree 2012)?

To address these contradictions, the University of California created the first quality-controlled system of education from kindergarten to the research university by the middle of the 20th century (Douglass 2000; Douglass 2007). Some called this system the "California Ideal," and it was later copied by most other state systems of education in the U.S., although unevenly (Douglass 2000).

The California system enabled all primary students to go to high school. It also promised the rising tide of high school graduates that they would be able to enter higher education, primarily through the low-cost and low-quality community college (Brint and Karabel 1989; Beach 2011a).

However, this did not mean that the California system fairly apportioned resources and adequately prepared all students for success. Most lower-class and ethnic minority students when to substandard high schools and, if they graduated, they went on to community colleges, where most students ended up dropping out or earning short-term certificates in order to enter the semi-skilled labor force.

The most talented students, a small, largely white and economically privileged minority, went to the best high schools with the most resources, and they were able to attend more selective universities, which offered a much better education than community colleges. Most academically accomplished, middle-class students would enter the system at the middle-tier California State Universities, while most elite, economically privileged students would enter the highly selective and expensive University of California tier, or private liberal arts colleges, like Stanford or USC.

Of course, the most talented and academically prepared students were also disproportionately the most economically and racially privileged, in terms of parental income, social status, access to the highest quality K–12 schools, and access to the many external resources that foster success in schooling (Grubb and Lazerson 1988; Douglass 2007; Golden 2006; Putnam 2015; Markovits 2019). Thus, the most exclusive tiers of the higher education system in California and the rest of the U.S. have always been able to maintain higher academic standards, consistent quality, and elite social status (Douglass 2007; Markovits 2019, 135).

At the same time, the lower tiers of the California system of higher education, especially the "open-door" community college, allowed academic standards to precipitously drop in order to accommodate new student populations entering college for the first time, most of whom were not prepared for success in college (Beach 2011a). Even with lower standards and an indulgent faculty, most community college students never graduate with a degree, earning this substandard institution various contemptuous nicknames, from "a high school with ashtrays" to "a halfway school for losers" (Beach 2011a, xx; see also Brint and Karabel 1989; McGrath and Spear 1991).

The California Ideal was promoted as a "magical" institution of democratic access and meritocratic success (Labaree 201, 154). But this ideal glossed over the traditional structural inequality of U.S. society, which was embedded in the system of schools from top to bottom (Beach 2011a). Neoliberal policy makers and school administrators thought they could have their cake and eat it too, but structurally, the California plan snubbed the neediest students and rewarded the most privileged, as most schools have always done.

The California Ideal diverted the most money and the best resources to elite institutions that would serve elite students. Considerably less money and resources were given to urban high schools and community colleges that would serve the vast majority of students, most of whom were underprivileged and in urgent need of remedial assistance.

In this way, higher education in the U.S. has mirrored the incoherence and structural inequality of K–12 schooling (Labaree 2012), which continues to be funded unequally, mostly by state taxes and local property taxes. Despite opening up education to all students, the American system of education is "messy, grossly inefficient, and deeply unfair" because it continues to preserve the advantage of privileged students, while offering the less privileged little besides false hope at a better life (Labaree 2012, 154).

In America, wealthy school districts have always had the best schools with the best teachers and the most educational and extracurricular resources, which helps to propel wealthy students into elite colleges and high paying jobs. Poor districts have always had dysfunctional schools with inadequately trained teachers and substandard resources. This is still the case in the 21st century, although there have been some nominal efforts to equalize funding across school districts from state and federal programs.

While the national average expenditure per public school student in the U.S. is currently about $12,000, this figure masks stark inequality, as one school district in Kentucky spends only about $8,000 per student, while a rich district in New York spends about $27,000 (Markovits 2019, 126–27). However, wealthy parents who send their children to exclusive private schools can spend up to $75,000 per student per year (126).

Elite private schools have student/teacher ratios of 7:1, compared to 16:1 or higher in public schools. Exclusive private schools also have "large, well-educated faculties" and "deploy vast physical resources in their teaching practices," to say nothing of their well-endowed facilities, like libraries, science labs, art room, theaters, and sports fields (Markovits 2019, 126).

While liberal reformers spent the 20th century trying to make schools more economically efficient by creating standards and accountability agencies, there has never been much effort to equalize the resources for schooling, especially in terms of providing adequately trained teachers in every classroom, so as to help eliminate traditional social and economic inequalities.

Accountability metrics have made good schools better and bad schools without resources much worse. As W. Edwards Deming pointed out, "it is not physically possible for humans or machines operating in the same system to produce more with less" (Aguayo 1990, 12). But that is exactly what many schools in the U.S. have been asked to do, especially those schools serving the neediest students. Thus, the inequality between the best-funded school districts and the least-funded districts has only gotten worse over the last several decades (Kelly 2020).

THE DISCOVERY OF HUMAN CAPITAL

By the middle of the 20th century, there was a significant reaction against the pseudoscientific determinism of many accountability reforms, especially I.Q. tests and school tracking, which were often used to reinforce racism, sexism, and socioeconomic inequality (on science and racism see Gould 1981; Jacoby and Glauberman 1995; Mukherjee 2016, 344–49; on racism and school tracking see Oakes 1988; Brantlinger 1993; Lucas 1999; Halpert 2012). Part of this realignment can be attributed to political events outside of schools, such as the fight against German fascism in WWII, the ensuing fight against Soviet fascism in the Cold War, the landmark civil rights ruling of *Brown vs. Board of Education* in the United States, and the later civil rights movements of the 1960s and '70s in the U.S. and Europe.

Scientists were also gradually discovering that student learning and intelligence were products of personal experience and socialization, not just heredity, which meant that natural intelligence was not the primary determinant of academic and labor market success. These scientific discoveries lead to several important pedagogical reforms in schools and helped lend authority to democratic political reforms.

Scientists realized that social groups and institutions, like parents, peers, schools, and churches, played an important role in the development of a student's knowledge, skills, and vocational capability (Mukherjee 2016, 346–47). Scientists also discovered that students were not born predestined by their biology as superior, average, or inferior types of people.

While humans do inherit genetic endowments from their parents, everyone interacts with physical and social environments through personal experiences, which amplify, delay, or inhibit biologically based capabilities (Gopnik 2009, 2016; Ridley 2003; Pinker 2002; Mukherjee 2016). Thus, scientists now know that every individual can learn a lot and accomplish a lot, if they are motivated to do so.

Given the brain's natural plasticity, especially during early childhood and adolescence, psychologists discovered we all have an innate ability to learn and grow by developing the neural circuitry of our brains and the biomechanics of our bodies (Gopnik 2009, 2016; Steinberg 2014; Mitchell 2018). More importantly, scientists discovered that there is no natural limit to how much learning a person can do because the more one learns, the more one is capable of further learning (Ericsson and Pool 2016; Brown, Roediger, and McDaniel 2014; Gopnik 2016; Mitchell 2018).

This discovery was a fundamental challenge to the archaic, traditional notions of natural intelligence, hereditary elites, and predetermined tracks at school, which had been propagated by bigoted psychologists and elitist school administrators for many decades. Since all students are capable of learning and developing their capabilities, the traditional pedagogy of mindless memorization and predetermined curricular tracks was increasingly attacked in the latter 20th century as unjust and counterproductive, not to mention overly restrictive and boring.

By the end of the 20th century, educational researchers and school administrators turned away from a rhetoric of ranked categories based on intelligence and socioeconomic status. Instead, they developed a new paradigm of student "development" and student "learning," which was meant for *all* students, not just superior students. This new emphasis also led to a revision of the measurable products of schooling.

By the 1970s and '80s, student learning was reconceptualized as discrete *bits of knowledge* that could be memorized and reiterated by students on standardized tests, which would accurately measure how much knowledge the student had in their brain (Brown, Roediger and McDaniel 2014; McNeil 2000; Schneider 2017, 16–24). Student learning was also re-conceptualized as discrete actions, often called *skills*, which could be physically demonstrated through movement, like push-ups or swinging a hammer, or through fabricated products, like producing an essay or conducting a chemistry experiment (Ericsson and Pool 2016, 131).

The purpose of schooling was now to fill students up with knowledge and skills, with some allowance made to let students choose what subjects to study based on their personal interests and career goals. All students were encouraged to build their knowledge and skills so they could enter college, earn degrees, and compete in the labor market for high paying jobs.

So instead of focusing on fixed levels of intelligence and static natural abilities, schools at the end of the 20th century started to focus on *developing* students' malleable bodies and brains to produce an open-ended amount of knowledge and skills that could be connected to college credentials and labor market outcomes. Accountability reformers now believed that *all* types of students could and should be taught the same fundamental curriculum, albeit with some measure of personal choice. Schools were supposed to leave "no child left behind," as famously stated in a national school reform program initiated in the early 21st century (Schwartz-Chrismer, Hodge and Saintil 2006).

But while the purpose of schooling, and the end products of schooling, were changing, student achievement was still being measured by standardized tests and labeled by numerical grades (Schneider and Hutt 2013). Students were also still being tracked for different levels of higher education and vocational goals, albeit the tests were updated to be less culturally biased, the tracking was more subtle and voluntary, and everyone was being encouraged to go to college. Schools also retained a traditional bias for abstract, conceptual knowledge over practical skills (Ericsson and Pool 2016, 137), which continued to put many groups of students at a disadvantage, especially in terms of preparing students for labor market success.

By the end of the 20th century, as psychologists re-defined the products of schooling more concretely, and measured these outcomes more accurately, economists were also able to monetize these educational products for the first time by statistically connecting educational credentials to labor market outcomes. Groundbreaking research by the economist Theodore Schultz and later Gary Becker, enabled social scientists to produce elaborate cost/benefit ratios to determine a clear picture of the economic value and efficiency of various forms of schooling (Schultz 1961; Grubb and Lazerson 2004; Beach 2009; Murphy 2017, 115).

One group of social scientists documented how student knowledge and skill symbolically transformed into various forms of capital, which was variously called "social capital," "cultural capital," or "human capital" (Bourdieu ([1984] 2010; Swartz 1997; Schultz 1961). These differing notions of capital were proxies for the social and economic value of a student's knowledge, skill, and productive capacity in the labor market. While social and cultural capital couldn't be directly measured by social scientists, economists could indirectly measure human capital by using various proxy metrics, like grades, diplomas, certificates, and degrees.

Economists could then study the average economic value attached to these metrics in the labor market so as to compute a relatively precise *Return on Investment* for different types of schooling, which is discussed at length in volume two of this series, *The Myths of Measurement and Meritocracy*. Economists could also measure the costs of schooling and compare it to this return on investment to determine which forms of schooling were most cost effective.

A separate, more critical group of social scientists studied the economics of schooling in a very different way because they were skeptical of the theory of human capital. Instead of seeing educational credentials as a measure of concrete skills or knowledge, these social scientists focused on the traditional relationship between schooling and the elite ideological product of "social status" (Collins 1979; Bourdieu [1984] 2010; Milner 1994).

These critics argued that the value of educational credentials was not a reflection of anything practical, like knowledge, skills, or economic productivity. Instead, the value of credentials came from possessing a scarce luxury good that gave its bearer elite social status, mostly due to the selective gate-keeping of expensive forms of schooling, especially private higher education and elite professional schools (Spence 1974; Collins 1979; Caplan 2018).

Some economists, like Bryan Caplan (2018), have argued that the value of educational credentials is based on both human capital and the signaling of social status (see also Labaree 1997a). Caplan (2018) argued that credentials allow students to access advanced levels of education, especially higher education, which enables further investment in more advanced forms of human capital, like graduate and professional schools, which then enable higher forms of elite social status.

More importantly, individuals use credentials as a type of currency that can be traded for money. Credentials allow students to leave school and enter the marketplace where they can use their credential as a social signal in order to barter for high-paid employment, which is where the *actual*, as opposed to the *nominal*, value of human capital has always been realized (Spence 1974; Collins 1979; Brown 1995; Caplan 2018).

Caplan (2018) argued that college credentials signal higher levels of schooling, which continues to be an exclusive luxury good, and these credentials also signal higher levels of knowledge and skills, which together increases the economic value of students in the labor market (see also Grubb and Lazerson 2004).

LOSING FAITH IN PUBLIC SCHOOLS

By the late 1950s and 1960s, the educational accountability movement in the U.S. became a *cause celebre*. But after a half-century of accountability reforms, most schools were not demonstrably better. In fact, many schools seemed to be getting worse. Thus, by midcentury, the national spotlight fixated on raising academic standards in K–12 schools and higher education. At this time, there was a heightened sense of geopolitical risk with the rise of global communism and the Cold War, and then the Soviet launch of Sputnik in 1957.

By 1958 the National Defense of Education Act sought to bolster American political and economic might through better schools, which would now focus more on science and mathematics. A year later in 1959, Admiral Hyman Rickover published *Education and Freedom*, where he argued, "schools must now . . . concentrate on bringing the intellectual powers of each child to the highest possible level. Even the average child now needs almost as good an education as the average middle-and upper-class child used to get in the college-preparatory schools" (qtd. in Ravitch 2000, 362).

In the U.S. a decade later, however, most public schools and institutions of higher education were not living up to Rickover's challenge. At every level, schools were dealing with increased numbers of more diverse and economically disadvantaged students, a situation which challenged academic standards. At the same time, schools were dealing with decreased government funding, increased state and federal accountability mandates, and they were charged with achieving new mandates, such as increasing STEM classes and desegregating schools. The end results? Dysfunctional schools, declining standards, and achievement gaps between rich, white students and everyone else.

By 1970 Ivan Illich (1970) lamented, "School has become a social problem; it is being attacked on all sides" (71). Surveying high school transcripts from 1964 to 1981, the U.S. Department of Education found a "systematic devaluation of academic (and some vocational) courses" (qtd. in Ravitch 2000, 405). Because of all this, in 1983 the National Commission on Excellence in Education Educational declared the U.S. was "at risk": "The educational foundations of our society are presently being eroded by a rising tide of mediocrity that threatens our very future. . . . Learning is the indispensable investment required for success . . . [those] who do not possess the levels of skill, literacy, and training essential to this new era will be effectively disenfranchised" (qtd. in Ravitch 2000, 411; see also Steinberg 1996; Berliner and Biddle 1995, 139).

Over the past half-century, educational researchers uncovered many problems with schools in the U.S., such as high rates of absenteeism, teachers low academic expectations, grade inflation, automatic social promotion, low levels of homework, watered down textbooks, low scores on national and international tests, especially in English and Math, declining SAT scores, high rates of remediation in college, and lots of college drop outs (Ravitch 2000, 403–405, 408–411; Steinberg 1996; Camara, Kimmel, Scheuneman and Sawtell 2003; Koretz 2017; MacPhail 2019; Melguizo and Ngo 2020). Educational historian Diane Ravitch (2000), in particular, has done an insightful job of documenting these diverse problems.

Scholars have also uncovered that students haven't been learning much in colleges and universities, and what students do learn doesn't really deserve the designation of "higher" education (Arum and Roksa 2011; McGrath and Spear 1991; Labaree 1997; Perkins, 1985).

In 1985, to address the systemic "risk" of substandard schooling, Tennessee governor Lamar Alexander declared that "the Governors want to help establish clear goals and better report cards, ways to measure what students know and can do. Then, we're ready to give up a lot of state regulatory control—even to fight for changes in the law to make that happen—if schools and school districts will be held accountable for the results" (qtd. in Schneider 2017, 37).

Since the 1980s, wave after wave of accountability reforms were proposed and put into practice, such as America 2000 in 1990, and then Goals 2000 in 1994, and then No Child Left Behind in 2001, and finally Every School Succeeds in 2015 (Schneider 2017, 37–44; Koretz 2017).

However, while all of these accountability initiatives helped intensify and politicize the criticism of schooling in America, they did nothing to actually fix schools or improve student learning. By the early 21st century, only 35 percent of fourth graders in the U.S. were proficient in reading, although in the two most populous states, California and Texas, only 30 percent of students were proficient ("Do Your Homework" 2019, 7). Even worse, this gap wasn't closing by high school. Researchers found that only 25 to 38 percent of high school graduates were proficient in reading or writing (Perin and Holschuh 2019).

And this bad news extended to higher education. While more students were going to college, most of these students were unprepared for success in higher education, with the most disadvantaged students the farthest behind. According to one study, about 73 percent of middle-class and upper-class students are unprepared for college, while shockingly, 93 percent of the most economically disadvantaged students are unprepared ("Do Your Homework" 2019, 7), which includes almost half of all Americans.

The average reading level of incoming college freshmen since the 1990s has been somewhere between 3rd and 6th grade levels, and math skills have been much worse. Because so many students are unprepared for college, there has been a huge spike in remedial education over the last several decades (Ravitch 2000, 410; Steinberg 1996, 38; Perin and Holschuh 2019; Melguizo and Ngo 2020). Increased remediation pushes four-year degrees into six-year degrees or longer, which increases the emotional and financial costs of college.

To make matters worse, many college students refuse to do much work in college so professors have been lowering standards and inflating grades (McGrath and Spear 1991; Johnson 2003; MacPhail 2019; Schneider and Hutt 2013, 16). But even with extensive amounts of remedial education, most students still drop out of college without ever earning a degree (Brint and Karabel 1989; Beach 2011a; McGrath and Spear 1991; Kirp 2019).

While institutions of higher education in the U.S. have never been exempt from the criticisms of the educational accountability movement, it wasn't until the 1990s that national accountability reforms were mandated for colleges and universities. These accountability efforts focused first on community colleges (Beach 2011a), and only recently in the past two decades, have they been applied to colleges and research universities.

However, reform efforts in higher education have been mostly focused on public, nonselective institutions. These schools receive the most public money and they have had the worst performance metrics, largely because they serve more disadvantaged students and because they receive less funding and have fewer resources than elite schools. Several critics have noted that nonselective colleges and universities in the U.S. have become "dropout factories" (Kirp 2019, 4, 11) because most students who attend these schools drop out and never earn a degree, many leaving with thousands of dollars of student debt.

Early in the 1990s, the National Governors Association (1991) announced that institutions of higher education would be treated no differently than public K–12 schools. The NGA declared, "The public has a right to know what it is getting for its expenditure of tax resources. . . . They have a right to know that their resources are being wisely invested and committed" (3).

Over the next twenty years the public was shocked when academic researchers and government agencies found "little consistent evidence to suggest that either postsecondary education in general or the type of institution attended in particular had a differential effect on knowledge acquisition for different kinds of students" (Pascarella and Terenzini 2005, 134; Keeling and Hersh 2012, 27).

The Spellings Commission (2006) on the Future of Higher Education noted the "lack of useful data and accountability" metrics by colleges and universities, which meant that there was "no solid evidence" for student learning or other outcomes (4, 13). To make matters worse, there were no agreements about what to measure, how to measure, or how to compare the data that could be found. According to the Spellings Commission, no one actually knew which colleges or universities "do a better job than others of not only graduating students but of teaching them what they need to learn" (vii).

The lack of evidence on the outcomes and efficiency of higher education shocked many critics, like Donald Levine, a former dean of the University of Chicago, who complained: "The scandal of higher education in our time is that so little attention gets paid, in institutions that claim to provide an education, to what it is that college educators claim to be providing" (qtd. in Delbanco 2007).

Over the last decade, and for the first time, according to historian and sociologist David Labaree (2010), educational reformers have been trying to create uniform academic standards and measurements, modeled on the No Child Left Behind legislation, that extend from K–12 schools all the way to higher education (Schwartz-Chrismer, Hodge and Saintil 2006; Koretz 2017). Colleges, universities, and community colleges are now spending large amounts to money to collect vast quantities of data in order to evaluate if teachers are doing their jobs, and also to evaluate if "students learn the content of the academic curriculum," just like K–12 schools have had to do since the 1970s (Labaree 2010, 187–88, 206; Burnbaum 2000, 84).

College administrators are trying to get past inflated college course grades so as to develop more accurate measures of student learning, as well as other student outcomes (St. John, Kline and Asker 2001; Brint 2008). And increasingly, college budgets are being tied to accountability data and performance-based targets (Dougherty et al. 2016).

By the end of the 20th century, academic credentials and degrees had arguably become more important than ever before. But most people had come to believe that schools were hopelessly broken. With endless denunciations of schools combined with round after round of new accountability initiatives, Americans finally lost faith in schooling by the 1970s.

Political scientist Aaron Wildavsky (1979) was one of the first social scientists to capture the souring mood. He explained how people believed that

> something basic is bad about public education—or, at least, some very bad things seem to be happening on the sites that our schools occupy. We do not know how educators are performing; even less do we agree on any viable criteria for measuring that performance or lack of it. As far as they can be discovered, practices and policies seem inconsistent, evanescent, wishy-washy. (309)

Professor of education Jack Schneider (2014) pointed out that in 1940 "85 percent of adults polled by George Gallup agreed 'that young people today are getting a better education in school than their parents got.' Three-quarters of a century later, however, the tides had shifted dramatically. Today, only 41 percent of Americans believe schools are improving; half believe them to be worse. In short, the bedrock of the American school system—public faith in a public good—is no longer what it once was" (210). Today, only about 29 percent of Americans express confidence in public schooling

American's declining faith in schooling has also been part of a larger trend of declining public trust in government, other established institutions, and most experts, especially economists (Drucker 1969; Wildavsky 1979; Kellerman 2012, 21, 25; Kellerman 2015, 77; Nichols 2017). People have become more aware of the fact that most government programs and regulations have been both very expensive and "extraordinarily inefficient" in terms of achieving their stated objectives (Sunstein 1997, 322, 128).

There has been a widespread "loss of faith" in professionals and "professional judgment," according to professor of education Donald A. Schon (1983, 4; see also Nichols 2017). Not only do Americans mistrust politicians, but they also mistrust teachers, professors, professionals, and any kind of expert (Schon, 1983, 4, 9; see also Kellerman 2012, 21, 25; Kellerman 2015, 77; Nichols 2017).

By the 1990s, only 17 percent of Americans polled believed that the federal government would "do what is right" most or nearly all of the time (Grossmann and Hopkins 2016, 22). Since the 1990s, the Harris Poll has reported that "the percentage of people reporting at least *some* confidence in the leadership of government, corporations, and Wall Street has plummeted from around 90% to 60%" (qtd. in Pfeffer 2015, 16).

Psychologist Laurence Steinberg (2014) recently argued that "American high-school students' achievement is scandalous. . . . It's not just No Child Left Behind that has failed our adolescents, *it's every single thing we have tried*" (author's emphasis, 144). Many lawmakers and taxpayers are now echoing neoliberal intellectuals, like Milton Friedman and Peter Drucker who asked why should taxpayers continue to support public schooling if educational institutions don't work? (Cohen, Spillane and Peurach 2018, 204).

Almost everyone wants schools to be held accountable by quantitative evidence to prove their value and efficiency, especially when they are funded by public taxes (Brint 2009; Beach 2011a; Hersh and Merrow 2005; Labaree 2017, 181; Buckman 2007; McPherson and Shulenburger 2006; Nettles and Cole 2001; St. John and Parsons 2004). There are "no simple faiths" anymore when it comes to schooling, "only demonstrable results" (Grubb and Lazerson 1988, 58; see also Drucker 1969, 338; Cuban 2013, ch. 3).

From kindergarten to college, demonstrating the effectiveness of schooling has become an urgent social and political problem "that needs to be solved" (Labaree 2017, 194; Berliner and Biddle 1995). This is especially true for educational administrators defending their budgets, which have been increasingly tied to performance-based funding, and for teachers defending their jobs. This urgency has affected all educators, even professors in the ivory towers of prestigious research universities (Berdahl and McConnell 1999, 82; Hersh and Merrow 2005; Hacker and Dreifus, 2010).

However, one important problem that has often been overlooked is that almost all accountability reformers and critics of schooling have held naive beliefs, based mostly on myths, about education and schooling. Most reformers have never actually understood the intricate and delicate process of student learning, and how this process is loosely connected to what a teacher does in the classroom (Cuban 2013).

In order to prove that a problem exists, let alone prognosticate about possible fixes, one would assume that critics of schooling would have presented detailed evidence and precise analysis to substantiate their claims of broken schools. But for a century, accountability reformers have been hurling half-truths, myths, and unsubstantiated accusations at teachers, students, and schools, often based on nothing more than anecdotes, political grievances, or fearful fantasies (Berliner and Biddle 1995, 345).

And because accountability critics don't really understand the problems they attack, these prognosticators often offer simplistic, half-baked remedies that have little chance of working (164). That is why almost every school reform has failed (Elmore and McLaughlin 1988; Tyack and Cuban 1995; Payne 2008; Cuban 2013; Labaree 2012; Koretz 2017).

Students and teachers in the classroom are supposedly at the center of the educational accountability movement. It is here where education emerges from nuanced interactions between teacher and learner. But when it comes to understanding the dynamics of teaching and student learning, valid evidence and understanding have been in short supply. In the late 1960s, Peter Drucker (1969) argued that there are no measurements for education. . . . No one knows whether the students learn anything, let alone how much. We pour money and efforts into education, but what we get out we have to take on trust and hope. . . . We still know very little about learning and teaching. But we do know that what "everybody knows" about learning and teaching is largely wrong. (338–39)

Up until the 1970s, educational researchers never spent much time studying the tenuous connection between teaching and student learning, mostly because there was no funding for such research. Up until then, everyone just assumed that students learned what they were supposed to learn as long as they did what they were told, got good grades, and graduated. Even up until the 21st century, economist and professor of education W. Norton Grubb (1999) explained, teaching has "never been the subject of sustained description or any analysis for what happens, or why it looks as it does" (11).

Over the last thirty years, we now have a lot more evidence on teaching and student learning than ever before (Lortie 2002; Cuban 1993; Cuban 2013; Darling-Hammond 2010; Kelly 2012). Increasingly, educational researchers have studied the interactions between teachers, students, and the curriculum so as to collect data on how education emerges within the "black box" of the classroom, and the even deeper black box of the student's mind (Green 2015, 147).

However, there is still a lot that researchers don't know, especially about the dynamic interactions between teachers, students, and the curriculum in the classroom, how these interactions influence student learning and development, how these interactions are mediated by influences outside of the school, and the long-term consequences of teaching on student's lives and maturation.

On a day-to-day basis, no one really sees what is happening in a classroom because teaching and student learning is "invisible" (Grubb 1999, 11; Lortie 2002; Sizer 1992). Attentive teachers are really the only ones who know what goes on in the classroom, but there is still so much that teachers can't see or don't understand. Even though they are the focus of schooling, students themselves don't see much beyond their limited subjectivity, and they don't fully understand what they do see and experience, as we will explore later in this book and in volume 2 of this series, *The Myths of Measurement and Meritocracy*.

The invisibility of teachers and students is much worse in higher education (Grubb 1999) because there has been almost no collegial or administrative oversight of college instructors, and much less peer-to-peer interaction between teachers, especially for poorly paid adjuncts who comprise the majority of college instructors in the U.S. (Childress 2019; Kezar, Depaola and Scott 2019).

So how exactly have accountability reformers sought to gather data on teaching and learning in order to judge the quality and efficiency of schools? And how successful have such efforts been? To that subject we now turn.

Chapter 3

What Do Grades Measure?

Investigating Grades as an Accountability Metric

For thousands of years, teachers, school administrators, and government officials have measured student performance in the classroom in order to sort and rank students. That has been the purpose of most schools in most cultures throughout human history: sorting and ranking students, not enabling student learning. The oldest method of assessing students has been the direct testing of rote knowledge, practical skill, or moral character.

This work was mostly done by teachers in the classroom through examinations and direct observation. Traditionally, teachers were the experts and students were apprentices or wards. Teachers managed the classroom, designed the curriculum, administered the tests, and promoted students to the next level of learning. But teachers did not give students a certificate or credential signifying processing or expertise. Credentialing was usually done by a political or religious official, or sometimes by a trade guild or other professional organization.

For most of human history in most schools, there were few, if any, immediate administrative intermediaries between teachers and students and the school itself. However, because most schools were embedded in religious or political organizations, there were many layers of administrative bureaucracy governing school practices, but these officials were usually far from the daily activities of most schools.

For manual training, there was often no school and no administrators because the teacher was a craftsman who trained the student as an apprentice in a workshop, which was usually attached to the teacher's home. Master craftsmen provided room and board for the student until the student was skilled enough to go out on his own.

In some cultures, however, like ancient China, there were a lot more immediate forms of administrative bureaucracy effecting the daily practices of schools. China was also the first culture to invent the standardized, high-stakes test to sort and rank students, which was designed and administered by government officials for political purposes.

For millennia most teachers created personalized assessments for students, which determined whether a student passed or failed a course of study. In the classroom, teachers either established rapport with their proteges, so as to coax out the best performance of each individual learner, or teachers would threaten students with punishments, or both. Teachers would usually require students to perform a task or recite memorized texts as the main method of instruction. Sometimes, teachers would ask questions or criticize a student's ideas in order to get that student to display knowledge, skill, or character.

While the teacher-student relationship was very personal, it was also structured within larger social and political institutions, which often guided, or even dictated, the criteria that teachers used to interact with and evaluate students. For example, in Europe for hundreds of years, formal schooling was an official part of the Christian church and teachers were ordained priests or ministers, so educational assessments were also religious tests of obedience, devotion, and piety.

Secular, state-sponsored mass schooling in Europe was invented by Protestants in the German state of Prussia in the 18th century, which later became a model for secular, public schooling for the rest of Europe and the U.S. Schooling in Prussia involved patriotism, supposedly nondenominational religious instruction, political conformity, and military training, often leading to work as a government bureaucrat or a soldier.

For most of history, human cultures have been oral cultures, which meant that most schools did not teach literacy. When literacy was first taught, as in ancient China or medieval Europe, the oral culture and oral skills were usually more important. Thus, educational evaluations were traditionally oral in nature, highly ritualistic, and focused more on the intricacies of the subject bound by the social context than on the abilities of the student (Stray 2005).

In oral cultures, students were trained to reproduce an oral traditional and accompanying social practice, which usually meant memorizing and reciting a ritualized text along with a ritualized behavior, like singing, marching, or taking a test. It wasn't until the development of Protestantism in Europe in the 16th century that literacy was taught as a primary skill for its own sake, so that children could read the Bible directly for devotional purposes (MacCulloch 2004; Ryrie 2017).

In some cultures, academic evaluations were public affairs where the student could be challenged not only by teacher but also by bystanders. In 18th century Europe, for example, many schools used an interactive and competitive performance, which "resembled a multiday academic tournament," where students were evaluated and ranked each day after each performance (Schneider and Hutt 2013, 3; Stray 2005, 79–80).

In the European liberal arts tradition, which informed schooling in the U.S. up until the late 19th century, evaluations were usually public debates between the student and critics, usually the teacher and other instructors, whereby the student had to defend his work against the objections of spectators (Stray 2005, 80; Reese 2013; Hutt and Schneider 2018, 236).

It wasn't until 18th century in Western Europe that examinations transitioned from oral, group performances into individual, written exercises, although examinations stayed mostly oral in Europe and the U.S. up until the late 19th century (Stray 2005). In Europe in the 18th century, numerical grades were introduced as a tool to evaluate student performances, and also to sort students by a hierarchical ranking scheme (Schneider and Hutt 2013, 4; Stray 2005).

At the American college Yale in the early 19th century, for example, students were graded from 4 to 0 with a score of 2 or higher representing a passing grade on an oral examination. Student grades were written down in the "Book of Averages," which was kept secret from students so they wouldn't be too focused on their scores during the semester (Schneider and Hutt 2013, 4).

At William and Mary college, student grades were not based on numbers, but on moral categories, with "first in their respective classes" designated for top students down to "orderly, correct and attentive" for average students, down to "very little improvement" and "learning little or nothing . . . on account of excessive idleness" for the lowest ranking students (4).

In ancient China and Korea, on the other hand, two of the oldest literature cultures in the world, examinations were traditionally written, and the most important examinations were always graded by government officials. Examinations were also standardized so they could be applied to large groups of students who were being processed for government jobs. In East Asia, school examinations were not so much a pedagogical tool as they were a political tool. China invented the standardized written test as a method to evaluate and sort students so they could enter the imperial bureaucracy (Mote 1971; Chaffee 1995; Jacques 2012, 96; Seth 2002).

Western Europe and the U.S. were late to adopt the ancient Chinese technology of written, standardized tests because relatively few students enrolled in Western schools up until the 19th century, and because schooling in Europe was more of a social enterprise focused on training clergy, and later for training sociopolitical elites. In the 18th and 19th centuries, the Prussian state adopted a new system of mass schooling, similar in nature to the ancient Chinese system, but the Prussians introduced a more bureaucratic system of age denominated grades, a broader range of academically and vocationally specialized schools and curriculums, and modern standardized tests, all managed by a special class of school administrators and government officials (Cremin 1980; Kaestle 1983).

By the 19th century, mass schooling was becoming widely practiced in Europe and the U.S. Most schools had adopted "fiscally, socially, and pedagogically efficient" methods to effectively sort and rank large number of new student populations who were being processed to fill civil service positions in newly developed nation states (Labaree 1984, 68). Thus, by the end of the 19th century, government officials in Europe and the U.S. had initiated standardized schools, standardized class rankings, standardized curriculums, standardized testing, and standardized grades, adopting practices very similar to schools developed in ancient China.

By the late 19th century, grades were standard practice in most Western schools. They took the form of "lettered systems, percentage systems and other numerical systems" and were often recorded in an official "report card" that tracked a student's progress through a specific curriculum (Schneider and Hutt 2013, 7). But while examinations and grades have been the primary way that teachers have evaluated, sorted, and promoted students within schools for thousands of years, these practices have always been highly idiosyncratic.

Educational reformers in the late 19th century wanted to create "standardized grading systems" that would enable a "unified and scalable mechanism for measurement and communication" (Schneider and Hutt 2013, 8), but this didn't really happen until the middle of the 20th century. However, some basic grading parameters were institutionalized by the early 20th century. By 1902, according to Francis Parker, a teacher and school administrator who helped initiate the progressive educational movement in the U.S., "parents in general measure school progress of their children by per cents on monthly report cards, by text-books finished, examinations passed, promotions gained" (qtd. in Schneider and Hutt 2013, 10).

Standardized grades have always been plagued by two, often mutually exclusive goals (Hutt and Schneider 2018, 235; Camara, Kimmel, Scheuneman and Sawtell 2003, 4). On the one hand grades represent a teacher's personal assessment of students within the context of the classroom. And as a personal assessment, grades are inherently subjective, idiosyncratic, and infused with both the emotions of the teacher and the behaviors and attitude of the student (Deming 1994, 145; Brackett, Floman, Ashton-James, Cherkasskiy and Salovey 2013).

On the other hand, grades are supposed to communicate objective and precise judgements about a student's character and the quality of their work. And the meaning of this supposedly objective rating is supposed to be transparently clear to a larger audience outside the classroom, and even outside the school.

For over a century, various government officials, school administrators, and reformers have sought the holy grail of "a common standard" that could clearly communicate "fairly exact measurements of ability or of performance" about students across classrooms, across schools, and even across national and international contexts. But educational evaluation and grading have always been, and continue to be, highly arbitrary and idiosyncratic practices that communicate just as much, if not more, about the teacher and the school than the student (Deming 1994, 145; Schneider and Hutt 2013, 11).

Grades are not, and have never been, a valid or objective measure of student learning, student knowledge, or student skill (Deming 1994, 145; Hutt and Schneider 2018; Rosovsky and Hartley 2002). While grades are loosely correlated with many metrics associated with student success, such as emotional intelligence, persistence through schooling, and earning a credential or a degree, grades do not directly or necessarily correlate to a student's actual knowledge or skill (Rosenbaum, Deil-Amen and Person 2006; Rosenbaum 2001).

Grades have always been a very imprecise measurement meant for social comparison and ranking rather than student learning (Deming 1994). Grades, as well as schooling in general, have always been more focused on social or political norms and imperatives, rather than educational ideals or practices, or in the parlance of social sciences, grades, and schooling have been more a product of social signaling practices rather than the development of human capital (Bourdieu [1984] 2010; Swartz 1997; Spence 1974; Hirsch 1976; Caplan 2018).

There are two main educational problems with grades, as with all other accountability metrics. The first problem is their lack of validity. Grades don't measure what they are supposed to measure. Grades don't measure student learning, student knowledge, or student skill. The second problem is the perverse and counterproductive incentives that grades and other accountability measurements produce. These incentives interfere with, and sometimes damage, student learning. Students and faculty are incentivized to get the highest grades, or highest accountability measurements possible, not maximize student learning or student development.

Many researchers have found that educational assessment measures, including grades, "lack validity and reliability" (Gaither, Nedwek and Neal 1994). Grades are supposed to measure student learning and knowledge, but they don't tell us much about these qualities. Thus, grades are fairly useless for educational purposes. According to Robert Birnbaum (2000), professor of higher education and former vice chancellor of the City University of New York, assessment metrics in schools have often been "established because data were available rather than because they reflected something of importance" (Birnbaum 2000, 81; see also Deming 1994; Aguayo 1990).

The practice of teachers assessing students has been around for thousands of years, so teachers have typically passed down traditional techniques because they have been customary, not because they were valid educational tools. Accountability reformers and school administrators in the early 20th century simply assumed that grading was a valid measure of student performance, so they formalized, intensified, and expanded the practice.

While grades don't tell us much, if anything, about student learning, they do help teachers and administrators sort and rank students into neat categories that are useful for social, political, and economic purposes, like processing students for credentials and the labor market.

Before the 20th century, grading was highly "idiosyncratic" and based on teacher's subjective preferences (Hutt and Schneider 2018, 236). Since then, grading has become more formalized and somewhat standardized; however, the practice is still highly subjective. W. Edwards Deming (1994) argued that "a grade is only somebody's (e.g., teacher's) assessment of a pupil's achievement on some arbitrary scale" (146).

It wasn't until the 1960s that educational researchers started to methodically investigate the nature and validity of teacher assessments and numerical grades. Now we understand grading practices better than ever. However, the practice of grading has not gotten any more valid or objective.

Over the last half century, educational researchers have asked some uncomfortable questions. What exactly are grades supposed to be measuring? Do grades measure student learning, test-taking skills, motivation, attendance, effort, sociability, all of the above, or other factors, like genetic inheritance or parental income? If teachers don't know exactly what they are measuring then how do they know if they are measuring anything at all? Or, of equal importance, how do teachers know if they are measuring accurately?

As W. Edwards Deming (1994) put it, a numerical accountability metric "accomplishes nothing" by itself; "only the method is important," not the number (31). If the method of measurement is not accurate, the number is meaningless. Researchers have found that many, if not most, grades are meaningless, especially in terms of student knowledge or learning.

The question of student learning, and the validity of grades as accountability measurements, has gained more salience over the past few decades because educational researchers now know that student achievement is highly correlated with many other variables beyond an individual student's ability or performance. Some of these variables are only indirectly connected to teaching, the classroom, or the school. Some of these variables have nothing to do with schooling directly, like parental wealth or local property values.

Since the 1960s, with the publication of sociologist James Coleman's report on education, researchers have known that schooling contributes relatively little to students' learning or their socio-economic mobility. Educational researcher Jack Schneider (2017) explained that after half a century of research on the ingredients of student academic success, "out-of-school factors account for significantly greater share of a student's academic achievement and attainment than do in-school factors" (90). This is why critics of schooling call grades, and other accountability metrics focused on students and teachers, "a farce" (Deming 1994, 25).

Grading can have perverse effects on the practice of education. Ranking people, according to W. Edwards Deming (1994), with short-term and invalid measurements, "demoralizes" both teachers and students: "Judging people, putting them into slots, does not help them do a better job," especially when the criteria used for judging is out of a student's or teacher's control (26–27).

Policy makers and the general public seem to think that schools are solely responsible for producing a student's success. However, educational researchers have found that teachers and schools account for only 10–15% of the variance in student achievement (Kelly 2012a, 10; Marsh and Dunkin 1992, 170).

This means that most of the variables that cause a student's success in school actually come from outside of the school. When scientists also focus on students' genetic influences, research has found "no statistically significant relationships between the school environment and academic achievement" (Asbury and Plomin 2014, 115). Despite popular beliefs, teachers and schools actually have very little effect on students' academic success.

Let's put this research in perspective. Studies of professional sports have found that coaches account for about 20–30% of the team's performance, although this contribution varies considerably by sport and the outcome being measured (Berry and Fowler 2019). Recent studies have demonstrated that teachers and coaches do have some impact on a student's learning, academic achievement (Konstantopoulos 2012), and noncognitive skills (Jackson 2016). However, the impact of teachers on students in schools, around 10–15%, is considerably less influence than accountability reformers and school administrators, or even teachers, would like to admit (Steinberg 1996, 50).

Interestingly, teachers have much less influence over student achievement than coaches have over a player's athletic achievement. There is one obvious reason why. Coaches are able to select only the best athletes to join a team, and coaches can usually cut a nonperforming player. But teachers usually have no control over which students they will teach. And yet, even though coaches have a significant impact on athletes, they still only account for a small slice of the achievement pie, which has more to do with athletes' personal attributes and environmental conditions.

For several decades, research has shown that the main variables that determine successful learning are found within the students themselves, or in the case of coaching, the athletes themselves (Steinberg 1996, 50). Academic achievement is partly determined by biology and partly by the unique personal experiences of a student, especially their choices and learning experiences, both inside and outside of the classroom. When it comes to learning and academic success, a students' social and economic environments matter just as much, if not more, than schools.

Most learning happens outside of school, especially the most important types of social learning. Students experience most of their formative interactions outside of schools, especially in early childhood (Tomasello 1999, ch. 2). These personal experiences later go on to effect students' performance in schools.

About 85–90% of student achievement in schools is the result of a student's biology combined with their unique personal experiences, which are influenced by their physical and social environments outside of schools. Even at successful charter schools with great teachers, lot of support staff, and an innovative curriculum, a student's personal characteristics and socio-economic background still account for most of their academic achievement (Henig 2008, 123–24).

Three of the most important variables that affect a student's school achievement are environmental. They occur outside of schools and affect children long before they ever set foot in a school. These three variables, which are deeply intertwined, are the social construction of race, parental income and wealth, and parental education, especially the highest level of schooling that parents achieve.

All three of these variables are proxies for a wide range of social and economic resources that can help students learn and succeed in school, such as parenting skills and child development, especially the time parents spend talking to and reading with children, proper nutrition, access to tutors and extracurricular activities, access to top quality schools with the best teachers, and also peer networks (Heckman 2013; Hochschild and Scovronick, 2003; Putnam 2015; Schneider 2017, 21).

Most policy makers and school administrators talk as if schools and teachers have complete control over the student learning process, but most of the important variables that determine student success, especially in terms of learning and graduating, are beyond the control of teachers or schools (Cuban 2013; Payne 2008; Labaree 2012).

If course grades reflect a host of extraneous variables, many of which are beyond the control of teachers, schools, and even students, then how is it fair or accurate to use grades as the primary measure to evaluate student learning, let alone the quality of teaching?

New methods, like "value-added" statistical analysis, seek to control some of these nonschool variables to better understand what specific "value" teachers add to student achievement over the course of a school year, but these methods are controversial because they are not entirely accurate, partly because they still rely on subjective grades as proxy measurements of student learning (Kelly 2012a, 13; Konstantopoulos 2012; Cuban 2013, 140–48; Koretz 2017; Schneider 2017, 59; Atteberry and Mangan 2020).

Some studies have tried to overcome this flaw by using other metrics to measure non-cognitive skills, but these studies do nothing to improve the limited validity of accountability metrics (Bowers 2011; Jackson 2016). As education professor Sean Kelly (2012a) explains, "It is not easy to develop a system of accountability that can *reliably and accurately identify teacher performance* and that the teacher workforce believes is fair and impartial" (17, author's emphasis).

The validity of grades as an accountability tool is fatally compromised by the issues of variability and subjectivity (Camara, Kimmel, Scheuneman and Sawtell 2003, 4). Grades can vary greatly due to the content of the curriculum, the difficulty of assignments, the motivation of students, the previous knowledge of students, and the quality of assessments, as well as between subjects, classrooms, departments, and institutions.

Researchers have found that different teachers in different schools use "different grading standards" (Woodruff and Ziomek 2004, 22), so a grade of A or F in one school does not mean the same thing in another school. As one researcher pointed out, there are "deep philosophical divisions" between teachers over the "meaning and purposes" of grades (Johnson 2003, 3).

Some teachers use relatively objective standards and rubrics to evaluate student learning, some use subjective measures, and some don't assess student learning at all, giving all students an A grade for reaching certain benchmarks or for just showing up to class.

For example, one English professor at California State University gave his students B grades just for coming to class (Kirp 2019, 7). Dr. Oliver Sacks (2015) is another example of subjective grading. He awarded all of his students A grades for uniqueness. For Sacks, subjectivity was the point. As he explained, "My A was not some attempt to affirm a spurious equality but rather an acknowledgment of the uniqueness of each student. I felt that a student could not be reduced to a number or a test, any more than a patient could" (181).

Some instructors assign relatively precise grades to match learning objectives on rubrics. Others use holistic grading. Some grade simply for effort or improvement. Some use grades as a motivational tool to keep students participating. Some don't assign any grades at all. Some, like W. Edwards Deming (1994) gave all their students A grades out of principle, or out of protest against having to assign grades (147).

Most teachers use grades as a "hodgepodge" metric that captures student learning and a host of other non-cognitive skills and behaviors that affect classroom performance (Bowers 2011, 141). For many teachers, "grades frequently reflect" whether a student is "cooperative and trying," not that the student has demonstrated any precise level of learning (Camara, Kimmel, Scheuneman and Sawtell 2003, 4). Go into any classroom and you'll find that most teachers mix and match several of these methods, often inconsistently.

Thus, while grades are supposed to communicate uniform standards that can be used to evaluate and compare students across multiple contexts, most teachers and schools use very different grading standards that make valid comparisons impossible (Woodruff and Ziomek 2004). An A grade in biochemistry at MIT does not mean the same thing as an A grade in pottery at a Bunker Hill Community College, nor does a B in creative writing at one high school mean the same thing as a B in creative writing at the same high school with a different teacher down the hall.

And while many studies have shown that grades do signal academic skills and predict future academic success, especially for high school students going off to college (Rosenbaum 2001; Rosenbaum, Deil-Amen and Person 2006; Pattison, Grodsky and Muller 2013; Gershenson 2018, 11), this correlation does not explain causation, nor does it prove the validity of grades as a measurement of student learning or academic success.

CAMPBELL'S LAW AND THE CORRUPTION OF SCHOOLING

There is a final problem with the validity of grades, and any other measurement used for evaluation. This problem is connected to the institutional use of high-stakes assessment tools that are tied to rewards and punishments for individuals and organizations (Walton 1986; Aguayo 1990; Deming 1994, 31). Administrators often use assessment metrics not just to evaluate and compare student academic success, but also to evaluate teachers and the school as a whole, which is tied to performance funding or other types of rewards and punishment.

As W. Edwards Deming (1994) pointed out, "Common sense tells us to rank children in school (grade them), rank people on the job, rank teams, divisions. . . . Reward the best, punish the worst" (38). This common-sense belief is wrong, especially, as Deming (1994) emphasized, when it comes to schooling where the objectives are supposed to be student learning and personal development (45, 47).

Educational historian Larry Cuban (2013) calls the unfortunate phenomenon of performance ranking "the shotgun marriage of metrics to high-stakes outcomes" (88; see also Koretz 2017). Over the past half century, social scientists have found that there can be many unintended and adverse consequences when high-stake metrics get linked to individual or institutional evaluations tied to punishments and rewards (Walton 1986; Aguayo 1990; Deming 1994; Koretz 2017).

This predicament is often called Campbell's Law (Campbell 1976). The psychologist and social scientist Donald T. Campbell (1976) explained, "The more any quantitative social indicator is used for social decision-making, the more subject it will be to corruption pressures and the more apt it will be to distort and corrupt the social processes it is intended to monitor" (85; see also Deming 1994, 31; Koretz 2017, ch. 4; Muller 2018, 19; Cuban 2013, 88). A British economist put it more bluntly, in what is now called Goodhart's Law: "Any measure used for control is unreliable" (qtd. in Muller 2018, 20).

Why does this happen? In technical terms, performance measures often create what economists call a "moral hazard" (Alston, Eggertsson and North 1996, 61). A moral hazard is created by a policy or regulation that encourages risky or unethical behavior because the risk taker will not have to bear the full consequences of his or her actions. A moral hazard can also happen when it becomes "too costly for one side to a contract to accurately measure the performance of the other side, which creates opportunities for cheating" (61).

Campbell warned that high-stakes accountability measurements, especially standardized tests, would corrupt education because they would become invalid measurement tools that would reward the wrong kind of behaviors. Campbell warned that high-stakes measurements create moral hazards and that catching cheaters would be very difficult. According to Campbell, "When test scores become the goal of the teaching process, they both lose their value as indicators of educational status and distort the educational process in undesirable ways" (qtd. in Koretz 2017, 39).

How have accountability measurements corrupted schools? Take high-stakes standardized testing as a perfect example. Many teachers now spend most of their classroom time teaching to the tests by giving students "tricks" to answer multiple-choice tests or "ways to game the rules used to score the tests" (Koretz 2017, 6, ch. 7; Kempf 2016; Berliner 2011; Nichols and Berliner 2005). Students engage in little, if any, real or useful learning.

Teachers have also been lowering their standards and inflating grades to make students look much more successful academically than they actually are (Koretz 2017, 46–47; Kempf 2016; Berliner 2011; Nichols and Berliner 2005). Some administrators have been manipulating the tested population of students to make sure the lowest performing students don't take high stakes tests (47). Sometimes this has taken the form of transferring low-achieving students to other schools or encouraging them to drop out of school. And most shamefully, some teachers and administrators have been engaging in "outright cheating" by falsifying student achievement scores (6, 46).

To make matters worse, because performance measures cannot be verified, judgments of quality are made on existing data, which can be manipulated, or can be partially or wholly fraudulent. This leads to "adverse selection" of personnel, whereby deceitful agents who post the best performance markers get rewarded, even though their numbers may be questionable, if not fraudulent.

Often, as professor of education Daniel Koretz (2017) pointed out, "the wrong schools and programs" get "rewarded or punished, and the wrong practices may be touted as successful and emulated" (7). The opposite is also true. Honest, hard-working, and effective teachers, with true but lackluster performance measures, are passed over for promotion, criticized, sanctioned, or fired. Such moral hazards create a perverse Darwinian scenario: Survival of the corrupt.

When performance goals are mandated from above without employee input, subordinates are forced to follow meaningless targets without any intrinsic motivation (Koretz 2017; Kempf 2016; Berliner 2011; Nichols and Berliner 2005). Thus, the only incentive for workers to succeed are extrinsic rewards, often money, which leads to shortcuts or fraud to get the monetary reward. Staff begin chasing performance markers for the monetary incentives without knowing about or caring about the fundamental purposes of the organization or the rationale behind accountability goals (Pink, 2009, 48–49).

Thus, when it comes to schools, whenever lawmakers or administrators institute a single, predictable measure of academic performance linked to extrinsic rewards, whether it be for students, teachers, or the whole school, someone somewhere will be cheating to game the system (Nichols and Berliner 2005; Nichols and Berliner 2007, 25–30; Ravitch 2010, 160; Koretz 2017; Kempf 2016; Berliner 2011).

The Atlanta scandal of 2009 is perhaps the best-known recent example. Teachers cheated on behalf of students in order to raise test grades and meet accountability standards (Mitchell 2017; Koretz 2017, 73). But there have been many such instances of educational fraud in the U.S. for decades (Nichols and Berliner, 2007, ch. 2 and ch. 4; Levitt and Dubner 2009, ch. 1; Koretz 2017, ch. 6).

In Chicago in the 1980s, teachers patted themselves on the back for receiving superior or excellent ratings every year, but only 5–6 percent of their students were performing at grade level (Payne 2008, 30). At a high school in Washington D.C., auditors discovered in 2018 that 34% of all diplomas were awarded under false pretenses, many to students who rarely even came to school ("Grad Inflation" 2019).

A 2013 Government Accounting Office report concluded that "officials in 40 states reported allegations of cheating in the past two school years, and officials in 33 states confirmed at least one instance of cheating. Further, 32 states reported that they canceled, invalidated, or nullified test scores as a result of cheating" (qtd. in Koretz 2017, 88). One scholarly study estimated that "serious cases of teacher or administrator cheating on standardized tests occur in a minimum of 4–5 percent of elementary school classrooms annually" (qtd. in Koretz 2017, 88). Psychologist Laurence Steinberg (2014) sardonically quipped, "Fudging data on student performance" has been "the only education strategy that consistently gets results" (144).

Administrators from K–12 schools to universities use grades and the earning of diplomas as the primary markers of institutional success, which in turn gets used by governments, consumers, and media rankings to gauge the quality of educational institutions, which in turn influences school enrollments and funding. It's a positive feedback loop: The higher the grades, the more diplomas; the more diplomas the more high-quality students who enroll; the more students who enroll the more funding and prestige; and so on.

Thus, overreliance on accountability measurements, such as grades and diplomas, have corrupted a lot of schools because so many teachers and administrators have cynically calculated, why go through the trouble of actually teaching students when you can just fudge some numbers and get the same rewards? Thus, grading has become further debased as an accountability metric because so many teachers are lowering their standards and inflating grades.

Nationwide in the U.S., we are seeing the consequences of this cynical calculation. For decades, researchers have documented rampant social promotion and grade inflation in K–12 schools and in most institutions of higher education (Camara, Kimmel, Scheuneman and Sawtell 2003; Nichols and Berliner 2007; Rosovsky and Hartley 2002; Johnson 2003; Sperber 2000; Koretz 2017, ch. 5; Gershenson 2018). Professor of education Daniel Koretz (2017) has argued that grade inflation is not only "pervasive," but also "severe," so much so that he argued that this type of subtle cheating is "central to the failure of American education 'reform'" (54).

In Houston, TX, to take one example, some high schools were officially reporting zero dropouts and 100% of their students planning to attend college, and yet one principal admitted, most of her students "couldn't spell college, let alone attend" (Nichols and Berliner, 2007, 82–83). While Texas pioneered accountability reforms in K–12 education, which became national policy through George W. Bush's landmark No Child Left Behind law, researchers have documented how those reforms led to the corruption of education in Texas. Policy makers and administrators lost sight of education in a push to fudge the numbers so they could secure public accolades, get more funding, and build bigger football stadiums (McNeil 2000; Ravitch 2010, 96–97).

And what is the impact of grade inflation on students? While students no doubt like high grades that they have not academically earned, they are actually harmed a great deal by such educational fraud (Koretz 2017, ch. 5). First of all, students are lulled into a "unwarranted sense of complacency" that stunts their future learning (Gershenson 2018, 10). Students aren't motivated to learn more because they already think they know it all, and when students are confronted with higher academic standards in the future, they are liable to wilt under the pressure and either blame themselves or the teacher for the difficulty of authentic learning.

To make matters worse, grade inflation affects disadvantaged students the most. Poor students and ethnic minorities, who are often segregated in the lowest performing schools in the poorest neighborhoods, often receive the most inflated grades. This is because their teachers often can't teach effectively due to various social, economic, and environmental conditions that obstruct the learning process (Koretz 2017, 67).

And what happens when academically underachieving high school students fail upwards and make it into college, mostly through the open-door community college? They are then confronted with the fact that they are unprepared for academic success (Gershenson 2018, 10).

Most freshmen in the U.S. have to start college with remedial classes because they were not adequately prepared in high school (Melguizo and Ngo 2020). Most of these remedial college students eventually drop out of college, for various reasons, never earning a degree, and often with substantial amounts of student debt (Kirp 2019). However, many are also just passed through the college system with inflated grades and little learning.

For decades, researchers have documented the lowering of academic standards and the inflation of grades at institutions of higher education all across the U.S. (Lucas 1994, 290–94; Nichols and Berliner 2005; Nichols and Berliner 2007; Ravitch 2010; Koretz 2017; Kempf 2016; Berliner 2011; Nichols 2017; Johnson 2003), especially at community colleges (McGrath and Spear 1991; Eaton 1994; Beach 2011a). Statistics professor Valen E. Johnson (2003) argues that grade inflation in college has become "a national, if not international, problem" (v).

Many researchers have found that students learn little, if anything, in college (Arum and Roksa 2011; Perkins 1985), and yet somehow most college students are passing their courses, with over 25% earning A grades (Sperber 2000, 119). To take one example at Duke University in the late 1990s, A grades accounted for over 45% of all grades, B grades accounted for around 40%, while C+ grades or lower accounted for less than 15% (Johnson 2003, 2). An astonishing 85% of Duke students were receiving A and B grades, which is certainly not what you would expect from a normal distribution pattern if students were being evaluated based on objective measures of knowledge or skill.

For most college professors, inflating grades and keeping students and administrators happy has been much easier and more rewarding than trying to keep high standards. As English professor Murray Sperber (2000) sarcastically explained,

> A professor who wants to grade hard embarks upon a very time-consuming and labor-intensive course of action: Throughout the semester, he or she must respond accurately and at length to the work of every student in the class. Moreover, to fight grade inflation, a faculty member must be prepared to answer complaints from students and their parents, inquiries from department heads and deans, requests to appear before various student committees, and even lawsuits. Predictably, few faculty members at research universities choose to go down this lonesome road. (120)

Recently an anonymous professor at an elite institution lamented, "To save themselves and their careers, many of my colleagues have decided that it is no longer worth it to uphold high expectations in the classroom. 'Lower your standards,' they advise new colleagues. 'The fight isn't worth it, and the administration won't back you up if you try'" (Anonymous 2019, para. 5).

Not only does grade inflation weaken standards, reward mediocrity, and encourage minimal effort, high grades seem to be inversely correlated with the main measure of student success in college, which is graduating with a degree. Currently, over 80 percent of all college students in the U.S. are earning A or B grades (Nichols 2017, 95; Johnson 2003), but less than half of students who enroll in higher education will actually graduate with a bachelor's degree (Beach 2011a; Rosenbaum, Deil-Amen and Person 2006; Rosenbaum 2001, 57).

As college admissions rose, graduation rates declined from the 1970s to the 1990s because standards remained relatively high. But as admissions continued to rise, graduation rates began to increase starting in the 1990s (Denning, Eide and Warnick 2019). Students were no more academically prepared, in fact, they were less prepared, so the increase in completion rates was mostly likely due to political and administrative pressure. New accountability reforms most likely contributed to a lowering of standards, especially at nonselective public colleges and universities.

Many college administrators no doubt believed that increased graduation rates were a positive development. However, lowering standards and inflating grades to increase accountability targets does not help students or society. In fact, it makes social and economic inequality worse, a topic which is discussed in the companion volume to this book, *The Myths of Measurement and Meritocracy*.

Educational researchers Ernest T. Pascarella and Patrick T. Terenzini (2005) pointed out that "only about 50 percent of all college graduates appear to be functioning at the most proficient levels of prose, document, or quantitative literacy" (145), which means that all those inflated A and B grades aren't translating into actual knowledge or skill, putting many college graduates at a disadvantage when they enter the labor market, and putting many firms at risk because they have hired ignorant and incompetent college graduates (Chen 2013).

Educational researcher Jack Schneider (2017) has shown how standardized tests and letter grades are "incomplete measures of school quality," at best (49). A grade "reduce[s] the complexity of education into something simple": a number or a letter (53). But this virtue is also a vice. Accountability tools, such as tests and grades, are "limited in what they reveal and are not entirely fair across racial, ethnic, and economic lines. They take up too much instructional time and overlook most of what we value in schools" (24).

While it is certainly reasonable for teachers to use tests and grades to evaluate and measure student learning, these tools are not easy to implement in a valid way that promotes student learning and development. As Schneider (2017) points out, "measuring something as complicated as student learning" is very difficult, even under the best of circumstances, but almost impossible when it has to be done in a "uniform and cost-restricted way" (50).

But the biggest problem with grades and standardized tests is that they are rarely designed and used for educational purposes. Their primary purpose of these instruments, as W. Edwards Deming (1994) and others have pointed out, is sorting and ranking students to create a competition where some students are winners and most are losers (148–49).

When used for the social and political purpose of sorting and ranking students and teachers, accountability metrics, like grades, are designed to "produce artificial scarcity" so as to create a class of winners who get the gold stars, which results in "humiliation" for the majority of students or teachers with middling to lower ranks (148). This type of environment creates fear and is not conducive to learning or high performance (Kohn 1992; Edmondson 2019).

Schooling doesn't have to be this way. Deming (1994) rightfully point out, "there is no scarcity of good pupils" and there is no scarcity of good teachers (148). Competition has nothing inherently to do with education (Kohn 1992). In fact, competition usually inhibits student learning.

Given the right organizational priorities with the right leadership, the right staff, and adequate resources, almost all teachers and students could be successful in one way or another, in the various meaningful ways that academic and personal success might be defined and measured by an educator. But most politicians, school reformers, school administrators, and even many teachers and students don't actually care about education.

It seems that most people want students to play school and do what their told, rather than learn or develop as human beings. Schools want to force students e to compete for scarce badges of social prestige rather than engage in the difficult and laborious process of education. And that is a primary reason why educational reforms repeatedly fail. Reformers never challenge the myths of schooling, the self-defeating bureaucracy of schooling, or the corrosive competition of socially ranking students rather than educating them.

Chapter 4

Education as a Social Practice

The Foundations of Teaching and Learning

What if accountability reformers really wanted to promote better teaching so as to enable more student learning? What would this look like? In order to get some answers, we would first need to ask a different set of questions: What is education and how is it different than schooling? Only then would we be able to explore how teachers and students can best practice education through specific teaching and learning techniques.

Most people confuse the concepts of education and schooling because they think education is simply a matter of common sense, tradition, and personal experience—you know it when you see it. But this inarticulate common sense has never gotten reformers very far. So, in order to understand, let alone accurately evaluate, the *means* and *ends* of education, we first need to have a proper conception of what education entails. That is what we will explore in this chapter.

The sociologist of education Willard Waller (1932) pointed out almost a century ago that the practice of education is not an objective, technical endeavor. It is hard to see the practice of education and verify that it is really happening. This predicament has made it hard for scientists to research education, especially the practices of teaching and learning. How do you know if a teacher is actually teaching or just pretending to teach? Most people can't tell the difference. And how do you know if a student is actually learning or just pretending to learn by playing school? Again, most people can't tell the difference.

Education is a subjective, social practice that is tied to our complex nature as human beings. There is no easy or quick way to study education, as Waller (1932) pointed out in his groundbreaking book on teaching. He wrote, "Children and teachers are not disembodied intelligences, not instructing machines and learning machines, but whole human beings tied together in a complex maze of social interconnections" (1).

Over the past century, educational researchers like Waller have taken many steps to demystify the "complex maze" of education, and these scholars have made a lot of progress, which we will selectively review in this chapter and the next. But this information has not gotten to the general public or policy makers, nor is it well understood by school administrators or even many teachers.

Conceptually knowing about education, while it is the important first step, will only get us so far in actually reforming schools. While we need to know what real education entails, we also need the political, economic, and social will to put real education into practice, which is no easy task.

EDUCATION IS A SOCIAL PRACTICE

In order to understand education, we first need to understand some basic things about the complex topic of human nature. At the most fundamental level of biology, human beings are programmed by DNA inside of genes. Genes are the "fundamental unit of heredity," the "basic unit of all biological information," and the basic "building block" of all biological life, according to Dr. Siddhartha Mukherjee (2016, 9). Our genome is "a set of genetic instructions" that determines how our bodies and brains develop (11).

Our genes give shape to our appearance, our personality, and our abilities, similar to how a recipe determines the outcome of a meal. But a recipe does not make a meal all by itself. A chef needs to enact a recipe with specific ingredients and tools by cooking in a kitchen. Without the cook's actions and decisions, the meal would never get made. Also, without the necessary ingredients and tools to cook, which are found in the environment, the meal would never get made.

Likewise, as individuals, we make our own decisions and take our own actions by utilizing ingredients and tools in our environment in order to create our own destiny. But our thoughts and actions are shaped by our genome, which is either enabled or constrained by the social and physical environments in which we live (Pinker 2002; Mitchell 2018; Mukherjee 2016; Richerson and Boyd 2005, 9).

While we can make our own decisions, we are never entirely free to think or do what we want. We are conditioned by our culture. And for most of human history, individuals were more or less "prisoners" of their social and physical environments (Hagel, Brown and Davison 2010, 100; Acemoglu and Robinson 2019). We interact with and imitate the people around us. We also interact with various social norms and traditions, which influence how we think and act by giving us a predetermined set of choices, which almost everyone follows (Richerson and Boyd 2005; Tomasello 1999; Tomasello 2016, 86, 97; Searle 1995).

Most of us most of the time stick to a script that was written for us by our culture. As psychologist Jerome Bruner (1983) explained, when we think or act, we never "go it alone" (3–4). Instead, we "commit ourselves to institutions and traditions" created by other people, often over centuries, which we then use as "tool kits" to achieve our own objectives as we live our lives (Bruner 1983, 3–4; see also Pinker 2002).

These cultural tools have a double edge. They "both amplify our powers and lock us in our path," according to Bruner (1983, 3–4). When we choose to follow one custom or cultural tradition, we are also choosing to ignore other ways of living. We begin to lock ourselves along a path of repetitive thought and behavior (Burke 1969a; Burke 1969b). We are creatures of habit, which is largely an energy saving technique so we don't get overloaded with thousands of choices, trying to reinvent the wheel every day (Clear 2018).

Culture is like a well-worn road full of people. The road enables us to get where we are going, but it also determines where and how we travel by limiting our choices. We all have to follow the road, and we have to follow the customary "rules of the road," which includes cooperating with all the other people going their own separate ways. Culture makes our lives a lot easier and more meaningful, but it also restricts our freedom because we have to coordinate with everyone else in our society.

While our genes and our culture largely program the default settings of who we are, we still have *some* freedom to act and think in new ways, which philosophers and social scientists call individual "agency" (Ortner 2006). Management professor Peter M. Senge ([1990] 2006) pointed out that "the nature of structure in human systems is subtle because we are part of the structure. This means we often have the power to alter structures within which we are operating," although we often "do not perceive that power" (44). While we are supposed to follow the rules of the road in our culture, we can choose *how* we follow these rules, we can choose to *change* these rules, we can choose to *break* these rules, or we can ditch the road, and the rules of the road, entirely in order to make our own path.

Or, to go back to the metaphor of cooking, while our biological recipe has been largely determined by our DNA and genes, the environment mediates how the meal will actually turn out in terms of the quality of the ingredients, the resources in the kitchen, and the decisions we have available as the cook. While we have some freedom to cook our meal as we see fit, we are rarely in control of the ingredients, the kitchen, or the recipe. While we have some degree of freedom, we are always constrained in our agency, both by our biology and by our physical and social environment, which includes the traditions and institutions of our culture, which are the existing ideas and practices that structure and predetermine our way of life (Burke 1969a; Hobsbawm and Ranger 1983; Tomasello 1999; Richerson and Boyd 2005).

Most people like to follow the crowd and participate in social traditions because it is easier, safer, and often more fun than trying something new because you are participating with everyone else. Inventing something new is often a difficult and lonely path. In order to do something new, you would first need to know what others have done, and then think about what novel idea or act might be possible. Then you have to take a big risk by actually doing something new and potentially failing to make it work.

As members of a culture, we are all taught to follow a similar script, which we call tradition, the "right way of doing things" around here (Tomasello 2016, 86). Traditions are past down from one generation to the next. Historian Gerda Lerner (1986) explained tradition as authoritative beliefs and practices that are assumed to be "universal, God-given, or natural, hence immutable. Thus, it need not be questioned. What has survived, survived because it was the best; it follows that it should stay that way" (16). Most of us, most of the time, stick to the traditional script. It's just easier.

And yet, humans are not the mindless robots that 19th century psychologists once theorized. We do not mindlessly follow "the crowd." We are all unique individuals who come together in multiple ways in many different places and times, so when we participate in a cultural tradition, we reproduce it and re-create it in a slightly different way each time, and sometimes in dramatically different ways (Tomasello 1999, 39; Ortner 2006, 133; Rogoff 1990, 197; Rogoff 2003, ch. 2). Culture is not "transmitted," developmental psychologist Barbara Rogoff (1990) argued. Instead, culture is "transformed in the process of appropriation" (197; see also Rogoff 2003, ch. 2).

Traditions might seem permanent, but they are in the process of changing all the time. Think about every time you make your favorite meal in the kitchen. It always turns out slightly different even though you are always following the same basic recipe.

As psychologist Michael Tomasello (2014) pointed out, "there are thousands of human cultures, and each of them has conventionalized, normativized, and institutionalized a particular set of cultural and communicative practices" (32). Each cultural tradition in every society on the planet is being reproduced every day.Each culture is also changing in countless ways every day because every individual creatively engages in, and protests against, the way of life that they were born into (Sen 2006, ch. 2).

Social scientists explain human society as a set of structured "social practices" or "cultural practices" in which "individuals coordinate with the entire cultural group via collectively known cultural conventions, norms, and institutions" (Tomasello 2014, 81; Tomasello 2016, 86). But culture is more than just coordination and conventions. The philosopher Alasdair MacIntyre (1981) emphasized the importance of values in human culture, what he called "standards of excellence" (175). Values constitute our social norms and inspire our traditions (see also Beach 2018, ch. 16; Engelke 2018, ch. 3).

MacIntyre (1981) defined a social practice as "any coherent and complex form of socially established cooperative human activity through which goods internal to that form of activity are realized in the course of trying to achieve those *standards of excellence* which are appropriate to, and partially definitive of, that form of activity, with the result that human powers to *achieve excellence*, and human conceptions of the ends and goods involved, are systematically extended" (emphasis added, 175). We don't just participate in our culture to survive. We want to live *more abundantly* by pursuing the *good life* and trying to *achieve excellence*. Culture enables our ideals, which make life worth living.

Philosopher David Bridges (2006) explained the three conditions that must be met in order to define a particular human activity as a social practice. First, the activity must be "socially established, cooperative, coherent, and complex" (371). Second, there are values or "goods internal to that form of activity, which are realized through standards of excellence that are partially definitive of that activity" (371). Third, the activity must involve and embody human standards of excellence, defined in terms of "human goodness or virtue," which are realized through participating in the practice (372). Thus, social practices not only serve useful purposes by helping us survive, they also imbue our lives with meaning and identity, which motivates us to live more fully.

Over time, social practices become institutions with rules and rituals, and these cultural institutions become an important part of our cultural identity: "This is the way 'we' have always done things; it is part of who 'we' are" (Tomasello 2014, 83; see also Hobsbawm and Ranger 1983; Tomasello 1999). When we participate in an institution, like a school or a church, according to anthropologist Sherry B. Ortner (2006), we are playing a "serious game" with formal rules, which can include how to talk, how to act, how to dress, how to eat, and how to interact with other people (129; see also Tomasello 2014, 91; North 1990, 3).

Each culture has its own set of serious games that everyone has to play, and each game has its own set of rules. It's not enough to pay a game, you must follow the rules—otherwise, there will be serious consequences, which can include corporal punishment or even death. While most people actively participate in traditional games, some people choose to break the rules or not to play, and some dare to invent their own new games. We often call these daring people revolutionaries or innovators because they break away from tradition to invent a new way of life, often at great cost to themselves and their followers.

Culture is complex social tapestry of symbolic meanings and structured behavior that we are born into and which shapes us and molds us our whole lives (Geertz 1973). We are woven into the fabric of our culture from the time that we are born (Rogoff 1990; Rogoff 2003). And yet, we also have the power as individuals to accept and reject our cultural conditioning. We participate, but sometimes we resist. We follow the script, but sometimes we innovate.

As political scientist and philosopher Michael J. Sandel (1996) explained, "Even as we think and act as freely choosing, independent selves, we find ourselves implicated in a network of dependencies we did not choose and increasingly reject" (202). Being human is a long process of negotiated enculturation, teaching and being taught, learning and sharing, knowing and doing, accepting and rejecting. As children we are brought up as "apprentices" in our various cultures as we "learn from observing and participating" with adults and with peers as they engage in the serious business of life (Rogoff 1990, 7, 16; Rogoff 2003, ch. 8; Gardner [1995] 2011b, 131).

Thus, in order to understand the concept of education, we must first understand that education is an activity, a way of living, and not just an idea (Geertz 1973; Rogoff 1990; Rogoff 2003). As educational philosophers have pointed out for over a century, "human life begins in doing, not in thinking" (Smeyers and Burbules 2006, 440–42). Education is tied to the biological foundations of being human. We are social and cultural animals.

Thus, education is a social practice infused with meaning, morality, and *standards of excellence*. And in most cultures, education is also an institution. Education is usually a serious game, and as such, it must be *played*, not just *known*, and rules must be followed. Education necessarily involves the combination of knowledge and action, often in coordination with other people (Rogoff 1990; Rogoff 2003). Education is usually a team game, although not always.

Different from the institution of schooling, education is a structured way of life infused with specific standards of excellence that focus on teaching and learning for the purpose of creating and using knowledge as a cultural tool to make life better and more meaningful for both the individual and the culture at large. Education can happen any place and any time where a person decides to learn something new or to practice previous learning.

Now, let us contrast this definition of education with the conventional, common sense notion of schooling. For the past two hundred years, when people think of education, they believe that it consists of students following the commands of a teacher in a school. This is a fairly recent conception, which became popularized in the 19th century, although the practice of schooling was invented by the ancient Chinese almost two thousand years ago.

When most people think of schooling, they think of teachers talking or commanding. Then they think of students memorizing the abstract knowledge that comes out of the teacher's mouth, or out of the textbook the teacher has selected. And what do students do with this memorized information? They take standardized tests with formulaic questions that require predetermined answers. This testing activity takes place in a room called a classroom in a special building called a school.

Each student's performance is then graded and ranked via standardized measurements called grades. These grades are recorded on official pieces of paper that determine the cultural value of each student. After spending a specific amount of time in the school accumulating these grades, a student then earns a magic piece of paper called a diploma or degree. This certificate allows the student to apply for a job so they can earn money. Importantly, many people believe that learning stops once a student earns a credential and leaves school.

The tradition described above is the definition of *schooling*, not education. While education can take place in a school, often it does not. Schooling does not require, nor usually reward, education. The social practice of schooling was invented by the ancient Chinese, as is discussed in volume two of this series. Schooling is a political and economic institution that was created by and for elites. Schooling creates and preserves elite privilege, and it helps maintain political and economic inequality.

The social practice of education is something much, much older and more important than schooling. The practice of education is an inherent part of our biology and the evolutionary development of our species (Tomasello 1999; Mercier and Sperber 2017, 69). It is also the foundation of all cultures and the glue that holds our societies together through time (Geertz 1973; Rogoff 1990; Rogoff 2003). Education is one of the most important biological and social traits that makes us characteristically human, although we share some basic elements of teaching and learning with other species (Tomasello 1999; de Wall 2016).

When we practice education, we learn not just *to know*, but more importantly, we learn *to act*—to skillfully and meaningfully participate in our culture by playing serious games with others to achieve standards of excellence. We are created by our culture through the practice of education. Sometimes education entails learning to participate in and reproduce the established traditions that everyone has always followed. But while we are taught to be like others in our culture, we also have the ability to change and re-create our culture, and ourselves, through our novel thoughts and actions, which is a different form of education.

We can learn through our novel exploration, experience, and creativity (Dewey [1916] 1966); Robinson 2001). While education is often focused on the reproduction of traditional cultural practices (Richerson and Boyd 2005; Rogoff 1990; Rogoff 2003), the philosophers Smeyers and Burbules (2006) argue that "interpretation and adaptation" are always possible (447), even when we are following traditional rules. When we enact traditional social practices, we always have the possibility of changing them, either intentionally or accidentally, or we can choose to simply break with tradition and try something new (Rogoff 1990; Rogoff 2003).

The Russian novelist Lev Nikolayevitch Tolstoy (Schon 1983, 65), the Russian psychologist Lev Vygotsky (1978), the American philosopher John Dewey ([1916] 1966), and the American social-psychologist George Herbert Mead ([1934] 1965), as well as many others, all helped pioneer our understanding of education as a transformative social practice that develops individual human beings and also reproduces and re-creates human cultures (Rogoff 1990, 13; Rogoff 2003; Wertsch 1991; Cole 1996). Both Tolstoy and Dewey were active teachers who designed their own schools and they both theorized on the revolutionary political implications of learning by doing (Gutmann 1987; Ryan 1995).

Dewey ([1916] 1966) explained that education should be understood as part of the natural biological and social development of all human beings, and as such, it is a process of discovery, personal growth, and social being, which should have "no end beyond itself" (50), although Dewey liked to frame the ultimate purpose of education as a tool to solve all of life's problems and thereby grow as individuals and as a species (Ryan 1995, 28).

If education is treated as a narrow means to a specific end, according to Dewey, especially if that end is dictated by powerful adults and has little relevance to the student, then personal development and deep learning will not happen. Under these conditions, the student will not want to learn. This is the ironic and tragic predicament of all schooling when it is used as a controlling social, political, or economic program. Schooling often stifles or destroys our motivation to learn.

Students lose motivation when they are forced to learn things that they do not want to learn in a place they do not want to be. Authentic and lasting learning requires "salience" (Rumbaugh and Washburn 2003, 204–34). Students must be interested and willing participants in the learning process. When students are powerless pawns being forced to learn things they are not interested in, they will not learn much, if anything, or they will learn the wrong lessons, like nothing matters, or just do whatever you're told.

This is especially true if a once vibrant social practice is stripped down into empty, abstract concepts in order to be regurgitated on a lifeless exam because a teacher forced you to do it. When education degenerates into a useless ritual, complex social practices become reduced to the meaningless custom called *schooling* or institutionalization. Playing school or being institutionalized is an oppressive, authoritarian ritual forced onto students for political and economic purposes, not educational ends.

Dewey ([1916] 1966) explained that "education is not an affair of 'telling' and being told, but an active and constructive process" (38). Education is the process of living a meaningful life through participating in authentic social practices in order to become a member of a culture (Konner 2010, 118; Tomasello 1999; Tomasello 2014). When a people become *educated*, they "acquire a habit of learning" and a way of being that situates them within a culture and enables them to become a contributing member (Dewey [1916] 1966), 45; see also Rogoff 1990; Rogoff 2003; Wertsch 1991; Cole 1996).

Countless scholars in many disciplines across the arts and sciences have endorsed this theory of education as an active and constructive process. Knowledge is not a thing and it cannot be measured, let alone assigned a ranking grade. Business professor Peter Drucker (1969) distinguished information from knowledge, noting that only when information is applied through action "does it become knowledge. Knowledge, like electricity or money, is a form of energy that exists only when doing work" (269).

Psychologist Michael Tomasello (2014) once explained that "*being* smart counts for nothing if it does not lead to *acting* smart" (author's emphasis, 7). The proof of education is not test scores, grades, or credentials. When people become authentically educated, they do not need a magic piece of paper to certify it. The confirmation of education lies in a person's success in reaching goals, meaningful relationships with others, and fidelity to personal values.

Education and learning are not fixed, known qualities that a teacher gives a student. Education and learning are unknown potentials that a student draws from within and demonstrates through action. As psychologist Anders Ericsson explains, "Learning isn't a way of reaching one's potential but rather a way of developing it" (Ericsson and Pool 2016, xx).

Learning leads to "personal mastery," a "lifelong discipline" of learning and achieving, as management professor Peter M. Senge explained it ([1990] 2006, 132). Learning produces knowledge and skill, which are byproducts of our physical and mental participation in the activity we are trying to learn. But our bodies must be in motion if we are truly going to learn (Tversky 2019). Simply seeing new knowledge or skills doesn't do much. We need to see and then act on our perception.

"Acting changes the brain," according to psychologist Barbara Tversky (2019, 17). The more we do, the more we learn and the more we know, and the more we know, the more we can do and the more we can learn. It's a virtuous circle. There is no biologically or culturally predetermined upper limit to what we can accomplish. Ericsson (2016) argues, "There is no point at which performance maxes out and additional practice does not lead to further improvement" (113).

When we engage in the process of education and truly learn, we discover and internalize a set of social practices through doing the same activities over and over again, usually over many years, making the practice part of our identity and behavioral repertoire. Learning is an emerging and continuous activity (Senge [1990] 2006). It is not a means to an end. When it comes to authentic learning, there are no rules or set boundaries on *where* we can learn, the *process* of learning, or *how much* we can learn (Ericsson and Pool 2016). In many ways, our abilities as humans are *limitless*, in the sense that we are not born with prescribed biological or social limits to how much we can learn or do.

Human leaning is not an isolated, individual phenomenon, as some cognitive psychologists like to think. And it definitely cannot be reduced to the memorization of abstract information for standardized, written tests (Brown, et al. 2014). Instead, learning is a socially constituted way of living and growing through interacting with other people, our environment, and our self (Tomasello 1999; Gopnik 2016; Mercier and Sperber 2017; Wenger 1998; Tversky 2019).

We learn how to think and act through participating in particular communities, which makes our life meaningful by giving us identity and purpose (Wenger 1998, 141, 226). The Latin origin of the word "competition" meant to "strive together" (Senge [1990] 2006, 138). When we compete, in this ideal sense of the word, we strive with other people to become the best version of ourselves that we can be. We strive as a team. We learn the best with others.

We are born to learn and we spend our whole life learning as we develop and struggle to survive. Students learn simple, fundamental cultural practices from their parents and then more advanced practices in K–12 schooling. When students move on to higher education, they focus on specialized knowledge and skills produced and practiced by academic disciplines and professions.

In higher education, students learn how to participate in formal learning institutions focused on specific methods for researching, thinking, constructing knowledge, and skillfully acting to solve real-world problems. But learning does not end in school. Students move into the labor market and spend their lives learning as they participate in various organizations in order to make a living and contribute to their culture (Senge [1990] 2006).

When we are engaged in authentic learning, we learn new information about the world we live in, especially through the books and lectures of experienced experts who have specific skills that they practice. But more importantly, we also learn more about who we are, or who we want to become. We identify with the thoughts, actions, and personas of other people who have studied what we are studying—other people who have done what we want to do. We learn to do a social activity by first watching others who have mastered the activity through a process called "observational learning" or "imitation" (Tomasello 1999; Richerson and Boyd 2005, 108–112; Konner 2010, 597; Tversky 2019, 22).

Imitation is a form of learning that is coded deep in our biological nature. While all primates can "emulate" a teacher or other kind of leader, most primates don't understand the details or purposes of the activity they are emulating, even our closest relative, the chimpanzee, with whom we share 97% of our DNA (Diamond 1992; Richerson and Boyd 2005, 110). Only humans can truly "imitate" a teacher by learning how to do an activity with skillful detail and purpose, which leads to the uniquely human ability to creatively repurpose and adapt imitative knowledge for a new end (Richerson and Boyd 2005, 110; Konner 2010, 597).

After we have watched and imitated an experienced expert, we then practice that activity on our own or with a group, often with the guidance of a teacher or coach. "Seeing is mapped to doing and doing is mapped to seeing. . . . Our experience performing specific actions modulate[s] our perception of the same actions performed by others," according the Barbara Tversky (2019, 22). Why do we need a teacher to watch us practice? A teacher demonstrates the proper practice of a skill so we can contrast their actions against our own as we learn to accomplish the same skill.

A teacher also helps push us so that we can find the limits of our own ability and eventually exceed those limits in order to grow (Ericsson and Pool 2016). A teacher also gives us feedback so we can practice a skill properly, and also to see and understand our mistakes, and thereby, learn to perform the task better (Senge [1990] 2006, 74). The more we practice and learn, the more we can see and understand when we watch others perform the same task, which enhances our own practice and performance (Tversky 2019, 23).

But no matter what a teacher does, or what the class as a whole does, each student has to do their own learning and understanding all on their own (Cuban 2013, 51). Students need to be able to "make sense" of cultural practices as they learn to do them, not just memorize abstract facts or ritualized actions (Fitzgerald and Palincsar 2019, 227). Sense making involves asking questions, making connections between knowledge or skills, being able to solve problems, and building skills through increasing levels of difficulty (236–370).

The Russian philosopher and literary critic Mikhail Bakhtin (1981) perceptively understood sense-making as it pertained to language. He wrote, "The word in language is half someone else's. It becomes 'one's own' only when the speaker populates it with his own intention, his own accent, when he appropriates the word, adapting it to his own semantic and expressive intention" (293).

As we become educated, we learn how to become ourselves by knowing who we are and what we are capable of, which in large part entails learning how to become a contributing part of our culture through the practice of our newly acquired knowledge and skills (Tomasello 1999). And as we develop our personal and cultural identity, which includes learning how to contribute to our society, we bring meaning and purpose to our lives and the lives of others—we learn to live a *good* life.

LEARNING IS WHAT THE STUDENT DOES

The psychologists Hugo Mercier and Dan Sperber (2017) point out that as human beings we all have a "biologically inherited disposition to learn"—a "learning instinct" (69, 291; see also Pinker 1997; Sternberg 1988; Stanovich 2009; Gopnik and Meltzoff 1997; Gopnik 2016; Brown et al. 2014). The philosopher of science Karl Popper explained this instinct as a "cognitive hunger," a "need for knowledge" about ourselves and the world we live in (Berkson and Wettersten 1984, 12).

Learning arises naturally through any experience where an individual consciously engages in an activity or social practice (Tomasello 1999; Gopnik 2016). We instinctively learn from interacting with our environment through a process called "emulation learning," which simply involves being aware of and adapting to our physical or social environment to achieve a goal (Tomasello 1999, 29). The "most powerful" learning experiences, which we retain the longest, management professor Peter M. Senge ([1990] 2006) explained, "come from direct experience," from "trial and error," and from "taking an action and seeing the consequences for that action" (23).

Because learning is a natural instinct, it is not something that can be controlled or forced by teachers or managers, although it can be motivated and guided (Brackett 2019, 126). As Etienne Wenger (1998) has argued, "Learning happens, design or no design . . . it can only be designed for—that is, facilitated or frustrated" by the teachers or schools (225). Students either want or do not want to be educated. There is little a teacher can do to make learning happen.

We learn through personal experience and participation in social practices. If we do not participate then we will not learn. If we are forced to participate against our will, then we will not learn. Or at least, we will not remember what we were forced to learn. Or we will learn the wrong lesson, like hating the person who forced us to learn.

Developmental psychologist and evolutionary anthropologist Michael Tomasello (1999) explained that there are three basic types of human learning (5). The first is imitative leaning, which is biologically based and comes natural to all human beings, especially while we are young. The second is instructed learning, which takes place whenever an experienced and knowledgeable person, usually an adult, explains conceptual knowledge or a physical practice to a student. We all have a basic instinctual drive to teach as well as to learn (Konner, 2010, 587). One scientist went too far as to suggest that our species should be designated *Homo docens*, or "teaching person," rather than *Homo sapiens* (587).

Finally, there is collaborative learning, which is done when we work together with other people to accomplish a goal or to solve a problem (Senge [1990] 2006). As Tomasello (1999) explained, "social learning comes from the 'bottom up,' as ignorant or unskilled individuals seek to become more knowledgeable or skilled," while "teaching comes from the 'top down,' as knowledgeable or skilled individuals seek to impart knowledge or skills to others" (33; see also Richerson and Boyd 2005). Humans are the only species to have developed the top-down, direct instruction of students, which, as Tomasello argued, is "one of the most significant dimensions of human culture" (80; see also Konner 2010, 586).

While teachers enable all three kinds of learning, especially instructed learning, teachers do not *cause* student learning, nor are teachers responsible for student learning. The educational psychologist Edward L. Thorndike explained "the commonest error" of inexperienced teachers, which is an erroneous belief widely propagated by clueless school administrators and cynical politicians: You cannot "expect pupils to know what they have been told ... telling is not teaching ... telling a fact to a child may not cure his ignorance of it any more than patting him will cure his scarlet fever" (qtd. in Olson and Hergenhahn 2009, 67).

Political scientists Arthur Lupia and Mathew D. McCubbins (2000) emphasized that "people choose what and when to learn" (51). Authentic learning cannot be controlled or forced. A teacher is just a knowledgeable and skillful person who consciously and deliberately plans for student learning by "design[ing] social infrastructures that foster learning" (Wegner 1998, 229; Bain 2004, 49). Teachers can artificially organize relevant and meaningful educational activities through which students *can learn*, but only if students actively engage in the social practice as a willing participant (Ryan and Stiller 1991; Duckworth 2016, 137; Steinberg 1996, 15).

Thus, Lupia and McCubbins (2000) emphasize, "learning requires persuasion" (48). A teacher always has to persuade a student to pay attention to, and actively participate in, a lesson. Learning requires a student's interest and trust (48). This also means that a student has the freedom to *not* learn, an ability which most students exercise liberally every day.

So, what is the purpose of a teacher or coach? Instructors have four main jobs. First, teachers must design a challenging curriculum with explicit and clear learning objectives. Teachers need to set up a stimulating learning environment to help students reach their learning goals. This is what psychologists and social scientists have called "guided learning" and "designed learning," which draws upon, but is different from, our natural inquisitiveness and our natural ability to teach ourselves through imitation and experience (Konner 2010, 659; Rogoff 1990, 86, 90).

A teacher needs to design learning goals that are specific and attainable, but also challenging and demanding. Learning goals need to be SMART: Specific, Measurable, Actionable, Relevant, and Timely (Heath and Heath 2010, 82). For more advanced learners, teachers need to explain how and why goals are set, so that students can take part in their own goal setting, with the objective being that students eventually create their own learning goals with little or no oversight from the teacher.

In order to reach learning goals, a teacher provides "scaffolding" so that new knowledge is presented piece by piece, which is an interconnected approach that can be behaviorally demonstrated, not just verbalized conceptually (Olson and Hergenhahn 2009, 115; Rogoff 1990, 94, 104, 106). Scaffolding prevents students from becoming overwhelmed with too much information. It allows students to take on more responsibility over the learning process as they gain more mastery (Konner 2010, 257, 586, 597; Rogoff 1990, 86, 106).

A teacher also needs to progressively make the learning process more and more difficult, what Vygotsky called the "zone of proximal development," in order to maximize student learning by pushing students towards, and past, their limits (qtd. in Rogoff 1990, 14; Rogoff 2003, 50; see also Tyler 1949; Wood, Bruner and Ross 1976; Steinberg 2014, 35).

Second, teachers must demonstrate and explain a new practice so that students can see it and understand how it is done (Olson and Hergenhahn 2009, 115). This is often called "social learning" (Tomasello 1999; Konner 2010, 513, 586). Observing an expert practice a skill is very important because most professionals "know more than they can say," according to professor of education Donald A. Schon (1983, viii, 51). Skilled practitioners have a lot of "tacit" knowledge, which they can't always explain, but they can show (Polanyi 1962; Polanyi 1967; Schon 1983, 49–53; Senge [1990] 2006, 153; Isaacs 1999, 51; Hagel, Brown and Davison 2010).

Because tacit knowledge cannot easily be explained, it is important for experts to demonstrate their knowledge rather than try to explain it verbally. Professor Ken Bain (2004) explains that effective teachers should be able to practice what they preach. Teachers should be able to perform "intellectually, physically, or emotionally what they expect from their students" (16). Watching a teacher perform a skill can often be much more instructive than simply hearing a verbal explanation. This is one of the most important distinctions between a teacher and a lecturer.

It's important for teachers to be able to demonstrate a practice because after observing a teacher, students must then practice the same skill in order to produce their own learning. Students thereby develop mastery as they copy, negotiate, create, and control the activity through deliberate and repeated activity (Tomasello 1999; Duckworth 2016, 137; Bain 2004, 52; Ericsson and Pool 2016).

Children are biologically engineered to be "imitation machines," especially during the crucial ages from one to three when their brains are especially impressionable (Tomasello 1999, 52; Konner 2010, 514, 586). A teacher facilitates "guided participation" so as to not only demonstrate the knowledge and skills that a student will learn, but also to guide the student through how to practice this new learning so the student can develop mastery on their own (Rogoff 1990, 8; Rogoff 2003).

Learning involves not just cognition, but also "embodied cognition" (Godfrey-Smith 2016, 74; Tomasello 1999). The body needs to learn as well as the brain. The human brain learns information and concepts, while the body learns how to use this information to act skillfully in order to accomplish a goal.

We are automatically learning whenever we engage in an activity, any activity, as long as we are aware of what we are doing and reflect on our actions during and after the activity. To attain mastery, it is important not only to do the activity we are trying to learn, but also to think about and reflect on what we have done. We also need to reflect on what we need to do in the future in order to perform the task better.

When a student leaves the practice field, learning does not stop. A successful student needs to engage in "mental simulation" when away from the activity by thinking through the activity, practicing it in their mind, and reflecting how that activity should be done correctly (Heath and Heath 2007, 212). When we engage in mental simulation, our body actually activates "the same modules of the brain that are evoked in real physical activity" (212).

One meta-analysis of thirty-five scientific studies on mental simulation, which included 3,214 participants, found that "mental practice alone—sitting quietly, without moving, and picturing yourself performing a task successfully from start to finish—improves performance significantly" (Heath and Heath 2007, 213). It appears that overall, "mental practice alone" produces about "two thirds of the benefits of actual physical practice" (213).

Even though learning is laborious, difficult, and often painful, learning physiologically changes the brain and the body so that eventually the learning and doing process gets faster, easier, and less painful. The new activity gradually becomes, as Dr. Oliver Sacks (2007) explained, "so ingrained in the nervous system as to be almost second nature, no longer in need of conscious effort or decision" (37; see also Steinberg 2014, 36).

The third duty of a teacher is to help students deliberately practice their skills by guiding students through the learning process and by motivating them emotionally (Deci and Flaste 1995, 92). It is especially important to give students critical feedback to reinforce properly demonstrated knowledge and to point out errors (Olson and Hergenhahn 2009, 116; Steinberg 2014, 35; Oettingen 2014, 112). This is also one of the most important distinctions between a teacher and a lecturer. Teachers actually help students practice.

In order to gain mastery of a skill, it's not enough to simply practice over and over again. Such simple repetition does not lead to successful learning and skill development. While simple repetition results in some learning, it is superficial, it does not last long, and it only leads to a basic level of "acceptable" performance, which marks one as an amateur (Ericsson and Pool 2016, 13). In order to master a skill and become an expert, a student needs to stretch beyond their limits by engaging in deliberate and "purposeful" practice, which entails focusing on specific goals to reach and learning from mistakes (14–17; see also Yin, Wang, Evans and Wang 2019; Wang, Jones and Wang 2019; Olson and Hergenhahn 2009, 209, 222; Senge [1990] 2006, 74–75).

It is also important to space out practice with ample periods of rest and reflection in-between (Olson and Hergenhahn 2009, 132). As law professor Daniel Markovits (2019) explained, "Quantity and quality both matter for education: practice doesn't make perfect; perfect practice makes perfect" (123). Most of us need help setting realistic goals, understanding our mistakes, measuring our progress, and staying motivated through this difficult process. These are some of the most important services that a teacher provides.

It's important to remember that purposeful practice leading to mastery is very difficult, time consuming, and painful, which is why most students don't really like learning, either in school or out of school. True learning is hard work. It takes not only effort, but "laborious preparation" (Pfeffer 2010, 45). Business professor Jeffrey Pfeffer (2010) argues that success takes both "will," the "drive to take on big challenges," and also "skill," the "capabilities required to turn ambition into accomplishment" (43).

Success also requires failing—a lot of failing! Why is failing so important? Because we have the ability to learn from our failure (Olson and Hergenhahn 2009, 291; Senge [1990] 2006, 143; Heath and Heath 2010, 162; Edmondson 2012, 154, ch. 5). Hedge Fund manager and entrepreneur Ray Dalio (2017) has argued that "the key to success lies in knowing how to both strive for a lot and fail well" (xii). Dalio (2017) learned to see failures as "opportunities to learn and improve" (61).

Failure can be "awful-tasting medicine," Dalio (2017) acknowledged, but it teaches "lessons that intimately" helps us to succeed, the most important of which is learning how to "take advantage of [our] strengths while compensating for [our] weaknesses" (37). Every successful person in every imaginable field of performance has failed a lot and learned to "fail well" (37). But learning from failure is very hard for most people to do (Edmondson 2012, 77). That is why most people want to hear inspirational and uplifting stories of successful people, rather than the rough truth of failure (Pfeffer 2015, 49).

In a recent scientific study trying to quantify the dynamics of success, one group of researchers argued, "The more you fail, the more you learn, and the better you perform" (Yin, Wang, Evans and Wang 2019, 4; see also Wang, Jones and Wang 2019; Pfeffer 2010, 41). One of the most important things a good teacher can spot is what psychologists call "meaningful failures" (Rumbaugh and Washburn 2003, 169). This kind of failure is either a specific concept or skill that is difficult for a student to learn, or it can refer to student learning that diverges from the pedagogical plan of the teacher (Rumbaugh and Washburn 2003, 169; Senge [1990] 2006, 143). In both cases, a teacher needs to help the student understand how and why the failure happened so that it will not happen again, or so it will happen less.

Authentic learning is often very uncomfortable for students because they are stretching beyond their limits. This often results in failure and confusion, which causes a lot of stress and pain. But the successful student will push through the pain and discomfort in order to learn from failure and in order to perform better on the next attempt.

Teachers have to inspire and push students outside their comfort zone so that students learn how to take risks and grow as human beings. As management consultant and former CEO Keith Ferrazzi and colleague Tahl Raz (2014) argued, "The choice isn't between success and failure; it's between choosing risk and striving for greatness, or risking nothing and being certain of mediocrity" (52).

Psychologists and evolutionary biologists have found that not only is stress necessary for our optimal development, but stress can actually be good for us physically and mentally (McGonigal 2015; Konner 2010, 540; Sapolsky 2004). Anthropologist Melvin Konner (2010) explained, "The notion that a goal for children should be the absence of stress contradicts all we know about evolution and the logic of our own experience" (540; see also Olson and Hergenhahn 2009, 291). He points out that while some kind of stress is harmful ("distress"), other kinds of stress are beneficial ("eustress") because it brings about "effective coping" and "enhanced long-term function," in addition to developing new knowledge and skill (540; see also Sapolsky 2004; McGonigal 2015).

Psychologist Kelly McGonigal (2015) argues that "stress is a biological state designed to help you learn from experience" by helping you adapt to "whatever challenges you face" (59). Even negative, traumatic stress can ultimately be a rewarding learning opportunity if approached with grit (Duckworth 2016) and a "growth mindset" (Rendon 2015; Dweck 2006; Goleman 2013).

As business professor Andy Molinsky (2016) argues, "if you're not outside your comfort zone, you won't learn anything" (para. 1). Stretching our limits and learning from painful experience and failure takes a lot of effort and time. It often requires many years of dedicated and deliberate practice to learn a skill, and many more years after that to master it.

During that time, you have to sacrifice a lot of other activities in order to devote yourself to learning and mastering your new skill, which means that successful students need concentration, dedication, and stamina to persevere in the face of adversity (Ericsson and Pool 2016, 93; Richerson and Boyd 2005, 73). If a skill is not continually practiced and actively reinforced then that knowledge will gradually be forgotten and replaced by some other knowledge or skill (Olson and Hergenhahn 2009, 213).

The talented few who learn to master a craft are not born that way. Neither did they get lucky. And they certainly didn't buy their talent. Experts have grit (Duckworth 2016) and they also have a "rage to master," as psychologist Scott Barry Kaufman explained, which he defined as "an intense and sustained drive for excellence" (Kaufman and Gregoire 2015, 18).

The novelist Stephen King once explained his craft as all hard work: "If you don't want to work your ass off, you have no business trying to write well" (144). Experts push themselves hard for many years in order to perfect their craft. No teacher can produce competence, let alone mastery. A teacher can only help a student who is willing to do the hard work and put in the time.

As psychologist Anders Ericsson explained, "If you never push yourself beyond your comfort zone, you will never improve" (Ericsson and Pool 2016, 18; Olson and Hergenhahn 2009, 291). When a student engages in purposeful practice, one of the most important skills successful students develop is the ability to "acknowledge their failures, even to embrace them, and to explore and learn from them," an attitude that creates and sustains long-lasting learning and personal growth (Bain 2012, 100, 120–21; Duckworth 2016).

And luckily, the more students push themselves through deliberate practice, the more their brains and bodies physiologically change, which makes further learning and growing much easier (Ericsson and Pool 2016, 40; Heath and Heath 2010, 175).

The final role of the teacher is to be a role model for the student. Not only should a teacher be able to practice what they preach, but teachers should also embody a set of moral values and behavioral norms that demonstrate goodness, as it is culturally defined by the context in which the teacher and students operate. As management professor and former business executive Andy Grove (2015) once explained, "nothing leads as well as example" (52). Leaders must be able to "visibly" embody not only their personal values, but also the values of the enterprise that they lead (52).

Now this last role might seem kind of quaint to many people in the 21st century. Some might even find this principle controversial because of the contested nature of values in multicultural organizations, especially in schools. But for thousands of years teachers in every culture have always been considered moral exemplars, as they represent not only knowledgeable leaders, but also the moral norms of a culture. One of the main jobs of a teacher has always been to transmit values and moral norms.

In fact, it is impossible to properly teach without referencing and demonstrating moral values of some kind. Values and behavioral norms are essential motivational tools, for both teacher and student. We must believe that our beliefs and actions have value in order to dedicate ourselves to the mastery of a skill. Thus, it's important for teachers to impart the values of mastery, knowledge, and dedicated practice, which only accomplished experts can really understand and demonstrate. A teacher can't just declare knowledge and skill, they must *be* knowledgeable and skillful, and they must be able to *demonstrate* hard work and dedication to a craft.

There is also an enigmatic quality to mastery that only experienced experts can understand and impart to novices. Mastery is always momentary. Success is often over far too quick. And failure is ever-present, lurking at the edges of every action. We are always less than perfect, even experts, so there is always opportunity for criticism and learning.

The process of expertise, of practice and perfecting, is a never-ending struggle (Lewis 2014, 7). We simply choose to stop at some point, often because we get too tired or bored to compete any more. Everyone has to accept the tragic condition of human limitations, especially our mortality. Whatever expertise we achieve in this life will one day decline once we stop pushing our self to perfection. Our expertise will gradually weaken and dissolve as our bodies and minds break down with age.

Too often educational administrators, policy makers, and even many teachers, make education seem quick and easy, as if it is a simple product that you can pass on to a student through a quick lecture, which they can write down on a piece of paper and regurgitate on a test. Even worse, many policy makers and administrators talk about education as if it were a product that can simply be bought and transferred to customer, like a can of baked beans.

According to human capital theory or the financial transaction version of schooling, a teacher is nothing more than a salesman or saleswoman who effortlessly and immediately delivers a standardized product to a student. This factory conception of schooling makes the teacher the most important factor in schooling because students are just passive recipients of knowledge (Cuban 2013, 12; Freire 1970/2003). This myth leads people to believe that teachers are in control of students' learning. This is utter nonsense. As educational historian Larry Cuban (2013) pointed out, "Teachers cannot carry alone the total responsibility for their students' well-being and achievement" (12).

Take athletic coaches, for example. Few believe that coaches are in control of athletes on the field, let alone controlling the outcome of a game. While coaches are held partially responsible for the outcome of a match, the main responsibility falls to the athletes who are on the field playing the game.

If anything, teachers have much less control than coaches. Athletes are carefully selected and trained, and only the best make it on the team, and only the very best make it on the field. More importantly, athletes want to be on the field competing. Athletes choose to play and compete. Most students are forced to go to school. Thus, most students are not prepared or motivated for success, and many resent their powerlessness at being forced to learn, which makes a teacher's job very difficult, if not impossible.

When it comes to learning, and gaining skill and knowledge, it is the student who is in control of the process, not the teacher. The student must choose to learn. No teacher can force learning, let alone control it. In order for learning and personal development to happen, a student needs to not only "use or lose" the practice they are learning, but also to "use and improve" their knowledge and skill through deliberate practice (Steinberg 2014, 34–35).

As professor of education Ralph W. Tyler (1949) noted over a half century ago, "Learning takes place through the active behavior of the student; it is what he does that he learns, not what the teacher does" (63; see also Ryan and Stiller 1991). Thus, for thousands of years, one of the hardest tasks of a teacher has been to get students to be actively involved in their own education. Philosopher Martha C. Nussbaum (1997) explained how teachers must "confront the passivity of the pupil, challenging the mind to take charge of its own thought" (28).

Teachers do *influence*, but never produce or control, student learning. Teachers play an important part in the learning process, but not the central role. The philosopher John Dewey was one of the first to formally explain that true teaching required a fundamental "equality" between student and teacher (Ryan 1995, 71).

Teachers embody the knowledge and skills of the particular social practices they are trying to impart to students, which they expertly demonstrate through pedagogical activities that will be conducive to student learning. Once a teacher has enacted and performed their knowledge and skill, then they move into their primary role, which is to help facilitate the learning of students by motivating, guiding, and critiquing students' practice.

But there is no guarantee that students will learn, let alone master an activity. Students have to *want* to learn. And, they have to *work* at learning. This is why little learning takes place in schools, and why most students never attain mastery of the skills that they do learn. Most students don't want to work at learning. Learning is hard work.

And furthermore, for teaching to be truly effective, the teacher must also be willing to learn. Not only does the teacher need to learn how to explain the curriculum clearly and effectively, but the teacher also needs to learn from the student. Perhaps most importantly and profoundly, the teacher learns how the student learns or isn't learning. This is a special kind of knowledge, which enables the teacher to facilitate the learning process by motivating the student to strive for higher levels of learning.

As professor Constance Weaver (2007) has explained, effective teaching demands "ongoing experimentation" (154) in the classroom, especially new ways to try to motivate students so they *want* to learn. Teachers must continually monitor, assess, and revise the curriculum and the educational environment in order meet the diverse and ever-changing needs of individual students.

Professor of education Mary M. Kennedy (2019) argues that "teachers are essentially tinkerers" (157) because the classroom dynamic is constantly changing every day, every month, and every year. Effective teaching is only ever measured in small gains each day, and these gains never last. Weaver (2007) went on to add, "Adaptations will usually be necessary as well as desirable" because "we must all to some extent reinvent the wheel of effective instruction" for every class (154–55). Not only is every student different, but every group of students is different, plus young people are constantly growing and changing every day.

Thus, there are no silver bullets with teaching. There are no certainties that a teacher will ever be effective, and even when they are effective, it doesn't last long. All teachers fail to get some students to learn each day. When practicing education, a teacher's work is never done.

With education, there is only hard work, dedication, and experimentation, which require not only knowledge and skill, but also vision and creative flexibility. For those who have actually studied education or practiced teaching, they know, as professor of education Sean Kelly (2012a) explained, "being a teacher is one of the most demanding of all careers . . . the task is so very difficult" (27).

TEACHING IS A COMPLICATED AND UNPREDICTABLE ENDEAVOR

School administrators need to carefully design and implement accountability measures in order to promote effective teaching and authentic student learning, as opposed to promoting mindless ceremonial rituals and the playing of school. But the problem with accountability initiatives is that student learning, as Theodore R. Sizer (1992) documented, is a "complicated and unpredictable business" that is hard to understand, and even harder to measure (2; see also Muller 2018).

This is why most schools have always rewarded the ritualized "telling" of information and the useless activity of taking standardized tests over the much more difficult practices of teaching and learning (Sizer 1992, 2, 109; Keeling and Hersh 2012). Playing school is easier to see and measure, so accountability metrics almost always focus on the lifeless detritus of schooling, rather than the messy activity of teaching or learning.

Like other social practices designed to change human behavior, teaching is a "process of thinking and feeling as well as overt action," as Ralph W. Tyler (1949) described in one of the foundational studies of teaching (5–6). Like social work, teaching is an unpredictable and low-yield endeavor. Sociologist Peter Rossi (1987) documented this difficult predicament and he formulated his "iron law of evaluation," which states, "The expected value of any net impact assessment of any social program is zero" (3–20; Labaree 2010, 107–8).

And it's not just social programs. Business professor Peter Drucker (1969) warned aspiring business managers, "the probability that any activity or program will fail is always greater than the probability that it will turn out successful, let alone that it will accomplish what it was designed to do" (195).

Changing the mind and behavior of a human being is a challenging business, in part because every human being is different. This is especially true with adolescents who don't want to participate in the serious games that adults want them to play. As every teacher knows, there are low rates of success with education, even under optimal conditions. Professor of education and sociology Gerald Grant (1988) documented how "teaching is often lonely, repetitive work in which a teacher is incessantly asked to give and ends the day emotionally drained" (140–41).

But rarely do teachers labor under the best of circumstances. Under less-than-optimal conditions, success is often impossible. Some students simply do not want to change their minds or their behavior, and there is nothing a teacher or a school can do.

Take for example health education. The U.S. government has spent many millions of dollars trying to educate teens on the subjects of drugs, alcohol, obesity, and sex.. For decades, adults have been trying to change adolescent behavior so teens would avoid dangerous risks, harming themselves and society (Steinberg 2014, 103). When you look at the statistics over the last forty years, there has been almost no change in teen behavior. The only exception has been a decrease in teen smoking, but smoking has gone down nationwide for all Americans, so it is not an indication that health education programs are actually working.

Psychologist Laurence Steinberg (2014) argues, "Clearly, whatever we are doing has not been very effective. . . . Most systematic research on health education indicates that even the best programs are successful at changing adolescents' knowledge but not in altering their behavior" (103–4). And it's not just adolescents.

Researchers have found that employee wellness programs don't produce any real benefits to either consumers or health care providers (Song and Baicker, 2019). These programs aren't producing any measurable health benefits for consumers and they don't reduce a worker's health care costs. Giving people information or other resources does not often produce results. It is very difficult to change human behavior, at any age.

With this in mind, teachers should never be held directly responsible for student learning. Most of the learning that students do (or fail to do) is largely outside of the control of teachers (Kennedy 2019, 141), especially given that most student learning takes place outside the classroom and is affected by many people besides the teacher, especially by parents and peers (Richerson and Boyd 2005, 36, 156). As Ralph W. Tyler (1949) explained, learning is "the interaction between the learner and the external conditions in the environment to which he can react. Learning takes place through the active behavior of the student; it is what he does that he learns, not what the teacher does" (63).

While teachers play an important role in facilitating student learning, students must do the actual learning on their own. A good teacher sets high standards and expects "more" from every student (Bain 2004, 17), but many students resent good teaching because they don't want to learn (Brint 2009, 18). And yet, a teacher interacts with a student for only a single year, for K–12 teachers, or for three to four months, for college instructors, so how much real learning can take place in such a short amount of time?

But no matter what the teacher does in this short period of time, each student must continually practice their skill and learn from their mistakes for years in order to reach competency and expertise (Ericsson et al. 1993; Ericsson 2003; Ericsson and Pool 2016; Duckworth 2016). This rarely happens. Thus, as historian of education David F. Labaree (2010) has pointed out, "the connection between teaching and learning is indirect at best" (134, 136).

When you examine the historical records, as Labaree (2010) has explained, the institution of schooling has "never really been about learning" (3, 74, 206; 2017, 53). Schools have always offered "low academic standards" in order to accommodate students who are not prepared or motivated to learn, even institutions of higher education (Labaree 2010, 3, 74, 206).

Professor of education Linda Darling-Hammond (2010) has argued that schools with "high-quality curriculum" in the U.S. have been "relatively rare" (54). Historian Laurence Veysey, describing early 20th century college norms, stated: "It would only slightly caricature the situation to conclude that the most important function of the American professor lay in posing requirements sufficiently difficult to give college graduates a sense of pride, yet not so demanding as to deny the degree to anyone who pledged four years of his parents' resources and his own time in residence at an academic institution" (qtd. in Labaree 2017, 93).

For many students in the U.S., especially in high schools and colleges, "the content doesn't really matter" because students don't really want to learn it (Labaree 2017, 93). So, what is a teacher supposed to do? The answer for most, sadly, is to play school instead of educate. And accountability metrics reinforce and reward this useless and destructive compromise.

Chapter 5

Nurture and Nature

The Ecology of Student Learning (On What Teachers Can and Cannot Do . . .)

Good teaching does matter. Teachers can help increase and improve a student's learning, academic achievement, and noncognitive skills (Kelly 2012b; Konstantopoulos 2012; Darling-Hammond 2010; Jackson 2016). But when it comes to documenting the educational process, especially for accountability measures, the practices of teaching and learning are difficult to see, and even more difficult to measure.

David F. Labaree (2010) warns, "We are unable to measure adequately the effects that teachers have on students. The things we can measure most precisely about teacher effects are the most trivial" (152). This puts the whole notion of accountability measurements on thin ice, that is, if one even cares about scientific validity, which most policy makers and school administrators don't.

Despite the challenge of validity, educational researchers have documented over the last couple decades some of the basic principles that good teachers practice in order to maximize student learning (Chickering and Gamson 1991; Kuh 2001; Bain 2004; Pascarella and Terenzini 2005, 115). However, the impact of good teaching should not be overstated. As we already discussed, teachers provide only the "scaffolding" for student learning (Wood, Bruner and Ross 1976), not the actual learning, which is solely the student's responsibility (Gopnik 2016, 176).

There is also evidence that scaffolding is unnecessary for some types of learning, like acquiring language (Konner 2010, 257). Pascarella and Terenzini (2005) have documented the many types of teaching behaviors that are correlated with student learning in higher education, but they warn that there is almost no evidence to prove that teacher behaviors "cause student learning" (117; see also Konstantopoulos 2012, 35; Asbury and Plomin 2014, 115).

In fact, some researchers who account for genetic influences have found "no statistically significant relationships between the school environment and academic achievement," and as some of these researchers have pointed out, "it wasn't for lack of trying" (Asbury and Plomin 2014, 115). Educational research shows clearly that learning is what the student does, not what the teacher does. Students bear most of the responsibility for learning, or not learning. Teachers play only a small part. Parents and peers are more important for student learning than teachers or schools.

Actually, students' peers play the most important role in the process of socialization and learning, an insight psychologist Jean Piaget pointed out back in 1926 (Rogoff 1990, 147). The main problem with student achievement is, as we have already discussed, many if not most students don't want to learn in schools, primarily because adolescent peer cultures do not value learning or academics.

Therefore, policy makers and school administrators need to rethink the whole notion of educational accountability that is focused on teachers and schools. Some educational researchers have perceptively noted that "school quality may be a red herring that has little or no causal relationship with academic achievement" (Asbury and Plomin 2014, 137). Thus, we need to rethink the notion of accountability. Who should be held accountable to whom and why?

MEASURING WHAT MATTERS?

There is a growing body of research that shows that education does not have the same effect on all students, and not all students learn when they are in school (Pascarella and Terenzini 2005, 134–150). This means that the success of even the best teachers is uneven, at best. Good teaching practices simply do not work with all types of students, as Remmers, Martin, and Elliot (1949) established nearly 70 years ago, nor do effective teaching techniques work all of the time (Pascarella and Terenzini 2005, 115). Seifert et al. (2014) recently documented that good teaching practices are "moderated" by the personal traits, knowledge, and previous experiences of students (555–557). Thus, "high impact/good practices may not constitute a broadly applicable 'silver bullet' for effective" education (555–557).

In their report, these researchers concluded: "The cognitive skills and orientations toward inquiry and continued learning students bring with them at college entry are the most powerful predictors of their skills and orientations at the end of their fourth year, suggesting the postsecondary environment and the experiences that occur within this milieu are less influential in contributing to student learning" (555–556). As we have already discussed, schools don't do much to increase student learning, and there is a growing body of scientific research to prove it.

Take for example the many studies that have confirmed the limited impact that college teachers have on various student skills (Arum and Roksa 2011; Roksa et al. 2017; Pascarella and Terenzini 2005; Perkins 1985). Educational researchers have known since at least 1966, with James S. Coleman's seminal study *Equality of Educational Opportunity*, that the social environments outside of schools, especially parents and peers, have the largest effect on student learning and their future socioeconomic success.

Wealthy and educated parents read to their children more, speak to their children more, are more openly affectionate, more consistent with discipline, and spend a lot more money on extracurricular educational activities for their children than middle-class or lower-class parents, which enables wealthy children to acquire greater cognitive and non-cognitive skills before they even reach the 1st grade (Markovits 2019, 120–24).

Teachers and schools have relatively little influence on academic achievement (Kelly 2012a, 10; Marsh and Dunkin 1992, 170; Berry and Fowler 2019). Even high-quality private schools don't produce much student learning, despite popular myths to the contrary (Ravitch 2000, 415; Steinberg 1996, 50; Schneider 2017, 81). In a recent study, professors of education Robert C. Pianta and Arya Ansari (2018) found that controlling for sociodemographic factors, like race and class, "all of the advantages of private school education were eliminated" (419).

As Jerry Z. Muller (2018) has pointed out, the late 20th century accountability movement has heaped a lot of blame upon teachers and schools "for their failure to accomplish what may be beyond their reach" (100). Thus, it is important for the educational community and policy makers to remember what historian, and former teacher and superintendent, Larry Cuban (1993) documented in his monumental study of teaching over the last century: "By learning more about the instructional quark that is the classroom, policymakers, practitioners, and scholars can come to have reasonable expectations about what teachers can and cannot do, what schools can be held accountable for and what is beyond their reach" (12).

David F. Labaree (2004) has pointed out that teaching is "an enormously difficult job that looks easy" (39; Labaree 2000). When you get past the superficial appearances of playing school, as Labaree (2010) points out, teaching is an act of "irreducible complexity" with "no established set of professional practices that have been proven to work independent of the particular actors involved and the particular time and place of the action" (151). As Waller (1932) perceptively pointed out almost a century ago, "rarely is it perfectly clear whether a teacher has succeeded or failed in his [or her] work. More often it is a debatable question" (29). Accountability measures have obscured our understanding of education, as Muller perceptively explained, because we can't really measure what matters and "not everything that can be measured can be improved" (101).

Teaching is a social practice permeated, and often undermined, by "chronic uncertainty," not least because every student is different and each person reacts differently to the same instruction (Labaree 2004, 151; Labaree 2000; Koretz 2017, 130). The psychologist Erik Erikson (1958) once described his patients as "a universe of one" because each was so different (72). Likewise, every student is a universe of one with their own unique wants and needs.

Developmental psychologist and philosopher Alison Gopnik (2016) explained how teaching is a lot like parenting. Both are difficult interpersonal relationships that require constant time and attention. They are full of "paradoxes" and "trade-offs," which defy easy understanding, let alone measurement or assessment (16). Instructing a child or young adult is a difficult and uncertain process with no guarantees, other than kids will always try to get what they want, even when they don't know clearly what they want.

Gopnik argued that education, like parenting, is "risky and often heartbreaking" (19) because the mind and behavior of a student cannot be predicted or controlled. In education, outcomes are always tentative, indefinite, and uncertain.

It is often impossible to see, let alone accurately measure, effective teaching. And what can be measured often does not tell us much about the act of teaching or the true reality of the learner's experience. It is profoundly ironic and interesting that one of the greatest and most insightful philosophers of education, John Dewey, was a terrible teacher. One of his biographers noted that Dewey was "a poor lecturer, unable to look his audience in the eye, unequipped with rhetorical tricks, and cursed with a dull, drawling delivery" (Ryan 1995, 220).

The brilliant economist Douglas C. North, who won the Nobel Prize in 1993, was also a terrible teacher, but he still reached some of his students intensely. According to one graduate student, who helped North teach economic history, "He is not terribly well organized in his presentation, in fact, sometimes he is very confusing. But he tosses out a wealth of ideas and suggestions, which often baffle the students. But he gets them to think" (Hughes 1982, 8).

Another student recalled, "North will argue about any thesis, and his personality can disturb the composure of almost anyone" (Hughes 1982, 8). This student went on to say, "It was the nature of the argument, his unwillingness to be convinced, and your gnawing fear that somehow North would turn out to be right after all" (7).

Many, perhaps even most, of Dewey's and North's students left class perplexed, and probably bored and dissatisfied. But some students were deeply and immeasurably taught a great deal. And these two men were able to reach and teach millions more through their published work, which is another inspiring form of teaching.

Some of North's students, especially his graduate students, not only learned a great deal, but were driven by North's arguments and compelled by his personality—so much so that they became distinguished scholars and teachers themselves, and they would later praise their former teacher many decades later for all he had done for them (Ransom, Sutch and Walton 1982).

Take another example, the philosopher Stanley Cavell. A couple of years ago, one of his students wrote a loving obituary about his former professor. He said, "According to the awful assessment measures of our awful times, [Cavell] was probably a lousy teacher, and yet he was the most exciting classroom presence I've ever experienced" (Benfey 2018, 1).

The profundity of learning is usually not something that can be seen because the effect of education often manifests itself long after the learning experience has ended—sometimes years or even decades later. Writing about himself in the third person, Henry Adams ([1918] 1961) quite elegantly explained the mystery of this process long ago: "Henry Adams had failed to acquire any useful education. . . . He must educate himself over again. . . . His course had led him through oceans of ignorance; he had tumbled from one ocean into another till he had learned to swim. . . . A teacher affects eternity; he can never tell where his influence stops" (195, 243, 300).

YOU DON'T NEED TEACHERS TO LEARN

In focusing on teaching effectiveness and school quality, there is important truth that often gets left out of the debate over school accountability, especially about the evaluation of teachers. While student learning can be facilitated with a great teacher, learning can also happen with a horrible teacher, or with no teacher at all. And learning doesn't have to happen in schools.

In fact, most learning happens outside of schools, often when we aren't even expecting to learn. Real learning can happen anytime and anywhere, without any teachers or textbooks or schools, because learning is a natural part of our human nature (Konner 2010, 350–51). We are born with the instinct to learn (Pinker 1997; Sternberg, 1988; Stanovich 2009; Gopnik and Meltzoff, 1997; Gopnik 2016; Brown, et al. 2014; Mercier and Sperber 2017, 291).

"In most of daily life," developmental psychologist Barbara Rogoff (1990) explained, children are "relatively free to manage their own learning"

(98–99). Thus, as Peter Drucker (1969) once argued, a teacher can be anything that helps spark learning in a student: "The teacher can be a book, a piece of music, perhaps even the student himself" (342). The human brain is naturally designed to learn from the social and physical environments that we interact with every day, as are all other animal brains, so much so that psychologists in the 20th century claimed to have discovered a basic repertoire of biological "laws of learning" (Konner 2010, 350–51).

In fact, not only does most learning take place outside of schools, but there is evidence that teachers and schools, even the very best, can actually "discourage" student learning and growth (Gopnik 2016, 174; Dweck 2002). In 1928 the psychologist Jean Piaget argued that it was "despite adult authority, and not because of it, that the child learns" (qtd. in Rogoff 1990, 148). English professor and creativity guru Sir Ken Robinson (2001) explained that "some of the most brilliant and successful people in all walks of life that I know—or know of—failed" in schools, but later "succeeded only after they'd recovered" from their schooling (6).

The philosopher John Dewey was one of the most important thinkers of the 20th century, especially in terms of his philosophy of education. He was a dedicated teacher for over 50 years. And yet, ironically, he always hated school. He thought it was boring and repetitive, focused on "endless rote-learned recitations" (Ryan 1995, 47–48). But Dewey loved to learn. His daughter explained that as a boy he was "interested in reading almost anything except [his] school books" (47).

The polymath Dr. Oliver Sacks (2017) is another case in point. As a boy, Sacks also "hated school" because he was "forced to listen passively to droning teachers" who he found boring and he also had "bullying schoolmates and a sadistic headmaster" (34, 103). Sacks didn't learn much in school, but he did learn a lot on his own in science museums because they opened up the world to him in way that schools never could (101).

Near the end of his life, Sacks explained that some children, "including some of the most creative, may be resistant to formal teaching; they are essentially autodidacts, voracious to learn and explore on their own" (130). For autodidacts like Dewey and Sacks "Nothing that is worth knowing can be taught," as the playwright and another autodidact Oscar Wilde ([1894] 1989, 570) once explained.

Learning is a natural extension of our biological and social development and it comes effortlessly to everyone during childhood. On the other hand, schooling is unnatural, boring, and difficult (Gardner [1995] 2011, 2; Brackett 2019, 14). For some children, school is a hard and unforgiving game to play. Schooling is an artificial social institution that is forced onto children by adults.

For most children, school turns learning into an empty and useless ritual of command and control. Schooling damages, if not destroys, our natural curiosity and love of learning, especially once children reach middle school. In many cultures without formal schooling, or with much less formal schooling than Western European countries or the U.S., developmental psychologist Barbara Rogoff (1990) argues that "children have the responsibility to learn and are involved with many other social partners in the process" of learning (133). These children learn to do real life activities, like cooking, cleaning, farming, or doing paid work rather than learning useless information in schools.

With this in mind, we need to acknowledge and break away from two dangerous myths about human learning. First, schools are *not* the primary place where students learn. Students naturally and continually learn from experience as they live and grow, and they learn from every social practice, tradition, and institution in their culture (Tomasello 1999; Rogoff 1990; Rogoff 2003), which includes schools, but should not be reduced to schools.

Second, teachers are *not* responsible for student learning. Nor are teachers the primary cause of learning. Children are biologically programmed to be little learning machines (Gopnik 2016; Rogoff 1990; Rogoff 2003). Nobody *needs* a teacher to learn.

Developmental psychologists, like Gopnik (2016), have demonstrated that "childhood is *for* learning—that's what children are designed to do" (51; Gopnik 2009, 8). She explained that children learn from every personal experience and social interaction, and she emphasizes that "very little" of childhood learning "comes through conscious and deliberate teaching" (Gopnik 2016, 88).

Therefore, educational administrators and policy makers should not overstate the role of teachers by holding them solely accountable as the main source of student knowledge and learning. Nor should schools be held completely accountable for student learning. If we are using a valid conception of how learning actually occurs for children and adolescents then accountability measures for K–12 students should be primarily focused on the students themselves, their parents, their peers, and their physical and social environment, which are the primary drivers of student learning (Richerson and Boyd 2005).

And for higher education, as students are transitioning into adulthood, most learning becomes self-directed and done outside of the classroom. Therefore, accountability metrics should focus primarily on students, their peer networks, and auxiliary student learning services. In higher education, teachers play a much smaller role in learning.

A recent memoir highlights the complicated truth of student learning detached from the mythical power of teachers and schools. Tara Westover

(2018) was raised in the woods of Idaho by fundamentalist Mormon parents who never let her go to school. Her father told his children, "All that really matters is that you kids learn to read. That other twaddle is just brainwashing" (46).

Westover (2018) learned to read the *Bible* and a few other books, but largely on her own because her father actively discouraged learning (61). Westover (2018) explained, "Learning in our family was entirely self-directed: You could learn anything you could teach yourself, after your work was done" (46). But her father, "made me think my curiosity was an obscenity, an affront to all he'd sacrificed to raise me" (61).

Eventually Westover (2018) rebelled against her parents and enrolled in college. She didn't have any formal schooling. She didn't have any perquisite skills or knowledge, other than the basics of reading and writing. In her first year of college, she struggled to "wrestle meaning" from lectures and textbooks because she lacked the background knowledge to make sense of many words and concepts, like "holocaust" and "civic humanism," which she called "black-hole words" (156–57).

She felt like a "freak" (157). Not only did he lack knowledge, but she also did not fit in socially or ideologically into college. She had never before set foot in a school or been a part of any social organization (157). She was viscerally "shocked" to learn "about my own ignorance," which challenged, and later upturned, her entire epistemological understanding of life: "I knew what it was to have a misconception corrected—a misconception of such magnitude that shifting it shifted the world" (157, 180, 197, 238).

Eventually, over the course of her freshman year in college, she learned not only how to learn, but the value of learning. She realized that learning was a tool to expand intellectual horizons. It helped her develop as a person. It opened up new ways of life and career opportunities.

She not only graduated with a B.A. from Brigham Young University, but she was awarded a competitive scholarship to study at Cambridge University where she earned an MPhil and later a PhD. She then went on to become a visiting fellow at Harvard University. Westover (2018) was able to overcome a massive knowledge deficit and direct her own learning as an undergraduate in college, often without formal instruction or help from teachers. She was able to learn how to learn, and thereby how to help herself. She achieved her educational success almost all on her own. It's a powerful testament to our natural ability to learn.

There is an important lesson here for all teachers, school administrators, and educational policy makers. Many autodidacts have made the same basic point, like Westover, Oliver Sacks (2017), Matthew B. Crawford (2009), and Nassim Nicholas Taleb (2012). Learning is a powerful tool, but it ultimately belongs to the student to develop and exercise at will—or not.

Discussing what readers bring to a work of fiction, English professor Jonathan Gottschall (2012) once explained, "A writer lays down words, but they are inert. They need a catalyst to come to life. The catalyst is the reader's imagination" (6). The same could be said for the lesson of every teacher. Education depends upon the catalyst of the learner's interest and determination. Only the student can bring education to life.

HUMAN ABILITY: DETERMINED BY NATURE AND NURTURE

While Westover demonstrates the natural learning instinct that we all have, few students could be as academically successful as she was if they had been forced to endure similar circumstances on their own. Why is this? Many people would never have found the motivation to leave their family or home in order to enroll in school in the first place, and for those that could, most likely they would have quickly given up on college after facing as many failures and setbacks as Westover did her first year. Most students drop out of college without ever earning their degree.

Westover's story demonstrates the difficulty in being an autodidact. You have to *want* to know. You have to *want* to achieve. You have to *want* to persevere. She wanted to go to college. But she recognized her own ignorance. She recognized her inability to fully teach herself all that she wanted or needed to know. Westover was hungry to learn, and she knew that she needed teachers.

Westover knew that there was only so much new knowledge or skills that she could teach herself. She understood that working on her own would take a lot longer than if she worked with experts. As Michael Tomasello (1999) and many others have explained, "The amount of knowledge that any individual organism can gain by simply observing the world on its own is extremely limited" (165; see also Richerson and Boyd 2005, 99).

This is why Westover sought out knowledgeable teachers in college. She needed people to help guide her self-directed path. She needed to be shown *how* to learn and *what* to learn. Peter J. Richerson and Robert Boyd (2005) argued that "teaching, imitation, and other forms of social learning allow us to inherit a vast store of useful knowledge while avoiding" the harder work and higher costs of trying to learn everything all on our own (99).

It appears that few people are willing or able to be autodidacts, like Westover (Taleb 2012, 242–43). While we all have a biological instinct to learn, most people need teachers to learn *effectively* and to maximize the potential of their learning. Even autodidacts can benefit from having a good teacher because there are limits to what we can learn all by ourselves. As psychologist Anders Ericsson (2016) explained, "Even the most motivated and intelligent student will advance more quickly under the tutelage" of an effective teacher (148).

There are two important recent examples that help demonstrate the limits of untutored learning. The first is the development of the World Wide Web, which was heralded as the dawning of a golden information age where everyone from anywhere could have more information at his or her fingertips than any previous university library could provide. Supposedly the Web was going to lead to the new enlightenment of humanity.

Instead, we have seen the proliferation of fake news and reactionary politics. Most people around the world have used the internet for gossiping with friends and family and entertaining themselves with cat videos, games, and popular music ("The Second Half" 2019, 25). While over half of humanity has used the Web for reading the news, only about a quarter have used it for educational purposes or to access healthcare information (Chart 2, 25). The internet has certainly not brought a new age of enlightenment.

Another example of the failure of untutored learning is Massive Open Online Courses, or MOOCs (Reich and Ruiperez-Valiente 2019). About a decade ago many educational administrators and policy makers thought that MOOCs would transform higher education and enable large numbers of students all over the world to graduate with high quality college degrees, especially poorer students in developing countries who didn't have access to quality schools or universities. But it didn't happen.

While millions of students around the world registered for MOOCs, less than half actually started the course. Worse, many dropped out after the first two weeks. Only a fraction of students who registered for a course, currently around 7%, completed the first year of study and returned for the second year. Even fewer of these students finished a course and actually earned a certificate of completion. It appears that most students struggle to motivate themselves, to stay focused, and to learn when they are by themselves. In order to stay focused and to learn effectively, most students need human interaction with trained teachers and motivated peers.

This raises an interesting question. Why are some people naturally gifted learners while others struggle? Why can some students effectively learn without teachers, or despite bad teachers, while others flounder even with the very best teachers?

To answer this question, we must turn to biology. As psychologist Steven Pinker (2002) argues, "Any theory of education must be based on a theory of human nature" (222) because all human behavior is informed and guided by biological processes. In his groundbreaking book on the subject, Pinker (2002) explained, "Far from being empty receptacles or universal learners, children are equipped with a toolbox of implements for reasoning and learning in particular ways . . . children are not indistinguishable lumps of raw material waiting to be shaped. They are little people, born with personalities" (223, 384).

While Steven Pinker (2002) and most other psychologists have admitted that the nature-nurture debate is "far from over" (372), over the last two decades there have been amazing breakthroughs in our understanding of genetics, human nature, and education. We now know that both nature and nurture shape human development in complex and interdependent ways throughout our life-cycle (Richerson and Boyd 2005).

As the biologist E. O. Wilson (2017) has explained, "Natural selection has programmed every bit of human biology—every toe, hair, and nipple, every molecular configuration in every cell, every neuron circuit in the brain, and within all that, every trait that makes us human" (102; see also Konner 2010).

While we are biologically programed, we are also social animals who live in distinct cultures where we are "suspended in webs of significance" that our societies have created over time (Geertz 1973, 5). These webs of significance create meaning and value that make our lives worth living. Many social scientists have documented how culture and biology have "co-evolved" through history, each playing a part in the development of every human being (Durham 1991).

The developmental psychologist Barbara Rogoff (1990) explained that scientists seeking to fully explain human thought and action must study not only "the nature of human nature," but also "the nurture of human nature" and "the nature of human nurture": "Biology and culture are not alternative influences but inseparable aspects of a system within which individuals develop" (3, 28; Rogoff 2003, 64).

And it's not just human beings. Natural selection has programed all living organisms on Earth with the same basic DNA and genes (Diamond 1992; Ridley 2003; Konner 2010, 26). We share around 96 to 98 percent of our DNA with the chimpanzee, our closest evolutionary relative (Diamond 1992; Richerson and Boyd 2005, 110; Wrangham and Peterson 1996). We share about 96 percent of our DNA with monkeys, 75 percent with dogs, and 60 percent of our DNA with fruit flies (Sapolsky 2017, 331–31; Hibbing, Smith and Alford 2014, 209).

We even share DNA with plants. For example, we share more than half of our DNA with bananas (Asbury and Plomin 2014, 19). We also share some of the same behavioral traits with plants, which are influenced by our genes, like our biological "circadian clock," which automatically tells both animals and plants when it's night or day (Panda 2018, 24; Chamovitz 2012, 25). Humans have about 20,000 to 25,000 genes in total, which is "1,796 more than worms, 12,000 fewer than corn, and 25,000 fewer genes than rice or wheat" (Mukherjee 2016, 322; Konner 2010, 159).

For all biological beings on Earth, from bacteria to mold, from plants to insects, from rats to chimpanzees to humans, as Dr. Siddhartha Mukherjee (2016) clarified, "Physics enable[s] chemistry, and chemistry enable[s] physiology" (142), and physiology enables the behavior and mental activity of an organism, although mental processes are dependent on an organism actually having a nervous system or a brain. "The difference between 'human' and 'breakfast cereal' is not a matter of gene numbers, but of the sophistication of gene networks," Mukherjee explained, "It is not what we have; it is how we use it" (322).

While all human beings share about 95 to 98 percent of the same genes there is still remarkable genetic variation between individuals due to that 2 to 5 percent difference (Hibbing, Smith and Alford 2014, 208; Mukherjee 2016, 266; Asbury and Plomin 2014, 19). Dr. Mukherjee (2016) argued that the human genome "accommodates enough variation to make each one of us distinct, yet enough consistency to make each member of our species profoundly different from chimpanzees and bonobos, whose genomes are 96 percent identical to ours" (325).

As psychologist and political scientist John R. Hibbing pointed out, "Even if variations exist in only the remaining 2 percent of the genome, that's still 64 million [nucleotide] base pairs—and change in a very small number of base pairs can dramatically alter behavior, physique, and health. . . . DNA provides approximately 64 million opportunities for variation from person to person" (Hibbing, Smith and Alford 2014, 208–9).

Over the past several decades, many scientists have documented how genetic differences influence a wide variety of human traits and behaviors, so much so that Hibbing et al. (2014) argued that "these different predispositions could indeed be viewed as different human natures" (212). Genetic differences between humans then get "amplified" by a person's physical and social environment, which leads to "distinct" predispositions underlying human thought and action (227).

Thus, when it comes to human learning, genetic differences combined with environmental influences can lead different people exposed to the same stimuli to learn "very different things" (139). However, it is important to remember, as Dr. Mukherjee (2016) pointed out, that when compared to other species on Earth, "the actual range of human genomic variation is strikingly low—lower than in many other species. . . . We are much more alike than unlike each other" (340).

Psychologists and brain scientists have found that heritable genes account for 40% to 60% of our personality traits, which includes intelligence and other traits associated with success in schooling (Mukherjee 2016; Hibbing, Smith and Alford 2014; Mitchell 2018; Pinker 2002; Asbury and Plomin 2014). However, just because certain traits are heritable does not mean that they are "easily inheritable" due to the wide variation caused by environmental influences and random chance (Mukherjee 2016, 346).

Although we have around 20,000 to 25,000 genes, "many or most are never activated in any given cell, and perhaps 20 percent are active at any moment" so environmental influences play a significant role (Konner 2010, 159). Genetic researchers stress there is a "fundamental interdependence" between genes, environment, and personal experience (Asbury and Plomin 2014, 30). Thus, John R. Hibbing argues, the study of genes enables us to understand that "people's differences run deep. We are not all born with the same 'slates.' We come into the world with much on our slate and the environment we encounter piles on its idiosyncratic touches" (Hibbing, Smith and Alford 2013, 86).

Based on current research, scientists have concluded that around 20% to 40% of our personal traits come from our unique interactions with various social and physical environments that we have encountered over our lifetime, especially with our peers and friends. Our personal experience is a product of both our biological predispositions and our ability to learn from our environment, in particular the people that we encounter and learn from. As Hibbing explained, "behavior results from a physical process initiated by the environment and shaped by genes" (Hibbing, Smith and Alford 2013, 197).

Biologist and neurologist Robert M. Sapolsky (2017) confirmed that "genes don't make sense outside the context of environment" (227). Take for example the ability to read. As psychologists Kathryn Asbury and Robert Plomin (2014) explain, "Schools are the reason children . . . learnt to read. Genes, however, are the primary reason why some of them are better readers than others" (29).

While the environment helps shape who we are, not all experiences are equal. Scientists have recently found that formal socialization, especially from our family, accounts for none to 15% of our personality traits. This includes schooling and other cultural institutions (Mitchell 2018, 25–30; Pinker 2002, 380; Tomasello 1999, ch. 2; Rosenberg 1988, 5). Our family environment actually contributes very little to our personality (Steinberg 1996; Pinker 2002, 391–92; Richerson and Boyd 2005, 36, 156; Harris 1999; Konner 2010, 197).

But a word of caution is in order. These figures are rough estimates, due to the limitations of current scientific methodology, because there is often a 10% to 20% measurement error for most studies (Mitchell 2018; Sapolsky 2017, 241–44). However, neurologist Kevin J. Mitchell (2018) argues that heritability figures most likely understate our innate biological physiology. This is because of the central role of DNA and genes as mediators of social processes. Our social nature is nurtured by our genes, and our genetic nature is nurtured by our social interactions.

Robert M. Sapolsky (2017) disagrees somewhat with Mitchell's (2018) emphasis on genes. Sapolsky (2017) argues that most research inflates heritability due to a lack of analysis of genetic traits in different environments over time (243–44). This disagreement highlights the inherent problem with measuring any marker of social or individual achievement, including success in schooling. As economist Fred Hirsch (1976) pointed out, it is usually impossible to separate "the effect of education from the effect of native ability and family background" (47). For human beings, genes and culture are completely intertwined.

But while our biological inheritance matters a great deal, genes do not determine our biological faculties so much as provide a blueprint or recipe that guides our development and must be enacted by each individual in particular physical and social environments (Waddington 1957; Konner 2010, 161). Each genetic blueprint must be enacted at both the cellular level and the level of the whole organism, through developmental processes and personal experiences, which includes cultural conditioning and individual learning (Richerson and Boyd 2005, 9; Tomasello 1999; Ridley 2003).

Every genetic blueprint is significantly effected by the environment. The external world either enables or constrains our biological predispositions. This is especially true for young children who are highly susceptible to change, due to neuroplasticity, and also completely dependent upon caregivers to deliver high-quality nutrients, safety, and emotional support.

Due to the nature of our evolutionary history, as Mitchell (2018) explains, our developmental process is "robust" and works "good enough" because it has created billions of human beings, all with that same basic functional parameters (76), albeit with some random variability. There is a lot of "wiggle room" at both the cellular level and the level of the whole organism, as we interact with our environment, which creates many random and unpredictable variations in our biology and physiology as we grow up (Mitchell 2018, 76–77).

There is a "developmental randomness" that is unique to every individual (73), which creates a "probabilistic nature" to our developmental processes and resulting traits and behavior (Mukherjee 2016). Anthropologist and Neuroscientist Melvin Konner (2010) emphasized the "rude fact that nothing in biology in 100 percent. If it's a biological law, it's fuzzy around the edges; all of the rules are probabilities" (77). He stressed that biological life is "marvelously messy" (77). Robert M. Sapolsky (2017) concurs. He explains, "genes aren't about inevitability. Instead, they're about context-dependent tendencies, propensities, potentials, and vulnerabilities" (265).

Genes do not create a deterministic and formulaic outcome as we develop and grow older. Genes merely guide our development within biologically based parameters that have emerged through millions of years of evolutionary tinkering (Mitchell 2018, 69; Mukherjee 2016; Richerson and Boyd 2005; Deacon 1997, 322). As we develop, Mitchell (2018) clarifies, "the genome cannot predict (and cannot specify) any cell's exact state" (68). There is always "noise in all the operating parameters of every cell," which helps to create the unique characteristics of every individual (68).

Plus, as we grow older, we are exposed to a lot of random events in our environment, including our own personal choices, and these external events interact with our personal genetic endowment to produce what is unique to us as individuals. Thus, the influence of genes is quite complex and highly idiosyncratic. As Dr. Mukherjee (2016) explained, "genes, environments, gene-environment interactions, triggers, chance, and opportunities" all come together in unpredictable ways to determine who we are and who we become (273).

Many, if not all, of our personal experiences are potentially shaped in some way by our genetic inheritance and our unique physiological nature. Thus, there is usually no clear demarcation between "nature" or "nurture" (Richerson and Boyd 2005; Asbury and Plomin 2014). We need to avoid the trap, first posed by Francis Galton in the 19th century, that either nature or nurture must be predominant with any specific human trait. Some scientists call this false choice "Galton's Error" (Wrangham and Peterson 1996, 95).

We need to embrace the messy reality that both nature and nurture operate simultaneously in highly complex ways all the time (Richerson and Boyd 2005). We need to see evolution the way psychologist James Mark Baldwin first described it: "Learning and behavioral flexibility can play a role in amplifying and biasing natural selection because these abilities enable individuals to modify the context of natural selection" (Deacon 1997, 322).

Our cultural experiences are affected by our genes, and our genes are affected by our culture and physical environment. All of our nurturing experiences with other human beings are partly affected by our genetic nature in what geneticists call "gene by environment (GxE) interaction" (Mitchell 2018, 122; Mukherjee 2016, 107), or what some biologists call "gene-culture coevolution" (Wilson 2017, 107, 119; see also Ridley 2003; Wrangham and Peterson 1996; Richerson and Boyd 2005).

We are born into particular physical and cultural environments that were somewhat chosen by our parents, what some scientists call an "ontogenetic niche," which is a highly significant inheritance that shapes us for the rest of our lives (qtd. in Rogoff 1990, 38; see also Tomasello 1999, 78–79). But even though we inherit choices made by our parents, like where we live, Mitchell (2018) argues that human beings also tend to "select and construct their own environments and experiences" as they grow older, which limits how much influence our parents or our cultures can have over us (81).

However, even when we make individual choices, how we choose and what we choose is "based on innate predispositions" (94). So even our social and cultural interactions have some genetic basis. It's complex, and messy.

When we interact with our physical and social environment through personal experiences, our environment shapes and constrains how our body enacts its genetic blueprint, which includes random chance happenings (Tomasello 1999; Richerson and Boyd 2005; Mukherjee 2016, 107). Studying how this process unfolds in the human brain, Gerald M. Edelman calls this developmental sequence "neural Darwinism" (qtd. in Sacks 2017, 175; Sacks 2015, 359–69). One action influences another action, which in turn influences the next action, and so on.

We reinforce our traits and behavior through continued experience, but we can also control or eliminate some traits or behaviors by changing our habits (Clear 2018). We can train ourselves to behave differently through changing our environment, practicing new skills, or simply through disuse and forgetting the old behaviors we want to discard. While we do have genetic programming, we also have a great deal of room to maneuver and make choices, as Dr. Oliver Sacks (2015) pointed out, "We make our own individual paths through life" (369).

But this does not mean that we have a lot of freedom to do whatever we want with our lives. While our brains are naturally plastic, designed to grow and change as we experience life and learn through interactions with our environment, Mitchell (2018) argues that "rather than overriding or flattening out their effects, processes of brain plasticity may reinforce and even exaggerate the widespread initial differences that arise due to both genetic and developmental variation" of each individual (86).

Each individual is often unconsciously drawn to select "situations, environments, and experiences" that emotionally *feels* right for that individual. Why? Because it reinforces both our "innate tendencies" (Mitchell 2018, 92–94) and the cultural way of life, or "habitus," in which we were born (Bourdieu and Wacquant 1992, 123–28; Tomasello 1999, 79). Most of us seek out environments and make choices in a habitual way that reinforces genetic dispositions, cultural programming, and past experiences.

We are born into a culture that gives us an extensive set of tools to understand and negotiate our instinctive tendencies. We have the ability to choose a way of living that cannot be reduced to biological determinism (Dennett 2003, 143). Many people misunderstand both the role of genes and the process of genetic evolution. Genes shape who we are, but they do not determine all of our traits or abilities, let alone determine our action on any given day.

"Predispositions are not destiny, but defaults," according to political scientist and psychologist John Hibbing, "defaults that can be and frequently are overridden" (Hibbing, Smith and Alford 2013, 13, 20, 23). As philosopher

Daniel D. Dennett (2003) explained very simply, "some of my genes fix some parts of my destiny" (157), but nobody actually believes that genes completely determine a human life.

Biologist and Anthropologist David Sloan Wilson (2002) explained that while many human features and traits are genetically evolved, there is still a lot of "open-ended potential" in terms of how our bodies develop and how any individual will think and behave because of the various influences of our physical and social environments (31; Hibbing, Smith and Alford 2013, 23). Our genetic programming and the much longer processes of genetic evolution are "genuinely open-ended" in terms of final outcomes (31). The future is not fixed.

Dennett (2003) optimistically explained, "I have never encountered anybody who claims that will, education, and culture cannot change many, if not all, of our genetically inherited traits" (156). While our genes play a part in determining who we are and what we are capable of, our physical and social environments also play an important part in determining our nature, as do our own choices and the random chance of events that we happen to encounter during our life. Dennett (2003) argued that knowledge of genes is "not an enemy of human freedom, but one of its best friends" (16–62). This knowledge allows us to truly understand, in a way that no previous generation of humans has understood, the "degree of freedom" we have to shape our own lives and society.

Knowledge of genes enables us to understand what we can and cannot change; thereby, giving us the ability to focus on those areas that are subject to modification. But our understanding of genetics is still incomplete. Dr. Mukherjee (2016) argues that scientists are in the "last mile" of genetics in terms of understanding how exactly "genetic propensities in the abstract" lead to the "concrete and particular personhood" of any given individual (388). But one thing is for sure, each one of us contributes a great deal to our personality and our fate, just not as much as most people would like to believe.

Thus, with a more accurate understanding of our biology, the social practice of education and schooling becomes both more liberating and more problematic, especially for those political activists who seek to use schools as instruments of progressive sociopolitical reform. On the one hand, evidence on the "Flynn effect" demonstrates that the widespread cultural adoption of schooling has had an effect on absolute measures of intelligence around the world, which has been steadily increasing over time (Mitchell 2018, 166; Richardson 1999, 51–52). While I.Q. is genetically based and heritable, the Flynn effect demonstrates that it can also be taught (Asbury and Plomin 2014, 91).

Academic intelligence is a cultural phenomenon. The Flynn effect is definitely not due to genes or personal experience. Instead, it seems to be solid evidence for the cultural effect of schooling on the development of intelligence, which is a rough and partial measure of human cognitive ability that is correlated with years of schooling (Ceci 1991; Richardson 1999, 50–51; Asbury and Plomin 2014, ch. 7). Schools produce the cognitive ability to score well on standardized tests administered in schools, a highly specialized, and rather useless, type of ability that psychologists often call I.Q. or general "intelligence" (Ceci 1991; Rogoff 1990, 43, 47), but it does give us a measure, however flawed, of human cognitive ability that can be learned through socialization and instruction.

However, it's important to note, a person's I.Q. levels are never static. Our general intelligence changes as we grow older, especially as children develop from toddlers into young adults (Asbury and Plomin 2014, 91). Thus, the whole notion of a stable I.Q. score that can be used to rank people in schools is simply nonsensical and not based on scientific research. But as a measure of learned ability that varies over time in relation to socialization processes, the notion of intelligence can be useful to scientists.

While schooling definitely has some effect on most students, there is evidence that schooling does not have an equal effect. Some students are more predisposed to be successful at the type of learning taught in schools and others less so (Asbury and Plomin 2014). Also, some students live in more accommodating or debilitating environments, which can increase the genetic influence of intelligence, or hinder it. Mitchell (2018) argues, "a rising tide lifts all boats, but some may still sit higher in the water than others" (168).

Gifted individuals who are genetically endowed with higher IQ or other innate capabilities might "benefit more" from education or schooling than nongifted students. Mitchell argues, "They may learn more readily and be able to apply that knowledge more productively. They may find education more interesting and rewarding and may therefore apply themselves more. They are more likely to be more encouraged by parents and teachers and thus choose to stay in education longer . . . the more you learn and understand, the easier it is to learn and understand even more" (168). Thus, schooling most likely exacerbates natural inequalities rather than ameliorating them.

The main educational lessons to be drawn from our emerging understanding of the human genome is that every person is unique, and that our biological nature and abilities are constantly changing, especially for kids. Medical health professionals are also drawing the same lessons ("Populations of One" 2020, 3). "Even within the normal range, children have distinctive brains, and not just owing to genetic or other prenatal causes," points out Melvin Konner (2010, 200). Thus, as education professor Daniel Koretz (2017) argues, teachers and school administrators need to stop "pretending that all kids are the same" (130).

For example, developmental psychologist Howard Gardner ([1983] 2011; 1993) has argued that there are at least eight different types of intelligence that a child can be born with, which can be nurtured and developed. Thus, there should never be a one-size-fits-all approach to any kind of learning experience, especially in schools (Asbury and Plomin 2014). Psychologists Kathryn Asbury and Robert Plomin (2014) argue that schools need to make "teaching and learning more personalized" for each unique student (150). They explain, "for partly biological reasons, all . . . children . . . are starting from different points and therefore need to take different steps to develop their understanding and their ability" (45).

With a proper understanding of the uniqueness of every individual, a teacher's job is "to gradually draw out each child's potential rather than aiming, as a class, at some arbitrary, externally imposed target," like national standards or average grades (Asbury and Plomin 2014, 45). Furthermore, just because some students are naturally gifted with potential talents does not mean that these students will be able to successfully nurture and train these talents into real skill and real achievement.

Genetic endowment and actual achievement are two very different qualities (Asbury and Plomin 2014, 92). Likewise, just because someone is not naturally endowed does not mean that they cannot acquire certain traits or skills. It just means that some people might have to work a lot harder and a lot longer to achieve a skill that may come more easily and quickly to a gifted student.

There is also evidence that the heritability of IQ is less powerful for young children and for people with lower socio-economic status (Asbury and Plomin 2014, 91; Mukherjee 2016, 347; Mitchell 2018). This means that biology matters less for young children, especially in the preschool years. It also means that genes matter less for underprivileged students who live in impoverished environments.

As Dr. Mukherjee (2016) explained, "Genes play a rather minor role in determining IQ in severely impoverished circumstances. If you superimpose poverty, hunger, and illness on a child, then these variables dominate the influence on IQ. Genes that control IQ only become significant if you remove these limitations" (347; see also Sapolsky 2017, 249).

Thus, in order to improve the outcomes of students from underprivileged communities, it is more important to focus on the cultural and physical environment rather than the natural biological endowments of individual students. Underprivileged students need quality food and healthcare, safe neighborhoods free of crime, economic opportunity, and good quality schools with highly trained teachers, especially preschools (Mitchell 2018, 166; see also Heckman 2013; Asbury and Plomin 2014).

Thus, it is important to remember that heritable measures of intelligence in populations with low socio-economic resources, or any other trait that social scientists tend to measure, are often confounded with, and influenced by, the child's lack of resources from the social and physical environment, such as access to safety, healthy food, libraries, good schools, trained teachers, or extracurricular activities, to say nothing of the negative influences of poverty and crime (Payne 2008; Kozol 1991).

Mitchell (2018) cited the example of the Irish in the 20th century who were a disadvantaged population in the U.K. and scored low on IQ tests for decades, and lower than the average for England. But as Ireland gained socio-economic status and wealth over the 20th century, IQ scores rose to become on par with English scores (167), which proves how important social and economic resources are when it comes to human development, especially during the first decade of a child's life (Heckman 2013).

But when it comes to performance in school, the intelligence of students only accounts for about 25% of academic performance, and even less when it comes to labor market success (Steinberg 2014, 117). Thus, the effect of natural, biological endowments should not be magnified or overstated, which is often the case when journalists report on this topic.

Soft skills, or what psychologists call non-cognitive skills, are much more important predictors of our success in school and in life (118; see also Heckman et al. 2006), but these important skills do not get as much attention from teachers, school administrators, and the media. And, unlike intelligence, no one is born with soft skills because they are mostly acquired through our culture and personal experience. These skills include hard work, grit, determination, perseverance, creating goals, self-regulation, relationship building, teamwork, and delaying gratification (Steinberg 2014, 118; Duckworth 2016; Mischel 2014).

These so-called soft "skills" are not really skills, as psychologist Laurence Steinberg (2014) argues. They are more like basic natural "capacities" that everyone has, like a muscle, that can either be strengthened or weakened by our physical and social environments, and through our deliberate practice (118). But unlike intelligence, soft skills are mostly cultural endowments. They need to be socially demonstrated and developed by parents, peers, and teachers, and these skills need to be actively perfected by students through personal experience. We aren't born a hard worker, or a good listener, or a goal-setter, or a team player. We learn these skills by watching others perform them.

Some of these non-cognitive skills have genetic components, but they are much less heritable than intelligence, and therefore, much more sensitive to environmental influences and personal experience. Most importantly, when it comes to schools, soft skills can be taught and learned much more readily than intelligence (Steinberg 123). Thus, while understanding the human genome is important, it is also important to remember that "next to nothing is determined by genes, and our environments are hugely powerful" in shaping who we are, who we become, and what we are able to achieve (Asbury and Plomin 2014, 96).

HOMO ADOLESCENS: A TRIBE APART

While our genetic inheritances are important, most of the natural endowments that we are born with must be activated and developed through our personal experiences, which means there is always a significant role for both socialization and individual agency. Even people born with so-called "natural talent" still have to choose to develop that talent through hard work and with critical feedback from a teacher. And people born without "natural talent" can still develop knowledge and skill with the right kind of motivation and training (Ericsson and Pool 2016, 208; Rumbaugh and Washburn 2003, 204–34).

Sadly, most adolescents in the U.S. are not learning to develop either cognitive or non-cognitive skills because these capacities have not been nurtured by their culture, in particular their peer cultures. Many American adolescents are simply unmotivated to learn. They do not want to develop their abilities. Why? Because their friends don't value learning and few teenagers want to risk looking uncool, especially at school.

As children grow up, they begin to socialize more and more with their peers. Older children also begin to "more actively select their own experiences and construct their own environments" (Mitchell 2018, 25–30), which decreases the influence of parents and adult institutions, like churches and schools (Richerson and Boyd 2005, 36, 156). When it comes to acquiring knowledge and adopting social practices, social scientists have demonstrated that peer groups have a much larger effect on adolescent behaviors than do parents or schools (Harris 1999; Sapolsky 2017, 164–69; Rogoff 1990, 188).

For example, young children begin learning and speaking the dialect of their parents and their teachers, but as they grow older, kids "almost always" switch to the dialect of their peers (Richerson and Boyd 2005, 36–38). Older children also move away from the culture of their parents and switch to the cultural practices and values of their peers.

When scholars talk about culture, it's easy to overgeneralize and forget that every culture has layers and layers of subcultures, classes, and castes (Hebdige 1979). Thus, when one is talking about children, especially adolescents, as Steven Pinker (2002) pointed out, we need to remember that "children have cultures, too" (390). Social scientists have studied the "separate culture of the young" for about a century (Waller 1932, 103), and it is a fascinating and strange subject.

Since at least the early 20th century, adolescents in the U.S. and other developed democracies have created what Patricia Hersch (1999) calls "a tribe apart," (11) focused on the social practices of partying, sex, drugs, recreational activities, and music. Teenagers live in a "separate world" from adults, and their adolescent cultural norms and objectives are often in conflict with the adult world, especially with teachers and schools (Hersch 1999, 11; Milner 2006, 33, 40; Twenge 2017; Waller 1932; Hebdige 1979).

Modern adolescents prioritize their own cultural norms, often in defiance of adult norms. Teenagers are focused on the maximization of pleasure and peer group status (Steinberg 2014, 74, 95). These norms often seem strange and irrational to adults because teenagers "glorify" stupidity (Steinberg 1996, 44), make irresponsible choices, and engage in "obviously reckless" actions (Steinberg 2014, 78). In Tom Wolfe's (2004) fictional portrait of modern college life, he satirized the "self-interest[ed]" teens and the "stupid, aimless, self-destructive things" that adolescents do (17).

As many critics have pointed out, like psychologist Laurence Steinberg (2014), students see high school and college primarily as a place to "socialize" with their friends, treating school as a "country club" where the "really important activities are interrupted by all those annoying classes" (142). Steinberg (1996) documented how adolescent peer culture in the U.S. denigrates "academic success and scorns students who try to do well in school (19).

When unmotivated high school students go on to college, these students are *not* focused on learning or earning a degree, but on enjoying themselves and playing with their friends. More and more, students see college as an "extended vacation or private club" where they can "drink, dance, scream, puke, pass out" (Matthews 1998, 95, 84), not as an institution for higher learning.

It's important to remember that what appears "stupid" to an adult can seem perfectly rational to a teenager. Sociologist Philip Cusick often asked high school students, "'which would you rather do, flunk a test or eat alone in the cafeteria?' Invariably the answer was, 'Flunk a test'" (qtd. in Milner 2006, 61). Sociologist Murray Milner Jr. (2006) has documented how "powerless" teenagers feel about their own lives. Students are controlled by adults, forced to go to school, forced be academically successful, then forced go to college, and finally, they are forced to get a job to support themselves (4, 30).

To claw back some autonomy, many adolescents rebel against the adult world and its rules by creating an "alternative status system" with its own "values and priorities" (30), which are not only distinct from the adult world, but also set against traditional adult values and priorities, like academic success and getting a job. Many students simply do not want to be academically successful and they don't want a job. They just want to have fun with their friends.

Thus, for many teenagers, developing and maintaining peer relationships and social status is more important than doing well on a test or earning high grades (Milner 2006, 21; Crosnoe 2011). It's important to remember that the need for social status is part of our evolutionary heritage, which we share with our closest biological relative, the chimpanzee (Wrangham and Peterson 1996, 191). Most teens are obsessed with social status. Few are obsessed with academics.

Many psychologists, like Laurence D. Steinberg (1996, 2014, 95), have explained how "peers shape student achievement patterns in profound ways, and that in many respects friends are more powerful influences than family members are," and both friends and family are much more important than schools when it comes to learning and academic achievement (Mercier and Sperber 2017, 295; Richerson and Boyd 2005, 36, 156; Harris 1999). As Steinberg (1996) explained in a large study of teens in the U.S.,

> For a large number of adolescents, peers—not parents—are the chief determinant of how intensely they are invested in school and how much effort they devote to their education. . . . Parents may influence their children's long-term educational plans, but when it comes to day-to-day influences on schooling—whether students attend class, how much time they spend on homework, how hard they try in school, and the grades they bring home—friends are more influential than parents. (138, 147–48; see also Pinker 2002, 391–92; Richerson and Boyd 2005, 36, 156; Harris 1999; Konner 2010, 118)

And perhaps even more important, when it comes to educational policy, friends are more influential on student learning than teachers or schools.

WHO SHOULD BE HELD ACCOUNTABLE TO WHOM?

Over the long term, psychologists have found that the effects of cultural experiences with our family, peers, teachers, and schooling, do not have a permanent influence on our personality traits or behavior. In particular, geneticists have found that the biological heritability of IQ increases with time, which means the influence of early socialization on our thought and behavior gradually decreases to zero (Mitchell 2018, 165; Pinker 2002, 392; Richerson and Boyd 2005, 37, 156).

Thus, Mitchell (2018) concludes that cultural institutions that seek to "influence cognitive performance," such as family, churches, and schools, seem to have only a "short-term" effect on cognitive development, and apparently no "long-lasting effects" (165). So why then are accountability reformers trying to hold teachers and schools as solely responsible for student learning and labor market outcomes? The reason, of course, is that accountability reformers, policy makers, and school administrators are playing politics. They simply don't understand the complex determinants of student learning and academic achievement—or they don't care. They are simply setting political priorities and forcing teachers and students to reach arbitrary standards.

If we are going to hold teachers and schools accountable to students, which in theory is a good idea, we need to have a much clearer and more accurate picture of how teaching and student learning actually works, which we just explored in the last two chapters. Learning is what the student does. Teachers only help.

Students should bear most of the responsibility for learning, or not learning. Teachers play only a small part in student learning. Parents, peers, and the culture at large play a much more important role. If we are going to gather accountability data on student learning, then we need to measure all of the most important influences that are responsible, not just the most politically expedient, which happens to be teachers.

The main problem, as we have already discussed, is that many students don't want to learn. This is primarily because adolescent peer cultures do not value learning, academics, or the adult world of responsibility. But what can we do about this?

Improving student learning, especially on a national level, would require deep cultural change, especially with youth culture, which would necessitate widespread social, political, and economic reforms, all beyond the scope or competency of school administrators and teachers. Therefore, in order to increase student learning and academic achievement, policy makers and administrators need to rethink who should be accountable to whom. They also need to rethink how best to practice accountability programs so as to fairly hold each party responsible for student learning, and most importantly, to promote real and useful education, rather than the empty ritual of playing school.

Chapter 6

A Managerial Coup d'État

There is a paradoxical problem at the heart of the educational accountability movement and the quest to make schools operate more like efficient businesses. And it's not just schools. This problem is endemic to the corporation as a business model, public or private. Charles Handy was a marketing executive at Royal Dutch Shell, an economist, and a business school professor. Handy wrote about this problem extensively. He called it the "curse of efficiency." When organizations "focus so much on efficiency" they almost always paradoxically "fail to be effective" (qtd. in "The Curse of Efficiency" 2019, 55). Why does this happen?

Handy (1993) argued that managers can forget that even the best organizations can be "only patchily efficient" (13). Part of the problem is that managers are always running from one failure to another, chasing illusory silver bullets, at great cost of time, money, and organizational resources. But running after holy grails never works because new ideas are not necessarily better ideas. Even the best ideas, Handy warned, rarely work as advertised (13).

Peter Drucker (1969) and Charles Handy (1993) were some of the first business school professors to stress that businesses are organizations founded on ideals, not just monetary objectives. But ideals can be mutually exclusive and they often come into conflict (Berlin 2000a; Drucker 1969, 191–92). Even more importantly, most managers forget that ideals are impossible ends. They can never be reached.

Thus, managers need to realize that the quest for efficiency is an ideal—an impossible ideal. Businesses can never reach perfect efficiency any more than a political system can reach perfect justice or equality. Therefore, an organization's means must justify its corporate goals because the means are all there is. Ideals will never be reached. While all businesses want to focus on efficiency and profitability, they also have to balance these ideals with other important goals, like following laws, developing corporate culture, maximizing shareholder returns, or operating in socially responsible ways.

THE CURSE OF EFFICIENCY

Handy (1993) warned that some managers become so obsessed with efficiency that they lose sight of all the other important corporate values they are supposed to be developing, especially the core values the business was founded upon. He called this particular type of blindness the "curse of efficiency." Instead of focusing on the most important goals of the organization, efficiency-minded managers often "pay attention to narrower measures, like cutting costs," because these accountability metrics are easier to see and measure ("The Curse" 2019, 55).

When an organization is obsessed with accountability and efficiency, short-term performance markers can take precedence over long-term organizational goals, to the detriment of the latter. If everyone is focused on short-term efficiency metrics, and competing against each other for the best numbers, then often those accountability markers get manipulated for personal gain, since long-term organizational goals don't really matter. If everyone is focused on selfish, short-term goals, then the organization crumbles from within.

Efficiency obsessed organizations also tend to treat their staff poorly. People become "human resources" to be controlled by management, rather than people that need to be personally and professionally developed for their own sake (Markovits 2019, 206). As a writer for *The Economist* points out, "Call someone a resource, and it is a small step to assuming that they can be treated like a thing, subject to being controlled and, ultimately, dispensed with surplus to requirements" ("The Curse" 2019, 55).

The former Soviet Union provides a perfect example of the "curse of efficiency." The USSR tried to create a complex accountability system for an entire country, but this quixotic quest went dangerously awry (Winiecki 1996). Communist officials mandated specific performance metrics for all state offices and state-owned businesses. These performance metrics were tied to complex central planning designs for the whole Soviet economy. However, it was impossible to understand, let alone measure, coordinate, and control, the entire Soviet economy and every organization in it. There are definite limits to administrative control and central planning.

Because it was impossible to measure all the important factors that contributed to economic growth and human welfare, Communist party officials and local managers substituted trivial metrics that could be easily measured and fraudulently manipulated. This allowed managers and officials to gain financially and politically in the short-term, all the while damaging long-term economic growth and stability, and putting people's health and well-being at risk.

Central committees "issued a general description of the planned products and watched select margins, such as quantity or weight, creating an opportunity for producers to ignore unmeasured qualitative margins" (Alston, Eggertsson and North 1996, 61). Perhaps the penultimate example of the curse of efficiency and the failure of accountability policies was the *Chernobyl* nuclear power plant accident in 1986, which put all of Europe and Asia at risk.

Economist Jan Winiecki (1996) explained how most Soviet managers and officials were "not interested in increasing efficiency but in showing improved *average* results from one year to another" (83; Aguayo 1990, 28). The Soviet accountability regime was simply a crooked numbers game. Short-term measurements mattered more than broader organizational or political goals. Manipulated numbers on an official form mattered more than the underlying reality of the business or the national economy. Thus, the Soviet economy and political system gradually disintegrated from within due to political corruption, organizational mismanagement, perverse incentives, and personal cynicism.

Sadly, the educational efficiency movement in the U.S. has degenerated into a Soviet-style numbers game. Like in Soviet Russia, American schools now strive to produce short-term measures so they can make political leaders happy and get performance-based funding (Deming 1994, 32; Koretz 2017, 46).

If schools in the U.S. were actually educational institutions then they would operate very differently (Deming 1994, 32). If schools were educational institutions, then they would focus on the complex practices of teaching and learning, rather than the cynical practice of playing school. But most schools in the U.S. are not educational institutions. Most schools are dysfunctional political and economic institutions focused on politically expedient short-term goals that have little to do with the long-term well-being of students.

And like the former Soviet Union, the problem with schools in the U.S. starts at the top. The main roadblock standing in the way of effective educational reform in the U.S. is clueless politicians and the administrative bureaucracy of state and local school systems. Political scientist and philosopher Michael J. Sandel (1996) has called this layer of professionals "the procedural republic" (209; see also Tyack and Hansot 1982). These groups of powerful people profit economically and socially by playing lip service to reform while keeping our dysfunctional schools the way they are.

In particular, school administrators and policy makers should be singled out for blame, a group that also includes a great many university professors who train administrators and policy makers. Most school administrators don't know what education is, let alone how to measure and assess it (Tyack and Hansot 1982; Ginsberg 2011; Cremin 1961; Labaree 2005). Many if not most administrators have never been teachers. Some university professors of education are brilliant researchers but horrible teachers who don't care about education. But many professors of education are mediocre researchers and mediocre teachers who prefer to play school rather than to teach, which sets a bad example for their students who go on to be teachers and administrators.

Many teachers are also part of the problem. They get paid whether they educate students or simply play school. Playing school is a lot easier to do. Many people who hold the job title of teachers, coaches, lecturers, and professors don't actually know how to properly practice teaching because they were never properly taught about the concept and practice of education, and because they don't have any passion to be educators (Labaree 2004).

There needs to be sustained reforms to address the "degraded professional culture" of teachers in the U.S. This would include reorganizing and restaffing not only K–12 schools but also community colleges, colleges, and universities as well, especially university schools of education (Payne 2008, 23, 81; see also Labaree 2004). This is a tall order that is probably impossible to accomplish.

So instead, educational reform goes like this: Incompetent people are given new mandates and sometimes more resources, and they are told to do better. The result, predictably, is that nothing changes, and often things get worse.

This is not a new argument against school reform. Many educational researchers, from Willard Waller (1932) to Charles M. Payne (2008) have decried the "dysfunctional bureaucracy" of schooling (Payne 2008, 23) and the difficulty of reform for almost a century (Tyack and Hansot 1982, Cremin 1961; Argyris 1993, 27–30; Labaree 2005). In many urban school districts, which tend to be impoverished and highly segregated by race and class, the dysfunctional bureaucracy of schooling can be "pathological" or "out-and-out corrupt" (Payne 2008, 45; see also Rogers 1969; Wise 1979).

Educational researchers Peurach et al. (2019) sardonically noted that the school bureaucracy seems "expertly designed to undermine" "collegial learning" and the development of competent teachers (40). School bureaucracy also demoralizes students and weakens their learning. Deeply ingrained sociopolitical and economic inequality dramatically compounds this problem (Markovits 2019, 25). Payne (2008) pointed out, "If we give people an enormously challenging task and only a fraction of the resources they need to accomplish it, sooner or later they start to turn on one another, making the job more difficult still" (24).

Most school administrators and policy makers in the U.S. don't understand the difference between education and playing school, just like former Soviet officials didn't know the different between sustainable economic growth and a fraudulent numbers game (Deming 1994, 32). Most school administrators can't tell the difference between real learning and pretending to learn, and they can't tell the difference between effective teaching and merely acting like a teacher, and this includes the many department chairs, Deans, VPs, and Presidents in higher education.

If an administrator doesn't understand what education is or how it's practiced then that person cannot see it to measure it accurately, let alone evaluate it fairly and validly. If an administrator doesn't understand what education is then that person cannot know what effective teachers look like, nor can they recognize authentic student learning. As business professor Peter F. Drucker (1969) once pointed out, an organization that has no clear vision and no clear objectives can't be efficient because "there will be no way to measure the results" and no way to "determine what effectiveness it has and whether it is obtaining results or not" (191).

ARE SCHOOLS EDUCATIONAL INSTITUTIONS?

Over the last couple of decades, the educational research community has reached a basic consensus over the concept of education and best practices for teaching and learning (see for example Lortie 2002; Cuban 1993; Cuban 2013; Darling-Hammond 2010; Grubb 1999; Bain 2012; Bain 2004). However, this information has not reached most school administrators or teachers, let alone policy makers. And *knowing how* to teach conceptually is very different from actually *teaching effectively.*

There have been many reasons for this failure of communication and dissemination of best practices, from the corrupt politics of public policy reform, petty academic disciplinary politics, the inability of ivory tower scholars to speak to the public, to the organizational dysfunction of university schools of education and the ineptitude of school administrators, especially at the district level, to a simple lack of time and will because the school year is devoted almost exclusively to standardized testing due to political mandates (Labaree 1992; Labaree 2004; Schneider 2014; Payne 2008).

What's the solution? To start, the educational community needs to move away from the traditional, top-down, bureaucratic model of running schools, from the research university down to the kindergarten classroom. This includes both the training of teachers in universities and the top-down professional development model for teachers in schools, which are just ritualized forms of playing school. Traditional professional development in schools, in particular, has never been an effective educational practice (Cuban 2013, 180–81; Kennedy 2019; Payne 2008, 81). Skilled and passionate teachers need to educate and train teachers and administrators, not bureaucratic PhDs, policy makers, or faddish gurus.

Both administrators and teachers need to be retrained by professional educators who knowledgeable, skilled, and passionate about education. These educators would teach teachers how to focus on the concept and practice of education, rather than playing school and playing politics. However, it is important to stress, this training needs to be the right kind of training and professional development that actually promotes student learning and teacher skills (Cuban 2013, 180–81; Payne 2008, 179). Most teacher training programs are "mediocre" at best (Wagner and Kegan 2006, 25). As psychologist Anders Ericsson (2016) has pointed out, professional development, as traditionally practiced, "is not exactly worthless," it's just "not doing much good" (134; see also Kennedy 2019).

For decades, policy makers, marketing gurus, and textbook companies have promoted a lot of faddist trends and silver bullets, all contributing to an endless parade of "differences which make no difference" (Smith 1969). Incompetent school administrators have fed this frenzy because they can't tell the difference between effective educational practices and fraudulent snake oil in fancy packaging. Educational researchers Garrett, Citkowicz, and Williams (2019) have pointed out that there have never been any silver bullets that have worked for educational institutions (131).

Teachers need to be trained by expert teachers, and teachers need to work with other skilled and passionate teachers in a community of dedicated practice. But this is rare. Educational professors Tony Wagner and Robert Kegan and their associates (2006) argue that "most of us in the profession of education have never been part of a system or community of practice dedicated to continuous improvement" (25).

But educators are not alone. To put this failure in context, the famous statistician and business management professor W. Edwards Deming once pointed out that most organizations and businesses have never sought to "improve constantly and forever" their core production processes or services (Walton 1986, 35; Aguayo 1990). Few organizations have ever been "learning organizations" focused on best practices and continual improvement (Senge [1990] 2006).

Ironically, and sadly, most schools have never been learning organizations. In order for schools to actually educate students and teach them to learn, and to love learning, these organizations must first become learning organizations. As such, they would need to be led and staffed by skilled and passionate educators who foster a community of dedicated practice.

But best practices will get us only so far. When researchers have found best practices that actually work in the classroom, there are always "wide variability of how much classroom practice actually changes through a given intervention or implementation" (Garrett, Citkowicz and Williams 2019, 131). This is also true for any organization, including businesses, which W.

Edwards Deming pointed out for decades (Walton 1986, 51; Aguayo 1990). What works in one place and time will not inevitably work in other places.

Educational professor Charles M. Payne (2008) has criticized the whole generalized notion of "best practices" (2, 63). He argued that having successful practices that can supposedly be replicated in any classroom is nothing but "decontextualized" nonsense (2, 63). There is no such thing as a replicable best practice in education. All best practices must be accompanied by "individual, personalized training" for teachers so they can adapt new practices to the specific context of their classroom and the individual needs of their students (Garrett et al. 2019, 131–32). In education, the wheel of instruction has to be reinvented anew every day in each classroom.

When best practices are found, teachers need help to create active learning opportunities so they can apply these new practices and find out what works or doesn't in any given classroom. Teachers also need training about how to conduct action research to generate student data to "inform their instruction" so they can empirically demonstrate what is really working or not working (Garrett et al. 2019, 131–32).

Why don't we already have skilled communities of practice in every school? Why are teachers and school administrators so ill-informed and incompetent? This is largely the fault of universities, which prize theoretical research over practical professional knowledge and skills (Schon 1983). Most university professors deliver highly generalized lectures about subjects they do not practice. This is especially the case with the subject of teaching. More particularly, it is the fault of dysfunctional Departments of Education across the U.S., which do not properly train teachers and administrators to be educators (Smith 1969; Labaree 2004).

As David Labaree (2004) pointed out in his groundbreaking study of Departments of Education, the training of teachers has always been treated with "disdain" by research universities because teaching is considered a "low-status" semi-profession, partly due to its traditional, stigmatized designation as "women's work" in the 20th century. In the U.S., teaching has traditionally had marginal relevance as a low-paid profession due to sexist and patriarchal prejudice (33–36). The sociologist Nathan Glazer (1974) famously called teaching a "minor profession" because of its ambiguous scientific foundations and non-rigorous academic requirements (346).

For most of the 20th century, scientific researchers were largely "embarrassed by education," according to psychologist and cognitive scientist Jerome Bruner (1983, 182). Researchers either ignored the subjects of teaching and student learning, because they were too subjective to study, or researchers investigated these subjects "in the abstract," cut off from complex empirical realities, which resulted in the false belief that "all learning" and all teaching was "basically alike" because all students learned in exactly the same way (Bruner 1983, 182).

Thus, the academic world largely overlooked the subjects of teaching and student learning until the 1960s and '70s, with the discovery of cognitive science and the development of the sociology and anthropology of teaching. However, breakthrough scientific research in these subjects did not really come until the end of the 20th century.

Institutions of higher education have also historically marginalized and denigrated the practices of teaching and learning (Grubb 1999; Kirp 2019, 28). Professors have traditionally focused on research and lecturing, rather than engaging in authentic educational practices. The practice of teaching and educating is very different from what most professors actually do for a living.

University professors have never been required to teach as part of their official job description, not even professors of education. This sad fact explains a lot when it comes to K–20 educational policy and practice. How can novice teachers learn how to teach from professors who have never taught and who cannot demonstrate real teaching? How can novice administrators learn how to manage and evaluate teachers when they don't know what teaching is or how its best practiced?

Furthermore, few professors have been able to clearly communicate their research so as to have an effect on educational policy or practice (Schneider 2014). Thus, as education professor Jack Schneider (2014) points out, teachers who pass through university departments of education are not well trained to read or understand scientific research, let alone successfully put this research into practice in diverse and challenging classrooms (184).

This situation has been made even worse over the 20th century by major economic transformations. Herb Childress (2019) explained how higher education administrators "systematically eliminate[d] an entire class of professionals" by purging full-time, tenured faculty and replacing them with low-paid, contingent adjunct instructors, many of whom live in poverty and depend on public assistance to survive (ix, 6; see also Kezar, Depaola and Scott 2019).

Most professors in the U.S. are no longer highly trained and accomplished tenured professionals, especially at underfunded and under-resourced state universities and community colleges. Most professors are poorly paid, short-term temp workers who have to work two or three different jobs to survive. Sometimes these adjuncts do not know what they are doing in the classroom. But most of the time, adjuncts know what to do but they are too poorly paid and overworked to put their expertise into practice.

Thus, the root of the dysfunction in our schools, especially in the U.S., lies within the research university, the supposed pinnacle of our system of schooling. The research university has become a labyrinth of bureaucracy and politics, with endless, arcane rules and useless rituals. University administrators have systematically devalued not only the practice of teaching and learning, but also the very concept of education (Aronowitz 2000; Childress 2019; Kezar, Depaola and Scott 2019). Universities produce research and sell credentials (and they offer football games and throw good parties). They do not educate students. Universities have debased student learning by reducing the college experience to the ritualized memorization of factoids, the hedonistic pursuit of pleasure, and the conferring of social status through inflated credentials.

Thus, presenting school administrators with valid information about teaching or learning won't do much good for anyone because this information will be misunderstood, ignored, and misused. Most school administrators with university degrees in school administration don't actually know how to manage an educational institution. All they did was buy a special piece of paper, which they framed and hung on their office wall. Most administrators just want to push around a bunch of papers and hold pointless meetings so that they can justify their extravagant salaries and bloated administrative budgets, while still looking important and "efficient" in the eyes of lawmakers and the public at large (Ginsberg 2011).

As many critics have pointed out over the past couple of decades, the current over-reliance on accountability measurements in schools, like grades, student evaluation surveys, and awarded credentials, are not focused on the authentic practice of education (Muller 2018; Birnbaum 2000; Peurach et al. 2019, 38). Accountability measures and procedures are about playing school, cutting costs, management gimmicks, and the illusions (if not delusions) of managerial authority.

Student evaluation surveys in particular, which are discussed over many chapters in volume two of this series, are a prime example of administrative malfeasance. Student surveys reflect a "cost-conscious" administrative decision to "outsource" management responsibilities onto the consumer so that administrators can save time and money, and pretend to look effective in the process ("Barely Managing" 2018, 65).

It is too difficult and too expensive for school administrators to actually evaluate teachers using valid measurement techniques, such as observing teachers in the act of teaching, or paying teachers to conduct classroom observations of each other, or setting up formal peer-to-peer discussions of teaching, or engaging teachers in quality professional development opportunities from trained experts instead of consultants pushing useless fads. Educational researchers have already identified effective practices to improve teaching and student learning, but school administrators simply choose not to implement or support these practices, often because they feel there is no time, money, or organizational will to do so.

DO ACCOUNTABILITY SYSTEMS EVEN WORK?

Supposedly the economic values of measurement, accountability, and efficiency help businesses maximize the bottom line (Doerr 2018). However, as journalist Adrian Wooldridge (2011) and many others have pointed out, the values of profitability and productivity can often "do more harm than good in the public sector" (324; see also Muller 2018; Birnbaum 2000). Rather than improve schools, accountability reforms have often been used to justify ineffective managerialism and the top-down authority of school administrators, while delegitimizing the professional judgment and skilled practices of teachers (Ginsberg 2011; Tyack 1974; Cremin 1961; Labaree 2005; Koretz 2017, 33, 203).

Statistician and business management professor W. Edwards Deming has made the same point about businesses. Typical "management by objectives" accountability measurements often do more harm than good for most businesses, not least because "the most important figures are unknown and unknowable" (Walton 1986, 36, 48, 93; Aguayo 1990; Deming 1994, 30). They also harm company morale and destroy productive work relationships. Deming (1994, 30) criticized accountability measurements as "management by fear" (Walton 1986, 90; Aguayo 1990, 27).

Accountability measures give school administrators an inflated sense of power and a "false sense of certainty" about the complex and chaotic institution that we call school. Student learning is continually in flux, and largely beyond the control of teachers or administrators (Birnbaum 2000, 198). Accountability practices are not only invalid, but they are also counterproductive because they often devolve into an "adherence to ceremony and ritual" rather than actual "evaluation and inspection" of teachers or students (198).

Accountability measures are also hypocritical displays of naked power. While administrators go on and on about organizational efficiency when talking about evaluating teachers and students, those same administrators never use their own logic to evaluate themselves and the massive growth of wasteful administrative jobs over the past couple of decades (Graeber 2018, 18). One academic Dean at a British university admitted that 90 percent of her job was empty "bullshit" that was "wholly and entirely disconnected" from the stated purpose of the school (qtd. in Graeber 2018, 55).

Accountability systems are also very expensive and most likely not worth the cost in terms of money, time, and the meager benefits they produce. There is also the damage that accountability systems can do to teacher and student morale because accountability practices can be socially corrosive (Gaither, Nedwek and Neal 1994, 83). Researchers have found over and over with businesses that punitive evaluation systems do not work. This failed method has been derisively called the "rank and yank" approach to management ("When Rank" 2020, 52).

When you evaluate and rank employees, and then discipline employees in the lowest rankings, it "hurts overall performance, not least by lowering productivity" because it saps employee morale ("When Rank" 2020, 52). When applied to schooling, as Birnbaum (2000) perceptively argued, "The irony of quantification [and evaluation] is that the more we are committed to measuring the effectiveness of [schools], the less effective we are likely to believe [schools] to be" (198). Our "obsession" with data driven rankings and economic metrics, according to economist Alison Wolf (2002), "has damaged our notion of what education is about" (254).

In order to validly assess teaching and learning, if indeed that is the goal of the current accountability movement, administrators actually need to observe teachers and students, and talk to teachers in order to understand their pedagogical justifications for what they do and why. Administrators would also need to promote and protect the principle of academic freedom for teachers, which is required for quality education to take place in classrooms (Ginsberg 2011; Whittington 2018; Fish 2019).

So many teachers are fearful of honestly talking to either students or administrators because they are scared of getting fired, especially marginalized adjuncts in higher education with no job security who can be let go at any time for any reason (Santoro 2018; Childress 2019, 11; Payne 2008, 44; Kezar, Depaola and Scott 2019).

AN ADMINISTRATIVE COUP

Let's be honest. The accountability movement in the U.S. is *not* about education. It's *not* even about accountability. It's about economics. It's about politics. It's about money, social status, control, and power. It's also about the administrative *coup d'état* of education, which started in the 19th century when America first created a bureaucratic system of common schools. It's about the "triumph of imbecile institutions over life and culture," as the economist Thorstein Veblen pointed out a century ago (qtd. in Breit and Ransom 1998, 31).

State politicians and social reformers in the mid-19th century sought to control teachers and students by creating "the one best system" of schooling for an industrialized, capitalist republic (Tyack 1974; Tyack and Hansot 1982; Callahan 1962; Cremin 1961; Labaree 2005). This managerial coup naturally entailed the "subordination" of teachers and students under the top-down leadership structure of a new class of managers called the school administrator (Callahan 1962; Tyack 1974, 60; Tyack and Hansot 1982; Cremin 1961; Labaree 1992; Labaree 2005; Ginsberg 2011; McNeil 2000; Graeber 2018).

The administrative control of education in the U.S. increased further at the end of the 20th century, as the bureaucracy of schooling exploded around the country, from kindergarten to college (Peurach et al. 2019, 37; Rogers 1969; Drucker 1969, 189; Wise 1979). To take one example, in higher education in the U.S. from 1985 to 2005, student enrollments increased 56 percent, while faculty appointments increased 50 percent, although most of these faculty jobs went to poorly paid adjuncts on temporary contracts who often had to work multiple jobs to survive.

At the same time, administrative jobs rose by 85 percent, while nonteaching staff jobs went up a staggering 240 percent (Ginsberg 2011; Graeber 2018, 161). And this administrative transformation wasn't just taking place in public colleges and universities. Administrative growth at public institutions of higher education grew by only 66 percent, while administrative growth at private schools grew 135 percent (Ginsberg 2011; Graeber 2018, 162).

A big part of the administrative takeover of schooling was the development of accountability programs, most of which were initiated in the 1960s and '70s to monitor the increased federal and state investments in education. As Jerry Z. Muller (2018) pointed out, the development of accountability systems in schools caused "a mushroom-like growth of administrative staff," as accountability metrics "diverted time and resources away from doing and towards documenting, and from those who teach and research to those who gather and disseminate data for the Research Assessment Exercise" (74).

These accountability programs were based on the old-fashioned, early 20th century management idea that organizations can be "precisely described and defined, and therefore carefully monitored and controlled" (Handy 1990, 130). Over the past half century, sociologists, historians, and business professors have proven this enduring myth of control to be a harmful fantasy (Handy 1990), but it endures as the guiding logic of most schools.

The political economist Thorstein Veblen was one of first social scientists to fully grasp the managerial transformation of schools in the early 20th century. In his critical study of education, *The Higher Learning in America*, published in 1918, he wrote, "It is further of the essence of this scheme of academic control that the captain of erudition should freely exercise the power of academic life or death over the members of his staff, to reward the good and faithful servant and to abase the recalcitrant" (qtd. in Spindler 2002, 53).

During the early 20th century, newly certified school administrators aspired to turn schools into factories (Tyack 1974; Tyack and Hansot 1982; Callahan 1962; Cremin 1961; Labaree 2005). They transformed the student into the raw material to be industrially processed and certified by the school. They also transformed the teacher into a deskilled manual laborer who was to be exploited as cheaply as possible and who needed constant micromanagement from above.

Veblen used the sardonic term "captains of erudition" for school administrators on purpose. It was a mocking swipe at the popular early 20th century deification of the new class of industrial managers, who many fawning admirers called "captains of industry," or as Peter Drucker (1969) called them, "the industrial engineer of scientific management" (272).

Armed with the power of the state and the latest management theory, just what have these captains of erudition accomplished over the past century? Arguably, they have done much worse than nothing. School administrators have jumped from management fad to management fad, leaving a trail of failed results and ruined lives (Birnbaum 2000; Best 2006).

And to make matters worse, administrators have squandered billions and billions of dollars away from the central activity that should be at the heart of all schools: Professionally trained teachers who have the creative freedom to develop the appropriate curriculum to meet the specific needs of students in a well-resourced classroom (Graeber 2018, 53).

And while we are focused on schooling, the dramatic rise in administers can be seen all across the labor market. Since 1983, *The Economist* pointed out, "the number of managers and administrators in the American workforce has more than doubled, while the employment in other occupations has gone up by only 44%.

The *Harvard Business Review* found that many people work in organizations with six layers of management, while in large organizations there are often eight layers or more. That same report also found that employees spent "an average of 27% of their time on bureaucratic chores" (Graeber 2015; Graeber 2018).

At this point it would be instructive to look at two enlightening metaphors that serve as good examples of the failures of school administrators and the corruption of education through the managerial bureaucratization of schooling. However, keep in mind, these examples could easily be extended to the damage done by cynical and corrupt executives in any public or private organization (Stewart 2009; Pfeffer 2015).

Sociologist Joel Best (2006) included this piece of office folklore in his recent study of crowd behavior and fads:

> The American rowing team and the Japanese rowing teach had a race. The Japanese team won by a mile! The American team became very discouraged by the loss and began to sag. Corporate management decided the reason for the crushing defeat had to be found. They established a continuous improvement

team to investigate the problem and recommended the appropriate corrective action. The result showed that the Japanese had eight people rowing and one person steering, while the American team had one person rowing and eight people steering. The American corporate steering committee immediately hired a consulting firm to do a study on this management structure. After some time and millions of dollars, the consulting firm concluded that too many people were steering and not enough people were rowing. The American team's management structure was then totally reorganized. The reorganized structure included three steering directors, three steering managers, two steering supervisors, and one rower. Included in the reorganization plan was a new performance standard which gave empowerment and enrichment to the rower in order to develop in him the incentive to work harder. The next year, the Japanese team won by two miles. To cut costs, the American team sold all the paddles, cancelled the capital investments for new equipment, ceased development of a new canoe, gave a superior performance award to the consulting firm, and distributed the money saved as bonuses to the senior executives. (as qtd. in Best 2006, 125)

Hopefully this story brought laughter before the deadly seriousness sunk in. This story applies to all sorts of management folly and bureaucratization in the public and private sectors. Since the middle of the 20th century, as Peter Drucker (1969) pointed out, people have taken it for granted that all organizations *must* be "managed by professionals, whether they are called 'managers,' 'administrators,' or 'executives'" (175).

But Drucker failed to understand that managers often enact policies or practices that serve the best interests of managers, rather than serving the interests of clients or the organization (Khurana 2002, 34; Stewart 2009; Pfeffer 2015; Rogers 1969; Wise 1979). Economists call this the "agency problem" (Khurana 2002, 34, 52; Pfeffer 2015, 19, 167). In higher education some have called this the "creating committees to deal with the 'too many committees' problem" (Graeber 2015, 150).

Whatever you call it, the problem of bureaucracy for the sake of bureaucracy causes inefficiency and suffering for all types of organizations around the world. In particular, it the core poison that has killed the educational ethos of public schooling in the U.S. (Rogers 1969; Wise 1979; Argyris 1993, 27–30).

But while mindless bureaucracy is an evil, there has been a much more pernicious and malevolent force at work: Autocracy and socio-political inequality. For most of human history, at least since the advent of agriculture, human organizations have been plagued by unequal distributions of power and resources, from the family all the way to the state. Socio-political and economic inequality has plagued schooling for centuries (Payne 2008; Kozol 1991; Markovits 2019). Public policy has always been a power play where the strong dictate and control the lives of the weak.

The business professor Peter Drucker (1954) once used a metaphor about the origins of surgery to explain the inefficient predicament of traditional power and authority. He wrote,

> Up until well into the seventeenth century, surgery was performed not by doctors but by barbers who, untaught and unlettered, applied whatever tortures they had picked up during their apprenticeship. Doctors, observing a literal interpretation of their oath not to inflict bodily harm, were too 'ethical' to cut and were not even supposed to watch. But the operation, if performed according to the rules, was presided over by a learned doctor who sat on a dais well above the struggle and read what the barber was supposed to be doing aloud from a Latin classic (which the barber, of course, did not understand). Needless to say, it was always the barber's fault if the patient died, and always the doctor's achievement if he survived. And the doctor got the bigger fee in either event (193).

For thousands of years, at the head of every social organization or institution, often with their names or busts engraved in granite, has been a powerful tyrant or an aristocratic elite who controlled for their own advantage the organization and all its resources, especially all of the lowly "human resources" who actually made the organization work, who for most of human history have been slaves, surfs, peons, drudges, grunts, and only more recently, wage-laborers.

During the industrial age, a new technocratic "intellectual elite" of managers and engineers reinvented this traditional "command-and-control" model of the firm, which placed the CEO at the top, like the captain of a ship, who commanded a hierarchically segmented group of managers and employees who actually did all the work (Kaplan and Norton 1996, 5, 16). The concept of leadership, as management professor Peter M. Senge ([1990] 2006) pointed out, has become synonymous with the "positional authority" of "top management" at the "top of the hierarchy" (319).

This belief implies that only top management should have the power to make decisions and affect change, and everyone else in the organization must do as they're told. Everyone seems to think "leader-centrically," according to management professor Barbara Kellerman (2012, xx; 2015, 2), that "being a leader is better and more important than being a follower" (xx). However, Kellerman pointed out that this common-sense belief is wrong. Followers are often more important than leaders.

During the 19th century, this command-and-control model was applied to the new institution of the modern, state-funded, "public" school system. University presidents, state bureaucrats, and school administrators each managed their own respective fiefdoms, all the while commanding an army of lowly grunts, the teachers, who were supposed to carry out the orders of their superiors while managing their pupils' academic success.

Teachers in turn presided as tyrants over the powerless peons in their classrooms, the students. For over a century, teachers have tried to command their classrooms like administrators commanded the school. But like the doctors in Drucker's example, teachers have always been controlled by their sociopolitical betters, taking the blame when schooling goes awry, and getting little praise when things go according to administrative plan. Even now, in the 21st century, teachers in the U.S. are still treated as ignorant barbers doing their masters' bidding.

However, this type of autocratic, managerial corporatism is not really an effective model for businesses, let alone for nonprofit organizations and public institutions, especially schools (Khurana 2002, 46; Stewart 2009). The widespread belief that corporate managers are in charge of businesses, or that administrators are in charge of schools, and that these leaders determine the performance of the organization, is simply false (Kellerman 2012).

The self-serving "myth of leadership" (Kelley 1992, 12), and the accompanying "cult of the CEO," the "romance of leadership," and the notions of managers as "corporate saviors" and "hero-leaders," have all been propagated by corporate managers, consultants, leadership gurus, and management professors since the late 19th century (Khurana 2002; Pfeffer 2015, 9; Kellerman 2008, 10; Kellerman 2012, 3). They are all hyperbolic nonsense. Even in the 21st century, there is still a widespread belief that the vague qualities of "leadership" and a manager's "charisma" somehow magically make organizations efficient and productive (Khurana 2002, xii–xiii, 68; Pfeffer 2015). They don't.

Business professors have found that CEOs and other business executives aren't very effective as corporate managers. One researcher summarized the scientific literature on effective leadership and found that "one of every two leaders and managers" is "estimated to be ineffective (that is, a disappointment, incompetent, a mis-hire, or a complete failure) in their current roles" (qtd. in Pfeffer 2015, 16). Another review of the literature concluded, "The base rate for managerial incompetence in any organization is quite high" (qtd. in Pfeffer 2015, 16).

Most managers don't actually know why a particular business model is successful, or not, despite what they pretend to know. This is due to "casual ambiguity," which refers to the complex, and largely unknowable chain of cause/effect within firms, between firms, and between firms and the broader social and physical environment (Pfeffer 1992, 144, 262; King 2007, 156).

No one really knows why some firms are successful and others not. As one business professor put it, "Outcomes in organizations are overdetermined in the sense that they have multiple cause. It is difficult, if not impossible, to ascertain which of the possible causes is the true source of the result" (Pfeffer 1992, 262).

But that hasn't stopped the corporate savior mantra from permeating the educational accountability movement, especially over the past two decades. Back in the 1960s, Peter Drucker (1969) noted the common myth that a "competent administration" can "cure" all organizational ills (214). Thus, for decades, almost all prominent school improvement proposals have involved giving more power to administrators who will drive innovative reforms by tightening their grip on staff (teachers), while pandering to the wants and needs of customers (students and parents).

Take for example a recent reform polemic written by education professor David Kirp (2019) who denounced the "college dropout scandal." His book is largely a cheerleading homage to various college administrators whose "forceful leadership is driving the campaign to improve graduation rates" (134; on the problematic measure of graduation rates see Kimbrough 2020). What's needed, according to Kirp, are "many more college presidents and provosts," like the ones interviewed for his book (134).

However, even Kirp admits, "these senior administrators, while admired by their colleagues for their boldness, remain rarities in the timid, status-quo-oriented world of higher education" (136). And what about faculty? They are the problem that needs to be fixed. Sound familiar?

As business professor Rakesh Khurana (2002) has argued, the myth of the corporate manager has become a "quasi-religious" dogma that has influenced every type of organization, and this dogma is widely believed with "virtually religious conviction" (71, 110) in both the private and public spheres. Khurana pointed out that CEOs are often deified as the main source of a company's success, and they are paid outlandish amounts of money.

In the 1980s, CEOs earned thirty times the salary of a typical company worker, but over the last couple decades CEO pay has grown tenfold to three hundred times the typical worker pay (Clausing 2019, 43). Since the 1970s, points out economist Kimberly Clausing (2019), "CEO salaries have increased over 900 percent," averaging about $15 million a year, while worker wages have risen only 10 percent (43, 152).

Many company directors, shareholders, and taxpayers have "blind faith" in the notion that a "charismatic CEO" has the mystical "power to heal" any problem with a struggling company or public agency (Khurana 2002, 21). But these irrational beliefs are not supported by facts. Khurana (2002) points out that "CEOs and other top executives have no statistically significant impact on firm performance, even when they make major decisions about strategy or structure" (22).

While some managers, like Jamie Dimon, who was detailed in Khurana's book, are highly effective leaders and worth their weight in gold, many administrators are incompetent and do real damage to their firms. Most managers, as business professor Clayton M. Christensen (2016) pointed out, are largely "powerless" and play only "symbolic" roles within an organization (102). As one honest hospital CEO put it, "I am the least important person in this building. This place would run without me for weeks, but the most important groups here are the people taking care of the patients" (qtd. in McShane and Glinow 2018, 285).

Sociologists and management theorists have traditionally believed that organizational leaders have earned their power because promotion was supposed to be based on "competence and experience," as famously theorized by Max Weber (Pfeffer 1992, 132; Kellerman 2015, 84). However, classical sociological theories turned out to be wrong—very wrong.

The professor of education Laurence J. Peter was one of the first scholars to explain how incompetent most corporate managers really are. His theory came to known as the "Peter principle" (Peter and Hull 2009). He stated, "Workers get promoted until they reach their level of incompetence" (Peter and Hull 2009; "The Promotion Curse" 2019, 50). Even competent professionals, once promoted, often become incompetent managers.

Why is this? To start, many, if not most, corporate managers are promoted for many reasons other than their knowledge or skill as managers. Recent scientific studies have uncovered that many corporate managers have been promoted largely due to their social connections, their ability to acquire power, and personal characteristic, such as likability, physical appearance, and attractiveness, not their leadership skills or competency at running a business (Pfeffer 1992; Pfeffer 2010; "The Eyes Have It" 2019, 60).

Many managers are good actors who know how to look like a leader. They use the right slogans. They push the right papers. But these managers simply do not know what they are doing. And the firm would be better off without them.

In particular, many educational administrators have been poorly trained in university schools of education (Labaree 1992; Labaree 2004). Educational leadership is certainly not a science. Many school administrators struggle to comprehend, let alone manage, the highly complex, "loosely coupled systems" of a school (Weick 1976; Meyer, Rowan and Meyer 1978). Incompetent school administrators often stand in the way of teachers and the learning of students, especially in higher education, with its endless labyrinths of administrative bureaucracy (Birnbaum 2000; Ginsberg 2011).

BEYOND THE "PUBLIC" VS. "PRIVATE" DEBATE

Organizational culture (Scott 1992; McShane and Glinow 2018) and politics (Stone 2002; McShane and Glinow 2018) are the main reasons why scientific research does not have much of an impact on public policy or institutional reform, especially the administrative and political priorities of managers and the culture they foster. This is particularly true of schools (Cuban 1993; Ginsberg 2011), which are highly institutionalized organizations.

Incompetence is a stubborn feature of all organizations, public and private. Because schools around the world have been strangled by inept and ineffective administrators for so long, it's doubtful that true educational reform, let alone more complex socio-political reform to address deep set inequalities, could ever happen in the U.S. or any other large postindustrial country (Tyack and Cuban 1995).

Many conservative critics could take this point about bureaucratization and administrative mismanagement and easily twist it as a weapon directed against big government so as to argue how the free market–oriented charter schools could do things much better than public schools (Henig 1994; Henig 2008; Smith 2003). Yes, free market initiatives are generally much more effective and efficient than government programs.

As Peter Drucker (1969) pointed out, public markets force businesses to pass a "test of performance" (237). They have to prove they can be profitable, similar to the idea of democratic accountability, whereby voters supposedly elect only competent leaders who produce results and force out leaders who do not.

The market system is predicated on the idea that businesses go bankrupt and their assets are reallocated when they are unprofitable. This risk of bankruptcy allows for the "creative destruction" of capitalism, which promotes constant change and innovation (Schumpeter 1950, 83). Holding nonprofit or government organizations accountable through a "test of performance" is logical in principle, as long as the test is valid and in sync with the organization's values and goals.

Charter schools are a good idea in principle because many of these organizations give control back to teachers and they put the focus of education on students. However, most charter schools have not been able to come up with valid accountability metrics to drive improvement. Thus, charter schools have not been shown to be any more effective than public schools (Henig 1994; Henig 2008; Cuban 2013, 125). Many charter schools have been just as bad as public schools in reproducing the disastrous policies and practices discussed in this book, especially for-profit charter schools, some of which are outright frauds designed to con unsophisticated consumers.

Governments also have a legitimate interest in controlling or managing schools in principle, especially democracies, as there is a definite democratic argument for public schooling and keeping schools accountable to democratic principles and processes (Gutmann 1987; Smith 2003; Borman, Danzig and Garcia 2012; Colby, Beaumont, Ehrlich and Corngold 2008).

Furthermore, private organizations can't always do things better than governments, especially where public goods and externalities are concerned. The political scientist Norton Long explained many decades ago that "governments are organizations" and that the converse is also true, "organizations are governments," so you will find organizational politics and inefficiencies everywhere, in every organization, public or private (qtd. in Pfeffer 1992, 8).

The Economist Robert H. Frank (1985) pointed out that neither the market system nor government work especially well at managing resources and both systems "will always be flawed" (244). Thus, political scientist Cass R. Sunstein (1997) argued that we need to "move beyond the increasingly tired and decreasingly helpful question of whether we should have 'more' or 'less' government or 'more' or 'less' in the way of free markets. These dichotomies are far too crude" (9; see also Giddens 1994).

Perhaps more importantly, for the purposes of this book, just because private organizations sometimes work better doesn't mean that they always work better, or necessarily work better. The growth of bureaucratization and management can be seen in all sectors of the economy since the late 19th century (Chandler 1977; Graeber 2015, 21; Graeber 2018, 149; Frank 1985, 245; Starr 2017; Giddens 1994).

Sociologist Paul Starr (2017) detailed the rise of bureaucracy in the American health care industry and he argued that bureaucrats had become "the overwhelming majority of professionals in the modern world" (420). Bureaucracy is a standard organizational feature of the modern world in both public and private organizations and firms.

In fact, as anthropologist David Graeber (2015) pointed out, it was private American and German business conglomerates who invented modern bureaucracy, not governments (8, 12–13; see also Chandler 1977). Private corporations have always been just as inefficient and bureaucratic, and just as much of a threat to the free market and individual freedom, as have governments or other political institutions (Giddens 1994; Stewart 2009; Graeber 2018, 16–19).

While noting the inefficacy of managed socialist economies, anthropologist David Graeber (2018) explained how both the public and private sectors in capitalist countries have also managed to create millions of "bullshit" jobs that serve no purpose to the firm or to society (17). Graeber (2015) call this phenomenon the "iron law of liberalism": "Any market reform, any government initiative intended to reduce red tape and promote market forces will have the ultimate effect of increasing the total number of regulations, the total amount of paperwork, and the total number of bureaucrats" (9). Most of the criticisms that conservatives use against big government can easily be turned against most businesses, especially multinational corporations.

Thus, the "public" vs. "private" dichotomy is simply not helpful in thinking about the inefficiencies and indignities of managerialism and bureaucratization in the 21st century. And neither is the traditional political dichotomy of "right" vs. "left" (Giddens 1994). Bureaucratic rationality, technocratic overconfidence, and good old-fashioned ineptitude can often do more harm than good in any kind of organization.

As economists Abhijit V. Banerjee and Esther Duflo (2019) argued, "The history of state-directed investments is not one that inspires confidence; judgments are frequently bad even when they are not actually deliberately distorted to benefit someone or some group, which is often. These are 'government' failures just as there are market failures, and there are so many instances of these that it would be dangerous to blindly rely on governments to pick the winners. But there are also so many market failures that it makes no sense either to rely on the market alone" (203).

Sociologist Anthony Giddens (1994) argued three decades ago, "bureaucracies everywhere," public and private, have become "inflexible and impersonal," and thus are a universal impediment to human well-being (18). Dr. W. Edwards Deming made the same point, but put the blame more squarely on corporate managers and failed accountability systems, which "destroy" people and organizations (qtd. in Senge [1990] 2006, xii; Aguayo 1990).

While bureaucracy is often associated with government programs, free-market bureaucrats destroy private enterprises all the time because clueless or greedy administrators lose sight of their business' core mission and core strengths. Just take General Electric for an example, a company which has collapsed from its glory days because of gross mismanagement by "GE jerks," which devastated both employees and stockholders (Pfeffer 2015, 37).

Sometimes the fallout is even worse, people can die, as the recent scandal at Boeing has highlighted. Boeing used to be highly praised company that was "run by engineers for engineers," but over the last two decades corporate bureaucracy corrupted the company, reduced the quality of its core product, and perhaps fatally damaged the company's reputation (Nocera, 2020, para. 5).

Two decades into the 21st century and it seems as if almost every type of business, nonprofit organization, and social institution has become bureaucratized and mismanaged by incompetent administrators, and this is clearly the case with many public schools, community colleges, and universities. Historian Francois Furstenberg (2020) took aim at his own institutions, John

Hopkins University, to explain how university leaders were "failing" due to their "ineptitude" (para. 1).

The bankruptcy of management principles, incompetent leaders, and bureaucracy was memorably demonstrated by the banking and finance industry, which caused a devastating global recession in 2009, but we see it again and again in every sector of the economy. According to anthropologist David Graeber (2015), we now live in an age of "total bureaucratization" (18), and bureaucracy creates not only inefficiency, but also incalculable financial and moral costs.

One recent study of the health care industry in the U.S. found that insurers and providers spent $812 billion in 2017, a single year, on just administrative costs, which represented 34.2% of all health care expenditures in the nation that year (Himmelstein, Campbell and Woolhandler 2020). Canada, which has a nationalized health care system, spent much less on health care administration that year. Only 17% of all health care expenditures in Canada went to bureaucrats in 2017. Hundreds of billions of dollars in the U.S. are wasted every year on bureaucracy, in just the health care industry, to say nothing of the rest of the economy, all the while millions of Americans fight for survival, struggling to find food, adequate housing, and pay for medical care.

The larger point here, which the metaphorical rowing story brilliantly describes, is that administrative control and bureaucracy is one of the central afflictions that plague organizations and institutions all around the world, especially in schools in the United States (Rogers 1969; Wise 1979; Argyris 1993, 27–30). Effective and lasting educational reform cannot come from, nor can it be managed by, school administrators, college VPs or Deans, corporate executives, management consultants, politicians, or policy wonks.

As business professor Charles Handy (1993, 19) and political scientist Aaron Wildavsky (1979, 131) have both perceptively asked over the last few decades about accountability reforms, "effectiveness for what or for whom"?

Clearly, the educational accountability movement, as we have examined in this book, has not benefited either teachers, students, or society. However, one group has benefited enormously from all these waves of accountability reforms. Administrative personnel at schools have proliferated over the last thirty years. In most school systems, administrators often outnumber teachers, and top administrative pay packages have become inflated beyond reasonable levels (Labaree 1992).

It's time to reimagine schools where real educational practices are the central focus of the organization. We can do without the paper pushers, bureaucratic machinery, and invalid accountability metrics. Schools need to reimagine and reprioritize their central purpose: The profound and immeasurable educational relationship between students and teachers who are trying to learn from each other. It's a simple notion with revolutionary implications.

Conclusion

Can We Deschool Our Schools?

Peter F. Drucker (1969) once pointed out that every yardstick used for accountability measurements "bespeaks a value judgment regarding the purpose" of the activity or the organization for which it was created (196; see also Kaplan and Norton 1996, 10; Koretz 2017, 203). Thus, many critics have pointed out how Andy Grove's (2015) celebration of efficiency metrics meant for profit-oriented businesses can fall short, very short, when used to evaluate the practices and outcomes of public institutions, like schools ("From the Cradle" 2020, 56).

In order for accountability metrics to work, and for broader school reforms to be successful, innovations must originate from within the classroom and be directed by committed and experienced teachers who are trying to reach the needs of specific groups of students. Schools should be managed by teachers, not administrators or business consultants. Teachers should hold themselves accountable to their students, just like students should be held accountable to their teachers. This is the only foundation for successful educational programs.

Toward this end, the reader needs to imagine something much more radical than administrative reform through faddish management theory, privatization, or government decree. Ivan Illich (1970) suggested a half-century ago that there was an important distinction between education and schooling. Illich argued schools were getting in the way of students' education, and so he proposed that educational reformers needed to think about how they might "deschool" our culture.

Illich argued that we "confuse teaching with learning, grade advancement with education, [and] a diploma with competence" (1). Further, he argued, "We cannot begin a reform of education unless we first understand that neither individual learning nor social equality can be enhanced by the ritual of schooling" (55).

While Illich had a bold educational vision (1970), he was a bit utopian and went too far in suggesting that all children, especially adolescents, could naturally become autodidacts on their own, which is a romantic fantasy that the French novelist and philosopher Jean-Jacques Rousseau popularized with his pedagogical novel *Emile* in 1762. In contradiction to Rousseau's and Illich's romanticism, modern psychology has clearly demonstrated that all children need "authoritative" parents and teachers to guide them into a responsible, constructive, and self-aware adulthood (Steinberg 1996; Steinberg 2014; Gopnik 2016).

In order to effectively educate our young, we still need teachers and schools. We still need professionally educated and caring individuals to be in control of both the classroom and the curriculum. Children need to be taught discipline and rules, as much as they need to be taught about creativity and autonomy. But as David F. Labaree (2012) pointed out, we all need to be a lot more pessimistic when it comes to the very possibility of reforming schools and improving educational practices. This is especially true when reforms are coming from agents at the top of the political pyramid, like government bureaucrats, school administrators, CEOs, or other powerful actors with a political agenda.

We also need to step back to look at the big picture in order to ask, what do we want out of our educational institutions and who can achieve those objectives under what conditions with what resources? In other words, what should "a good school do" (Schneider 2017, 94)? This conversation needs to be open to everyone and led by teachers and students, not administrators.

Management professor William Isaacs (1999) pointed out that "it is a contradiction in terms to use a top-down, control-oriented approach to try to *manufacture* learning and empowerment instead of creating conditions where they naturally emerge" (author's emphasis, 337–38). When managers dictate the circumstances of teaching and student learning then learning becomes "a standard to impose, not a process to germinate" personal growth (338).

Would-be educational reformers need to have a dichotomous, if not schizophrenic, frame of mind. On the one hand, reformers need to think more deeply about how to change our educational institutions in order to promote real learning, real competence, and real personal development—in short, a *real* education, which would empower individuals and transform society, rather than reinforce and reproduce existing socioeconomic inequalities through ritualized schooling.

This entails both rethinking and reimagining schooling. It also entails reducing schooling so that this overburdened and dysfunctional institution can allow education to be practiced more meaningfully outside of the formal school system, which has monopolized the concept and practice of education to the detriment of all.

On the other hand, reformers need to pay close attention to cynical scholars like David F. Labaree (2012), who insightfully pointed out how almost every educational reform has failed. He has reasonably argued that educational reformers need to be a lot more cynical and pessimistic. He has warned would-be reformers to not "assume you have the answer," and perhaps more importantly, to assume that your "reform might actually make things worse" (159).

Labaree (2011) has also cautioned that we cannot measure what matters most with education. And even when researchers can uncover meaningful insights into education or schooling, this information rarely makes it to teachers or administrators, and even less frequently has any real or lasting impact on educational practice (Labaree 2011; Labaree 2012; Schneider 2014, 12).

Successful educational reform needs to be driven by empirical evidence-based practices; the accountability movement gets that much right. However, accountability measures need to be focused on the activities of real teachers and students engaged in education in real classrooms, rather than measures dictated by ideology, politics, or administrative expediency (Labaree 1992; Henig 2008; Schneider 2017). And there needs to be a "broad portfolio" of tentative, low-stake measurements to assess student learning and school quality (Schneider 2017, 96).

Education professor Linda M. McNeil (2000) has pointed out, "The language of accountability seems, on a commonsense level, to be about professional practice that is responsible to the children and to the public. . . . Behind the usage of these terms in educational policy, however, is a far different political and pedagogical reality" (10; see also Labaree 1992).

If we are going to use accountability measurements to evaluate schools then these metrics must be "reframed" by real educators so they can be valid and useful for educational purposes (Schneider 2017, 251). However, this is easier said than done. Reliable and useful information on schooling costs a lot of money and takes a lot of time to produce (Labaree 2011; Schneider 2017).

It's ironic that the accountability movement in the U.S. has often been accompanied by calls for fiscal austerity and budget cuts. As Nobel Prize winning economist Douglass C. North (1990) explained, it takes a lot of resources to measure social programs accurately; thus, the costs of accountability measurements are often "prohibitive" for many organizations (29–31).

North also stated that it is often "too costly to be comprehensive or fully accurate" when conducting accountability evaluations (29). To make matters worse, evaluations require enforcement mechanisms, which add even more costs to the equation (32). Thus, most organizations take shortcuts and act without full knowledge or the proper oversight to ensure employee compliance. The unscrupulous go even further and "cheat, steal, or lie" to take advantage of the inevitable information asymmetry, as we already discussed (30; see also Akerlof and Shiller 2015).

But even more importantly, business professors have found that performance reviews of employees simply don't work. It's impossible to measure every meaningful facet of an employee's job and almost all performance evaluations are full of rater "bias and subjectivity" (McShane and Glinow 2018, 160). Most studies conclude that "performance reviews are stressful, morale sapping, and dysfunctional events that typically descend into political arenas and paperwork bureaucracies" (McShane and Glinow 2018, 160). It's time to question whether accountability metrics, for either employees or whole organizations, are merely political power plays or ritualized Kabuki management theater (Wildavsky 1979).

Take for example the quantification and evaluation of teaching and student learning in schools, which sounds on the surface like a perfectly logical and useful management activity. But these two idealistic goals are largely intangible, so they are very hard to put into practice (Labaree 2011). And ironically, when managers actually try to quantify and evaluate teaching or learning, these metrics easily lead to the corruption of the very practices they are meant to objectively evaluate (Koretz 2017).

No one, not even the best educational researchers, can accurately or fairly quantify or evaluate teaching or student learning. It's simply impossible. First of all, researchers can't fully understand, let alone see or measure, either activity in its fullness. While a researcher can see some aspects of teaching, it is much harder to observe student learning. There is no way to fully or fairly evaluate either practice.

And to even try, you would need many skilled professionals with PhDs who would need a lot of resources to set up a valid study, which would take months or years. And that's just measuring the teaching and learning practices in just a single classroom. What about the costs of measuring a whole school or a whole school system? Accurate measurements and valid evaluations would be very expensive in terms of money, human resources, physical resources, and time.

This is why about two-thirds of U.S. businesses don't fully measure or evaluate employee performance ("Staff" 2019, 55). Employee evaluations are too difficult and expensive because it's very hard to judge the quality of a worker (Banerjee and Duflo 2019, 28). Ironically, businesses in the U.S. spend a lot of money and time on evaluating and interviewing applicants, but they inefficiently use the wrong tools to do this work so they often do not hire optimal employees ("Staff" 2019; Brafman and Brafman 2008, 77). And to make matters worse, firms rarely monitor and evaluate those employees once they are hired ("Staff" 2019, 55).

All of this should make you wonder which clueless administrator had the brilliant idea of measuring and evaluating teachers as employees when most businesses shudder at this dauntingly expensive task? Of course, the administrative solution to this paradox is simply to cut corners by doing incomplete and invalid measurements, which lead to biased and misleading evaluations, or to just commit fraud and hope that no one notices.

CAN WE MEASURE WHAT MATTERS MOST?

The practices of empirical research and evidence-based evaluation in both theory and practice are very important and useful. Most types of educational evaluation could be much more structured, rationally organized, and empirically minded. However, this does not mean that all educational processes and outcomes can or should be measured by scientists or school administrators, especially for evaluative, as opposed to epistemological, purposes.

There are some things that just cannot be measured. A lot of powerful people need to learn this simple lesson. Policy makers and school administrators need to learn how to be more comfortable with our collective ignorance about teaching and learning, and what that means for the management of schools.

Economics can serve as a cautionary example. As Nobel Prize winner Robert Solow explained, we simply can't measure the "total factor productivity" of an economy. Thus, Gross National Product, one of the most important accountability metrics ever invented, has always been a weak estimate of the strength of an economy because it doesn't really measure much of the actual economy, and what it does measure is not very accurate.

Solow famously explained that the notion of total factor productivity was "a measure of our ignorance" because there are just too many known variables that cannot be measured by experts, and there are also many unknown variables that experts cannot even comprehend (Banerjee and Duflo 2019, 148).

Thus, the holy grail for economists, understanding economic growth, has always been a pipe dream. After a hundred years of intense study, according to economists Abhijit V. Banerjee and Esther Duflo (2019), "We don't understand very well what can deliver permanently faster growth. It just happens (or not) . . . we have no accepted recipe for how to make growth happen . . . no general principles" (179, 186).

As one economist, Bill Easterly, sarcastically pointed out about the 2006 World Bank Commission on Growth and Development, "After two years of work by the commission of 21 world leaders and experts, an 11-member working group, 300 academic experts, 12 workshops, 13 consultations, and a budget of $4 million, the experts' answer to the question of how to attain high growth was roughly: we don't know, but trust experts to figure it out" (qtd. in Banerjee and Duflo 2019, 186).

Like economists, educational accountability reformers have been overconfident in their own expertise, using "bad measures of school quality"

(Schneider 2017, 4) without knowing just how bad most educational accountability measurements actually are. This has led to not only ineffective reforms, but real damage to the lives of students and teachers.

As business professor Jeffrey Pfeffer (2015) pointed out, "Measuring the wrong thing is often worse than measuring nothing, because you get what you measure" (29; see also Deming 1994; Aguayo 1990). Corrupted measurements lead to corrupted organizations and ruined lives.

And some things are really hard, if not impossible, to measure accurately. Take Gross National Products or economic growth as examples. These index measurements are notoriously imprecise. Likewise, it is exceptionally hard to quantify educational practices and outcomes, especially student learning and student success. As Peter F. Drucker (1969) pointed out fifty years ago, "Knowledge work is not easily defined in quantitative terms, and may indeed be incapable of quantification altogether" (288).

And social policies designed to change human behavior are notoriously ineffective. By one estimate, only 10 percent of social intervention policies actually work, but only 1 percent reach "significant scale" to actually do much good (Banerjee and Duflo 2019, 188). If we applied this ratio to public schooling, one of the most ambitious social policies ever invented, we can begin to understand what educators are up against.

But just because we can't measure every educational practice or outcome, this doesn't mean that we can't evaluate some educational practices, personnel, or institutions in limited and valid ways (Labaree 2011; Koretz 2017). This is what economists do. They are able to measure some parts of the economy in order to make limited interventions that do some good for organizations or the economy as a whole.

Like economic interventions, educational accountability reforms should be done with full knowledge of valid methodology, knowing that all measurements, whether inside or outside of the classroom, are incomplete approximations, at best. More importantly, accountability reforms need to be done with full knowledge that most initiatives will fail to do any good at all, and that some might be counterproductive and dangerous. But that doesn't mean that we should stop trying to improve schools and educational programs.

We all need to be a lot less ambitious. We cannot substitute technocratic engineering and management for the messy and imperfect personal judgments of professional educators, who need to be part of the process of evaluating their work as teachers (Lefstein, Vedder-Weiss and Segal 2020; Koretz 2017, 33, 203; Wagner and Kegan 2006).

Even in the business world, managers need to balance between "objective, easily quantified outcome measures and subjective, somewhat judgmental, performance drivers" (Kaplan and Norton, 1996, 10). Competent managers should also take more of the blame than their employees for poor organizational performance (Aguayo 1990, 15).

Thus, we should not expect teachers or schools to perform magic with all students in all classes in every school in all neighborhoods. Teachers cannot control students and definitely cannot dictate outcomes. Education doesn't work like that. Thus, teachers should not be held fully, or even mostly, responsible for student achievement. If anyone should be held accountable for poor student achievement, its school administrators and politicians, not teachers.

We need much more realistic expectations about what teachers and schools can do, which should include more realistic expectations about the roles of parents and students when it comes to student learning. Remember, teachers and schools account for only 10–15% of the variance in student achievement (Kelly 2012a, 10; Marsh and Dunkin 1992, 170).

Even coaches of professional sports teams only account for 20–30% of the variance in a team's success (Berry and Fowler 2019). Parents and students are primarily responsible for student learning and success, not teachers, coaches or schools, but we must also acknowledge that even parents play a limited role in the long-term education of their children (Harris 1999).

We also need to examine the limits of market values and organizational processes for educational institutions. This includes criticizing the widely believed myth that the "consumer is always right," which business professor Clayton M. Christensen (2016) questioned in the late 1990s in his groundbreaking study, *The Innovator's Dilemma*. Christensen (2016) found that most mature businesses become trapped by the "dictates of their customers" and "powerless to change the courses of their firms against the dictates of their customers" (102). This becomes a fatal problem as markets change, especially due to the invention of "disruptive technologies" (xvi–xix).

Customer satisfaction can "mislead" businesses and lead to the eventual destruction of a firm (Christensen 2016, 48) because managers become unable or unwilling "to put their careers at risk" by challenging the status quo and introducing new products or trying to invent new markets (156). The world is always changing, and capital and consumer markets seem to change more quickly than most other social institutions, so individuals and firms must be able to adapt to new environments in order to survive, if not thrive (Kaplan and Norton, 1996, 14).

Christensen (2016) argued that successful firms need to be able to "plan for learning" in order to prepare for disruptive technologies and adjust to new markets (156; see also Kaplan and Norton 1996). Schools as organizations also need to "plan for learning." This means that schools need to be evaluated for reaching learning objectives that are tied to social and political goals, not just the performance of teachers and students.

Education is perhaps the most powerful disruptive technology ever invented. Properly understood and deployed, an education can completely transform not only the life of the student, but also the life of the teacher and the structure of the educational institution hosting these people. While education has often been reduced by rigid bureaucrats into a stultifying ritual of soulless social reproduction, the practice of education in schools should not be a useless ritual. As John Dewey ([1916] 1966) pointed out, properly practiced, education in schools could help transform the world into a better, fairer, and more productive place. If businesses need a "plan for learning" in order to survive the rapidly changing modern world, as Christensen (2016) pointed out, then so too do students, teachers, and schools. How can we do this?

LEARNING HOW TO LEARN

For several centuries, progressive philosophers and educators have pointed out, including radicals like Ivan Illich and more conservative educators like business professor Charles Handy (1990), that "education needs to be reinvented" in order to meet the changing needs of the present moment (211). Given what we have discussed in this book, what might the reinvention of education look like?

In order to successfully educate our young into mature, productive, successful, and satisfied adults, we need teachers who have the freedom to creatively experiment with practices that promote student learning in a wide range of diverse contexts to meet the complex requirements of the contemporary, global world.

Some educational practices will work, at least momentarily. Some practices will fail, and some will fail spectacularly. Some of these practices will be universally praised, but most will at times displease administrators, students, parents, or politicians, all of them combined.

And while schools are important, we also need parents and students to be full and willing participants in the process of education, both inside and outside of schools, if learning is going to be effective and useful, especially since students spend the majority of their life outside of schools (Steinberg 1996, 102, 120). And, yes, there is a role for school administrators, but it should always be an auxiliary and advisory role.

The primary mission of schools should be focused on teachers teaching in their classrooms. Administrators should come last in the organizational hierarchy, on par with the custodial and grounds-keeping staff, as administrators are really just a bunch of bureaucratic custodians in suits who push papers instead of brooms.

We also need to step away from the legally enforced framework of playing school to reimagine what learning really means in the context of the perennial human condition and the diverse roles that students will play in their various cultures to survive, make a living, and hopefully thrive (Tomasello 1999; 2014). Law professor Daniel Markovits (2019) argues that "deep reflection and an intrinsic love of learning are becoming historical curiosities" (154), a trend which is disturbing and tragic.

We need to reconceptualize learning as more than studying for a test in a school so a student can earn a credential (Senge [1990] 2006). Our schools, our businesses, our governments, and our very planet depend upon our ability to learn real knowledge and real skills. We also need to be able to learn better and faster than previous generations.

Business professor Charles Handy (1990) looked back to an older concept of learning as an active and never-ending process of exploration, understanding, testing the usefulness of our knowledge and skills, and reflecting on what works and what doesn't so we can live a better and more meaningful life (58–59; see also Dewey [1916] 1966; Argyris 1993; Robinson 2001). Handy (1990) went on to explain,

> learning is *not* the same as study, nor the same as training. It is bigger than both. It is a cast of mind, a habit of life, a way of thinking about things, a way of growing. Learning is *not* measured by examinations, which usually only test the theory stage, but only by a growth experience, an experience understood and tested. Learning is *not* automatic, it requires energy, thought, courage, and support. It is easy to give up on it, to relax, and to rest on one's experience, but that is to cease to grow. . . . Learning is *not* finding out what other people already know, but is solving our own problems for our own purposes. (author's emphasis; 63)

Biological anthropologist and psychologist Terrence W. Deacon (1997) explained that learning is not a "general process" because it "always occurs in a particular context, involving particular senses and types of motor actions" (48). He stressed that real learning is not a scholastic exercise in rote learning and memorization (66). Learning is an active process that involves not only understanding but also judging information in order to figure out "what is relevant" to the learner and the context of learning (48).

Learning also requires what Deacon (1997) called "habits of attention" because learners have to decide what to pay attention to and what to ignore, often in the context of comparing our current experience with past experiences and cultural common sense (48–49; see also Panda 2018, 121–122). True learning is not passive. It requires relearning what we know, reprogramming how we know, inferring what information we are missing, and thinking in new ways that go against the grain of our previous experiences or the traditions of our culture (Deacon 1997, 49; see also Clear 2018).

There needs to be a "fundamental shift or movement of mind," an "awakening" or "transcendence," as management professor Peter M. Senge ([1990] 2006) explained in his book on learning organizations (13). Deacon (1997) stresses that the effectiveness of learning depends "on the match between the learning process," the previous learning experiences of the student, and "the structure of the patterns to be learned" (108, 128). Thus, he concludes, "What provides efficient learning in one situation may be very inefficient in another" (128). Learning is always context dependent. There is no one best system and there never will be (Payne 2008, 2; Labaree 2012; Schneider 2017, 6).

Education and sociology professor Gerald Grant (1988) concluded his classic study of the high school by saying that we need to move away from the notion that all educational problems can be fixed by authoritative administrators "devising technical solutions" and "improved techniques" (158). The key to educational reform, which goes against the grain of schooling as it has been traditionally practiced for thousands of years, is trying to keep a structured, yet flexible educational atmosphere that gives teachers and students most of the control over the learning process.

Teachers and students need to be the focus of learning organizations. Teachers and students need to be able to explore and develop their natural love of learning and intrinsic motivation to engage in the learning process together as partners cooperating as a team (Argyris 1993, 30; Lortie 2002; Deci and Flaste 1995, 158; Rumbaugh and Washburn 2003, 204–34; Baker 2020, 61; Lefstein, Vedder-Weiss and Segal 2020; Edmondson 2012).

And this process cannot be forced. You cannot force a student to learn, especially to learn how to develop personal mastery (Senge [1990] 2006, 161; Baker 2020, 61–62). Students must want to learn. Good teachers struggle to ignite student interest and passion. This is what makes education so fragile, indeterminant, and exciting.

One of the biggest problems with schooling, as developmental psychologist Howard Gardner ([1995] 2011) pointed out, is that teaching students to *really* learn has never "been a high priority for educational bureaucracies" (8). Politics, bureaucracy, and accountability systems destroy the delicate educational dance of responsive teaching and authentic learning. As psychologist Edward L. Deci (1995) explained,

> In a way, it is all quite ironic. Parents, politicians, and school administrators all want students to be creative problem-solvers and to learn material at a deep, conceptual level. But in their eagerness to achieve these ends, they pressure teachers to produce. The paradox is that the more they do that, the more controlling teachers become, which, as we have seen so many times, undermines

intrinsic motivation, creativity, and conceptual understanding in the students. The harder the teachers are pushed to get results, the less likely it is that the important results will be forthcoming. (158; see also Baker, 2020, 61–62)

The biggest problem with schooling is the widespread belief that managers, researchers, supervisors, committees, consultants, and accountants—the bureaucratic professionals!—are all more important than the lowly worker who does the thinking and doing at the heart of the enterprise.

Peter F. Drucker (1969) expressed this sentiment perfectly in the late 1960s, back when the modern accountability movement for schooling was just getting started: "Education has become too important to be left to the educators" (313). Imagine if reformers said that "health care was too important to be left to doctors" or "taxes are too important to be left to accountants" or "bridge building is too important to be left to engineers." It's interesting to think about how such nonsense could be widely believed.

Almost every accountability reform has failed, especially the widespread use of standardized tests, and as Daniel Koretz (2017) pointed out, the "evidence of these failures has been accumulating for more than a quarter century" (7). Most educational problems are not getting better, especially for the most disadvantaged students in the worst schools (Schneider 2014, 210). It is impossible to ignore, Koretz (2017) argues, "the absurdities and failures of the current system and the real harms it is causing" (8).

And while critics have attacked everyone associated with schools, teachers have taken most of the blame over the last thirty years. Professor of education Theodore R. Sizer (1992) documented this several decades ago when he wrote, "Educators, so often criticized, are defensive."

> Behind top-down regulation lies a distrust of American teachers. The argument is simple: the fate of an adolescent cannot be left in the hands of a semicompetent adult, however well-meaning. So, supervise and carefully control that teacher and, by necessary bureaucratic extension, *all* teachers. (218–19)

Attacking teachers is nothing new (Labaree 1992). They have been blamed for the failures of schools in the U.S. for over a century. This blame has been tied to a widespread, long-standing belief that teachers are solely responsible for student learning outcomes, and that the effectiveness of schools depends more upon the performance of teachers than it does on the performance of students.

The Economist recently reiterated this popular belief stating, "The quality of teachers determines the performance of students" ("Do Your Homework" 2019, 8). Because of this pervasive myth, teachers have taken most of the blame when students don't learn what they are supposed to. But has blaming teachers ever helped reform schools?

No, blaming teachers has only made the underlying problems in schools worse because the real problems never get fixed (Labaree 1992). As the bureaucratic control of teachers has tightened, budgets and programs have been cut, leaving teachers with larger class sizes, more troubled students, and less resources, especially in urban schools with high concentrations of historically segregated ethnic populations (Payne 2008; Kozol 1991). Most teachers are overwhelmed by issues outside of their control. So why are they getting all the blame?

Most of the educational problems that critics have uncovered over the past century have nothing to do with teachers. The most important problems are highly correlated with students, their parents, and the political-economy of the nation, such as race, class, and the "unequal allocation of school resources" (Darling-Hammond 2010, 30; Payne 2008, 24; Kozol 1991; Markovits 2019). In the U.S., these issues are deeply connected to a systemic history of racial segregation, sociopolitical inequality, and economic exploitation. So, again, why are teachers getting all the blame?

Teachers and students are the heart and soul of the practice of education (Lortie 2002), not the bureaucrats or the politicians (Rogers 1969; Wise 1979; Argyris 1993, 29–30). We need refocus schools and realign priorities. As W. Edwards Deming (1994) argued, we need to create a "system of education in which pupils from toddlers on up through the university take joy in learning, free of fear of grades and gold stars, and in which teachers take joy in their work, free from fear in ranking" (62–63).

Teachers and students need to be allowed to concentrate on the art and science of learning without too much interference from outsiders, especially know-nothing administrators and mindless bureaucrats. We need to get away from the belief that teachers control and produce student learning, and that school administrators control and manage teachers. "When the school's organization becomes centered on managing and controlling," Linda M. McNeil (1986) explained, "teachers and students take school less seriously. They fall into a ritual of teaching and learning that tends toward minimal standards and minimum effort" (xi).

LET'S GET RID OF THE MIDDLE-MEN

Instead of an organization focused on command and control, educational institutions need to be focused on creating mutually beneficial relationships that promote learning, which in turn promotes individual and organizational change (Argyris 1993; Senge [1990] 2006; Kellerman 2012; Keltner 2016).

The philosopher John Dewey was one of the first educators to point out that while teachers need to guide students, they don't need to command and control students (Rogoff 2003, 207).

Instead, in order to maximize learning and human development, teachers and students need to be able to freely form a reciprocal relationship focused on a "joint understanding" of the learning task in the shared learning environment (Tversky 2019, 28). And teachers need to be able to discuss and evaluate their own work with other teachers (Lefstein, Vedder-Weiss and Segal 2020), without interference from administrators.

If we really want to fix our schools and to educate our young, then we need to strip away all the unnecessary political and bureaucratic detritus, which have "corrupted" the ideals of education (Koretz 2017, 6), especially the corrosive and counterproductive top-down command style of most administrative systems. Teachers, the skilled craftswomen and craftsmen in the classroom (Sennett 2008; Crawford 2009), need to be in charge of schools so they can patiently and lovingly polish the stone of student learning until a rough gem emerges that can eventually shine on its own. Education is too important to be managed by administrators and bureaucrats.

The sociologist Philip Selznick ([1957] 1984) famously argued long ago that administrators are "dispensable" (24). The most important work of an organization is done by the skilled employees, not the paper-pushers. Many types of organizations do not need managers or bureaucrats.

Psychologist Barbara Tversky (2019) points out, "An orchestra needs a conductor, but a string quartet does not. Jazz improve can be beautifully coordinated as can comedy improv, without scores or scripts or a leader. At the core of joint action is joint understanding, shared knowledge of the goals and subgoals of the task and the procedures needed to accomplish it" (28). Education is a cooperative enterprise by skilled experts, just like a string quartet. No administrators or managers are required.

Authentic learning is a collaboration between teachers and students. The art of education cannot be commanded or controlled, especially by mindless bureaucrats. Thus, educational organizations should be more of an "upside down" hierarchy, very unlike traditional schools, where the needs of teachers come first, the needs of students come second, and the needs of management come last (Nayar 2010, 40). Educational organizations should have "reverse accountability," whereby managers are accountable to the teachers and the students, and to the organization as a whole, rather than the other way around, which is more typical of most schools (103).

To be truly effective, education organizations should only be managed by skilled and experienced educators. Why? Because education is not a technical enterprise that can be observed, rationalized, controlled, and bureaucratized. Thus, very little of teaching or learning can be measured or objectively assessed. To measure and assess teachers or students accurately and fairly, one needs to understand the ambiguity and uncertainty at the heart of the educational enterprise.

Think about the predicament of managing ballet dancers, pianists, physicists, Navy Seals, basketball players, or F1 race car drivers. Only experienced professionals in these domains would be qualified to manage other, active professionals or students training to become professionals.

Part of the reason is that skilled practitioners have a lot of "tacit" knowledge (Polanyi 1962; Polanyi 1967; Schon 1983, 49–53; Senge [1990] 2006, 153; Isaacs 1999, 51) that cannot easily be explained or demonstrated to outsiders (Hagel, Brown and Davison 2010). You have to tacitly know what it means to *do* that kind of professional activity and to *be* that kind of professional. And this knowledge comes only through years of professional practice.

But more importantly, only an experienced professional can know what can't be known or done in a professional domain. Perhaps physics provides the best example of this predicament. The revolution in quantum mechanics during the 20th century has really brought to the forefront the limits of science and human knowledge (Du Sautoy 2016, 156–57). For one, modern physicists have demonstrated empirically that "to observe is to alter behavior" (149). Once you start observing and measuring, you can only capture a small, inert piece of the phenomena you want to understand. And the data you can capture is only a tiny part of the larger puzzle.

Physicists have also demonstrated the "probabilistic character and uncertainty" of the physical world (Du Sautoy 2016, 153). As professor of mathematics and philosopher of science Marcus Du Sautoy (2016) has asked, "What if reality is random and not as deterministic as I might want" (158)? We simply can't know many things that we would like to know. In many domains, we can at best only approximate probabilities.

Thus, Sautoy concluded, with the help of physicist Werner Heisenberg, "Our inability to know is actually an expression of the true nature of things. As Heisenberg put it: 'The atoms or elementary particles themselves are not real; they form a world of potentialities or possibilities rather than one of things or facts'" (179).

When it comes to teaching and learning, there is a lot that we don't know and will never know. There is also a lot that we cannot control or predict. A teacher never knows exactly which students are learning and how much and when this learning actually takes place. Likewise, a student never knows how much they learned from a teacher, nor when that learning might be relevant or useful.

Even when students fail, or when teachers fail, there can be a lot of meaningful learning that is taking place. Psychologists call these types of situations "meaningful failures" (Rumbaugh and Washburn 2003, 169). These ordinary, inconspicuous, and often uncomfortable situations usually do not fit the pedagogical assumptions of either the teacher or the student. That is why most people miss them, until later, sometimes days, months, or years later.

There is simply no way to know for sure when learning is happening. Nor can anyone know how much, how significant, or how long it will last. Education is an inherently indeterminate activity. Until school administrators and policy makers acknowledge this inconvenient truth, there will be no real progress in reforming our schools.

Epilogue
Learning to Learn—Revising the Liberal Arts

I have presented a modest proposal with revolutionary implications. But I'm just a scholar and this book is just a conceptual exploration of the practice of education. And yet, even though this is just a humble work of scholarship, I firmly believe, as historian Gerda Lerner (1986) once explained, that ideas can help to "create a consciousness" that can "liberate" (37) people and inspire profound personal and social change.

I firmly believe that our institutions, especially the institution of schooling, needs to be "recrafted to serve the needs of individuals," rather than individuals serving the needs of institutions by conforming to outdated and often useless traditions (Hagel, Brown and Davison 2010, 8). I resisted and rebelled against being institutionalized by schools my whole life, and in the process, I fell in love with the practice of education because it enabled me to understand and change my life, and later, the life of my students and my son.

This is the notion at the heart of *the liberal arts* (Nussbaum 1997), an ancient and noble practice that has always sought to teach students "how to be a human being"—the "cultivation of the whole human being for the functions of citizenship and life" (14, 9). The liberal arts tradition might sound quaint, but I believe that this powerful ideal is still relevant to the 21st century.

We live in a fast-changing, multicultural, globalized world that is becoming transformed by automation and artificial intelligence. We live in a complex "knowledge economy," as Peter F. Drucker (1969) perceptively pointed out a half-century ago, which places unprecedented demands on workers and citizens, especially those in the highest paid industries (Markovits 2019). In such a world, as Drucker (1969) warned, "The only meaningful job security is the capacity to learn fast. The only real security in an economy and society at flux is to know enough to be able to move" (305).

But more importantly for citizens of democratic countries, there is another reason for the continued relevance of the liberal arts tradition. Because we are living in a time of fake news, corruption, and authoritarian populism, the importance of a knowledgeable citizenry is essential to the preservation of democracy in the 21st century. As political scientists Steven Levitsky and Daniel Ziblatt (2018) explained, we are living in a period of "democratic recession," and they warned that democracies can die (205), even in the United States of America.

Many observers have recently questioned whether we are witnessing the death of American democracy in the age of Trump. In times like these, we would do well to remember the words of the statesman, doctor, and founder of Dickinson College, Benjamin Rush (1806). He wrote in his 1786 plan for the establishment of public schooling in Pennsylvania, "Freedom can exist only in the society of knowledge. Without learning, men are incapable of knowing their rights, and where learning is confined to a few people, liberty can be neither equal nor universal" (1).

We need to put learning and the learner at the center of all of our educational endeavors, especially schooling in whatever form it may take. This is especially true of democracies. We need to empower all people to understand their unlimited potential as learners and to foster diverse spaces for people to learn and practice at their own pace for their own purposes. To paraphrase and revise something Howard Gardner (1993, 178) once said, schools spend "far too much time ranking individuals and not nearly enough time helping them."

We need to reenvision education as helping students help themselves to become not only what they are, but also what they can aspire to be. There are no limits to learning, not until we reach and try. And we will continue to need accountability programs to evaluate and guide our schools, but they need to be accountability programs, according to Daniel Koretz (2017) that "produce students who are more capable—not just higher-scoring on a few tests but more knowledgeable, more able to learn on their own, more able to think critically, and therefore more successful, not only in their later work but also as citizens" (9).

Our economy, our democracy, and our future as a species depend upon the ability of our children to learn—especially learning from the mistakes of the past. May we find a way. I hope the ideas in this book help.

References

Acemoglu, Daron, and James A. Robinson. 2020. *The Narrow Corridor: States, Societies, and the Fate of Liberty.* New York: Penguin.

Adams, Henry. 1961. *The Education of Henry Adams: An Autobiography.* Boston: Houghton Mifflin, Originally published 1918.

Aguayo, Rafael. 1990. *Dr. Deming: The American Who Taught the Japanese about Quality.* New York: Carol Publishing Group.

Akerlof, George A., and Robert J. Shiller. 2015. *Phishing for Phools: The Economics of Manipulation and Deception.* Princeton: Princeton University Press.

Alston, Lee J., Thrainn Eggertsson, and Douglass C. North, eds. 1996. *Empirical Studies in Institutional Change.* Cambridge, UK: Cambridge University Press.

Anonymous. 2019, March 25. "What Happens after Rich Kids Bribe Their Way into College? I Teach Them." *The Guardian.* Retrieved from www.theguardian.com

Argyris, Chris. 1993. *Knowledge for Action: A Guide to Overcoming Barriers to Organizational Change.* San Francisco: Jossey-Bass.

Aronowitz, Stanley. 2000. *The Knowledge Factory: Dismantling the Corporate University and Creating True Higher Learning.* Boston, MA: Beacon Press.

Arum, Richard, and Josipa Roksa. 2011. *Academically Adrift: Limited Learning on College Campuses.* Chicago: University of Chicago Press.

Asbury, Kathryn, and Robert Plomin. 2014. *G Is for Genes: The Impact of Genetics on Achievement.* Chichester, UK: Wiley Blackwell.

Atteberry, Allison, and Daniel Mangan. 2020, June/July. "The Sensitivity of Teacher Value-Added Scores to the Use of Fall or Spring Test Scores." *Educational Researcher*, 495: 335–349.

Bagley, William Chandler. 1912. *Craftsmanship in Teaching.* New York: Macmillan.

Bain, Ken. 2004. *What the Best College Teachers Do.* Cambridge, MA: Harvard University Press.

———. 2012. *What the Best College Students Do.* Cambridge, MA: Harvard University Press.

Baker, Wayne. 2020. *All You Have to Do Is Ask: How to Master the Most Important Skill for Success*. New York: Currency.

Bakhtin, Mikhail M. 1981. *The Dialogic Imagination.* Austin, TX: University of Texas Press.

Banerjee, Abhijit V., and Esther Duflo. 2019. *Good Economics for Hard Times:* New York: Public Affairs.

"Barely managing." 2018, June 30. *The Economist*, 65.

Beach, Josh M. 2007. "Ideology of the American Dream: Two Competing Philosophies in Education, 1776–2006." *Educational Studies: A Journal of the American Educational Studies Association*, 41 (2): 148–64.

———. 2009. "A Critique of Human Capital Formation in the US and the Economic Returns to Sub-Baccalaureate Credentials." *Educational Studies: A Journal of the American Educational Studies Association,* 45 (1): 24–38.

———. 2011a. *Gateway to Opportunity*: *A History of the Community College in the United States.* Sterling, VA: Stylus Publishing, LLC.

———. 2011b. *Children Dying Inside: A Critical Analysis of Education in South Korea.* Austin, TX: West by Southwest.

———. 2018. *How Do You Know? The Epistemological Foundations of 21st Century Literacy*. London: Routledge.

Benfey, Christopher. June 20, 2018. "Stanley Cavell, 1926-2018." *The New York Review of Books*. Retrieved from www.nybooks.com

Berdahl, Robert O., and T. R. McConnell. 1999. "Autonomy and Accountability: Who Controls Academe." In Philip G. Altbach, Patricia J. Gumport, and Robert O. Berdahl, eds. *American Higher Education in the Twenty-First Century: Social, Political, and Economic Challenges.* Baltimore: The Johns Hopkins University Press. 70–88.

Berkson, William, and John Wetterstein. 1984. *Learning from Error: Karl Popper's Psychology of Error*. La Salle, IL: Open Court Press.

Berlin, Isaiah. 2000a. "The Pursuit of the Ideal." In *The Proper Study of Mankind: An Anthology of Essays*. New York: Farrar, Straus and Giroux.

———. 2000b. "Historical inevitability." In *The Proper Study of Mankind: An Anthology of Essays.* New York: Farrar, Straus and Giroux.

Berliner, David. 2011. "Rational Responses to High Stakes Testing: The Case of Curriculum Narrowing and the Harm That Follows." *Cambridge Journal of Education* 41 (3): 287–302.

Berliner, David C., and Bruce J. Biddle. 1995. *The Manufactured Crisis: Myths, Fraud, and the Attack on America's Public Schools.* Reading, MA: Addison-Wesley.

Berry, Christopher R., and Anthony Fowler. 2020. "How Much Do Coaches Matter?" *13th Annual MIT Sloan Sports Analytics Conference, MIT*. Boston, MA. Paper ID: 12549.

Best, Joel. 2006. *Flavor of the Month: Why Smart People Fall for Fads*. Berkeley, CA: University of California Press.

Birnbaum, Robert. 2000. *Management Fads in Higher Education: Where They Come from, What They Do, Why They Fail*. San Francisco, CA: Jossey-Bass.

Bok, Derek. 2009. *Universities in the Marketplace: The Commercialization of Higher Education*. Princeton: Princeton University Press.
Borman, Kathryn M., Arnold B. Danzig, and David R. Garcia, eds. 2012. *Review of Research in Education: Education, Democracy, and the Public Good*, 36. American Educational Research Association.
Bourdieu, Pierre. 2010. *Distinction: A Social Critique of the Judgement of Taste*. London: Routledge. Originally published 1984.
Bourdieu, Pierre, and Loïc JD Wacquant. 1992. *An Invitation to Reflexive Sociology*. University of Chicago Press.
Bowers, Alex J. 2011. "What's in a Grade? The Multidimensional Nature of What Teacher-Assigned Grades Assess in High School." *Educational Research and Evaluation* 17 (3): 141–59.
Brackett, Marc. 2019. *Permission to Feel: Unlocking the Power of Emotions to Help Our Kids, Ourselves, and Our Society Thrive*. New York: Celadon.
Brackett, Marc A., James L. Floman, Claire Ashton-James, Lillia Cherkasskiy, and Peter Salovey. 2013. "The Influence of Teacher Emotion on Grading Practices: A Preliminary Look at the Evaluation of Student Writing." *Teachers and Teaching* 19 (6): 634–46.
Brafman, Ori, and Rom Brafman. 2008. *Sway: The Irresistible Pull of Irrational Behavior*. New York: Crown Business.
Brantlinger, Ellen A. 1993. *The Politics of Social Class in Secondary School*. New York: Teachers College Press.
Breit, William, and Roger L. Ransom. 2014. *The Academic Scribblers*, 3rd ed. Princeton: Princeton University Press.
Bridges, David. 2006. "The Practice of Higher Education: In Pursuit of Excellence and of Equity." *Educational Theory* 56 (4): 371–86.
Brint, Steven. 2008. "No College Student Left Behind?" *Research & Occasional Paper Series*. Center for Studies in Higher Education, University of California Berkeley, CSHE.9.2008
———. 2009, Dec. "The Academic Devolution? Movements to Reform Teaching and Learning in US Colleges and Universities, 1985–2010." *Research & Occasional Paper Series*: *Research and Occasional Paper Series*, Center for Studies in Higher Education, University of California Berkeley, CSHE.12.09
Brint, Steven, and Jerome Karabel. 1989. *The Diverted Dream: Community Colleges and the Promise of Educational Opportunity in America, 1900-1985*. Oxford: Oxford University Press.
Brown, David K. 1995. *Degrees of Control: A Sociology of Educational Expansion and Occupational Credentialism*. New York: Columbia Teachers College Press.
Brown, Peter C., Henry L. Roediger III and Mark A. McDaniel. 2014. *Make it Stick: The Science of Successful Learning*. Cambridge, MA: Harvard University Press.
Bruner, Jerome. 1983. *In Search of Mind: Essays in Autobiography*. New York: Harper and Row.
Buckman, Ken. 2007, Fall. "What Counts as Assessment in the 21st Century?" *Thought & Action*, 23: 29–37

Burke, Kenneth. 1969a. *A Grammar of Motives*. Berkeley, CA: University of California Press. Originally published 1945.

———. 1969b. *A Rhetoric of Motives*. Berkeley, CA: University of California Press. Originally published 1950.

Callahan, Raymond E. 1962. *Education and the Cult of Efficiency: A Study of the Social Forces That Have Shaped the Administration of Public Schools*. Chicago: University of Chicago Press.

Camara, Wayne, Ernest Kimmel, Janice Scheuneman, and Ellen A. Sawtell. 2003. *Whose Grades Are Inflated*. Research Report no. 2003-4. New York: The College Board.

Campbell, Donald T. 1979. "Assessing the Impact of Planned Social Change." *Evaluation and Program Planning* 2 (1): 67–90.

Caplan, Bryan. 2018. *The Case Against Education: Why the Education System is a Waste of Time and Money*. Princeton, NJ: Princeton University Press.

Ceci, Stephen J. 1991. "How Much Does Schooling Influence General Intelligence and Its Cognitive Components? A Reassessment of the Evidence." *Developmental Psychology* 27 (5): 703–722.

Chaffee, John W. 1995. *The Thorny Gates of Learning in Sung China: A Social History of Examinations*. New Ed. Albany, NY: State University of New York Press.

Chamovitz, Daniel. 2012. *What a Plant Knows: A Field Guide to the Senses*. New York: Farrar, Straus and Giroux.

Chandler Jr, Alfred D. 1977. *The Visible Hand: The Managerial Revolution in American Business*. Cambridge, MA: Harvard University Press.

Chen, Pauline W. 2013, Feb 29. "Why Failing Med Students Don't Get Failing Grades." *The New York Times*. Retrieved from well.blogs.www.nytimes.com

Chickering, Arthur W., and Zelda F. Gamson. 1991. *Applying the Seven Principles for Good Practice in Undergraduate Education*. San Francisco: Jossey-Bass.

Childress, Herb. 2019. *The Adjunct Underclass: How America's Colleges Betrayed Their Faculty, Their Students, and Their Mission*. Chicago: University of Chicago Press.

Christensen, Clayton M. 2013. *The Innovator's Dilemma: When New Technologies Cause Great Firms to Fail*. Boston, MA: Harvard Business Review Press.

Clausing, Kimberly. 2019. *Open: The Progressive Case for Free Trade, Immigration, and Global Capital*. Cambridge, MA: Harvard University Press.

Clayson, Dennis E. 2009. "Student Evaluations of Teaching: Are They Related to What Students Learn?" *Journal of Marketing Education* 31 (1): 16–30.

Clear, James. 2018. *Atomic Habits: An Easy & Proven Way to Build Good Habits & Break Bad Ones*. New York: Avery.

Cohen, David K., James P. Spillane, and Donald J. Peurach. 2018, April. "The Dilemmas of Educational Reform." *Educational Researcher* 47 (3): 204–212.

Cohen, Lizabeth. 2003. *A Consumers' Republic: The Politics of Mass Consumption in Postwar America*. New York: Alfred A. Knopf.

Cohen, Nancy. 2002. *The Reconstruction of American Liberalism, 1865–1914*. Chapel Hill, NC: Univ of North Carolina Press.

Colby, Anne, Elizabeth Beaumont, Thomas Ehrlich, and Josh Corngold. 2008. *Educating for Democracy: Preparing Undergraduates for Responsible Political Engagement*. San Francisco, CA: Jossey-Bass.

Cole, Michael. 1996. *Cultural Psychology: A Once and Future Discipline*. Cambridge, MA: Harvard University Press.

Collins, Randall. 1979. *The Credential Society: An Historical Sociology of Education and Stratification*. New York: Academic Press.

Crawford, Matthew B. 2009. *Shop Class as Soulcraft: An Inquiry into the Value of Work*. New York: Penguin.

Cremin, Lawrence A. 1961. *The Transformation of The School: Progressivism in American Education, 1876-1957*. New York: Vintage Books.

———. 1980. *American Education, The National Experience, 1783–1876*. New York: Harper and Row.

———. 1990. *Popular Education and its Discontents*. New York: Harper and Row.

Crosnoe, Robert. 2011. *Fitting In, Standing Out: Navigating the Social Challenges of High School to Get an Education*. New York: Cambridge University Press.

Cuban, Larry. 1993. *How Teachers Taught: Constancy and Change in American Classrooms, 1880–1990*. 2nd ed. New York: Teachers College Press.

———. 2013. *Inside the Black Box of Classroom Practice: Change Without Reform in American Education*. Cambridge, MA: Harvard Education Press.

Dalio, Ray. 2017. *Principles: Life and Work*. Simon and Schuster.

Darling-Hammond, Linda. 2010. *The Flat World and Education: How America's Commitment to Equity Will Determine Our Future*. New York: Teachers College Press.

Dawley, Alan. 1991. *Struggles for Justice: Social Responsibility and the Liberal State*. Cambridge, MA: Harvard University Press.

De Waal, Frans. 2016. *Are We Smart Enough to Know How Smart Animals Are?* New York: W. W. Norton.

Deacon, Terrence William. 1997. *The Symbolic Species: The Co-Evolution of Language and the Brain*. New York: W. W. Norton and Company.

Deci, Edward L., and Richard Flaste. 1995. *Why We Do What We Do: Understanding Self-Motivation*. New York: Penguin.

Delbanco, Andrew. 2007. "Scandals of Higher Education." *New York Review of Books*, March 29, 2007. Retrieved from www.nybooks.com

Deming, W. Edwards. 1994. *The New Economics for Industry, Government, Education*. 2nd ed. Cambridge, MA: The MIT Press.

Dennett, Daniel C. 2003. *Freedom Evolves*. New York: Viking.

Denning, Jeffrey, Eric Eide, and Merrill Warnick. 2019. "Why Have College Completion Rates Increased?" Working Paper No. 19-77. Annenberg Institute at Brown University. Retrieved from www.edworkingpapers.com/ai19-77

Dewey, John. 1966. *Democracy and Education*. New York: Free Press. Originally published 1926.

Diamond, Jared M. 1992. *The Third Chimpanzee: The Evolution and Future of the Human Animal*. New York: Harper Perennial.

"Do Your Homework." 2019, June 22. *Special Report: California and Texas. The Economist.* London: Author.

Doerr, John. 2018. *Measure What Matters: How Google, Bono, and the Gates Foundation Rock the World With OKRS.* New York: Portfolio/Penguin.

Domjan, Michael. 2010. *The Principles of Learning and Behavior.* 6th ed. Belmont, CA: Wadsworth.

Dougherty, Kevin J., Sosanya M. Jones, Hana Lahr, Rebecca S. Natow, Lara Pheatt, and Vikash Reddy. 2016. "Looking Inside the Black Box of Performance Funding for Higher Education: Policy Instruments, Organizational Obstacles, and Intended and Unintended Impacts." 2016. *RSF: The Russell Sage Foundation Journal of the Social Sciences* 2(1): 147–173.

Douglass, John Aubrey. 2000. *The California Idea and American Higher Education: 1850 to the 1960 Master Plan.* Stanford: Stanford University Press.

———. 2007. *The Conditions for Admission: Access, Equity, and the Social Contract of Public Universities.* Stanford: Stanford University Press.

Drucker, Peter. F. 1954. *The Practice of Management.* New York: Harper and Row.

———. 1969. *The Age of Discontinuity: Guidelines to Our Changing Society.* New York: Harper and Row.

Dweck, Carol S. 2006. *Mindset: The New Psychology of Success.* New York: Ballantine Books.

Eaton, Judith S. 1994. *Strengthening Collegiate Education in Community Colleges.* San Francisco: Jossey-Bass

Ebenstein, Lanny. 2015. *Chicagonomics: The Evolution of Chicago Free Market Economics.* New York: St. Martin's Press.

Eberhardt, Jennifer L. 2020. *Biased: Uncovering the Hidden Prejudice that Shapes What We See, Think, and Do.* New York: Penguin Books.

Edmondson, Amy C. 2012. *Teaming: How Organizations Learn, Innovate, and Complete in the Knowledge Economy.* San Francisco: Jossey-Bass.

———. 2019. *The Fearless Organization: Creating Psychological Safety in the Workplace for Learning, Innovation, and Growth.* New York: Wiley.

Elmore, Richard F. and Milbrey Wallin McLaughlin. 1988. *Steady Work.* Santa Monica, CA: Rand.

Elson, Ruth Miller. 1964. *Guardians of Tradition: American Schoolbooks of the Nineteenth Century.* Lincoln, NE: University of Nebraska Press.

Engelke, Matthew. 2018. *How to Think Like an Anthropologist.* Princeton: Princeton University Press.

Ericsson, Karl Anders. 2003. "Development of Elite Performance and Deliberate Practice." In J. L. Starkes and K. A. Ericcson, eds., *Expert Performance in Sports: Advances in Research on Sport Expertise.* Champaign, IL: Human Kinetics.

Ericsson, Anders, and Robert Pool. 2016. *Peak: Secrets from the New Science of Expertise.* New York: Mariner Books

Ericsson, Karl Anders, Ralf Th. Krampe, and Clemens Tesch-Romer. 1993. "The Role of Deliberate Practice in the Acquisition of Expert Performance," *Psychological Review* 1003, 363–406.

Erikson, Erik H. 1958. "The Nature of Clinical Evidence." In D. Learner, ed., *Evidence and Inference*. Glencoe, IL: The Free Press.

Fawcett, Edmund. 2014. *Liberalism: The Life of an Idea*. Princeton, NJ: Princeton University Press.

Ferrazzi, Keith and Tahl Raz. 2014. *Never Eat Alone: And Other Secrets to Success, One Relationship a Time*, expanded and updated ed. New York: Crown Business

Fish, Stanley. 2019. *The First: How to Think About Hate Speech, Campus Speech, Fake News, Post-Truth, and Donald Trump*. New York: One Signal Publishers.

Fitzgerald, Miranda Suzanne and Annemarie Sullivan Palincsar. 2019, March. "Teaching Practices that Support Student Sensemaking Across Grades and Disciplines: A Conceptual Review." *Review of Research in Education: Changing Teaching Practice in P-20 Educational Settings*, 43: 227–248.

Foster, William T. 1911. "Scientific Versus Personal Distribution of College Credits." *Popular Science Monthly* LXXVIII, 388–408.

Frank, Robert H. 1985. *Choosing the Right Pond: Human Behavior and the Quest for Status*. Oxford: Oxford University Press.

Fredrickson, George M. 1981. *White Supremacy: A Comparative Study in American And South African History*. Oxford: Oxford University Press.

———. 2002. *Racism: A Short History*. Princeton University Press.

Freidson, Eliot. 1986. *Professional Powers: A Study of the Institutionalization of Formal Knowledge*. Chicago: University of Chicago Press.

Freire, Paulo. 2003. *Pedagogy of the Oppressed*. New York: Continuum. Originally Published 1970.

Friedman, Milton M. 2002. *Capitalism and Freedom*. Chicago: The University of Chicago. Originally published 1962.

"From the Cradle to the Grove." 2020, Feb 1. *The Economist, 56*.

Furstenberg, Francois. 2020, May 19. "University Leaders Are Failing: The Pandemic Reveals Ineptitude at the Top. Change is Needed." *The Chronicle of Higher Education*. Retrieved from www.chronicle.com.

Gaither, Gerald., B. Nedwek, and J. E. Neal. 1994. *Measuring Up: The Promises and Pitfalls of Performance Indicators in Higher Education.* ASHE-ERIC Higher Education Report No. 5. Washington, D.C.: George Washington University, Graduate School of Education and Human Development.

Gamble, Andrew. 2016. *Can the Welfare State Survive?* Cambridge, UK: Polity Press.

Gardner, Howard. 1993. *Multiple Intelligences: The Theory in Practice*. New York: Basic Books.

———. 2011a. *Frames of Mind: The Theory of Multiple Intelligences*. New York: Basic Books. Originally published 1983.

———. 2011b. *The Unschooled Mind: How Children Think and How Schools Should Teach*. New York: Basic Books. Originally published 1995.

Garrett, Rachel, Martyna Citkowicz, and Ryan Williams. 2019. "How Responsive Is A Teacher's Classroom Practice to Intervention? A Meta-Analysis of Randomized Field Studies." *Review of Research in Education: Changing Teaching Practice in P–20 Educational Settings*, 43 (1): 106–137.

Geertz, Clifford. 1973. *The Interpretation of Cultures: Selected Essays by Clifford Geertz*. New York: Basic Books.
Gershenson, Seth. 2018. *Grade Inflation in High Schools 2005-2016*. Thomas B. Fordham Institute. Ohio: Author.
Geyer, Denton Loring. 1922. *Introduction to the Use of Standardized Tests*. Chicago: Plymouth Press.
Giddens, Anthony. 1994. *Beyond Left and Right: The Future of Radical Politics*. Stanford University Press.
Ginsberg, Benjamin. 2011. *The Fall of the Faculty: The Rise of the All-Administrative University and Why It Matters*. Oxford: Oxford University Press.
Glazer, Nathan. 1974. "The Schools of the Minor Professions." *Minerva* 12 (3): 346–364.
Glenn, Charles L. 2011. *Contrasting Models of State and School: A Comparative Historical Study of Parental Choice and State Control*. New York: Continuum.
Godfrey-Smith, Peter. 2016. *Other Minds: The Octopus, the Sea, and the Deep Origins of Consciousness*. New York: Farrar, Straus, and Giroux.
Golden, Daniel. 2006. *The Price of Admission: How America's Ruling Class Buys its Way into Elite Colleges—and Who Gets Left Outside the Gates*. New York: Crown.
Goldrick-Rab, Sara. 2016. *Paying the Price: College Costs, Financial Aid, and the Betrayal of the American Dream*. Chicago: University of Chicago Press.
Goleman, Daniel. 2013. *Focus: The Hidden Driver of Excellence*. New York: Harper.
Goodman, Nelson. 1978. *Ways of Worldmaking*. Indianapolis, IN: Hackett Publishing Company.
Goodwin, Craufurd D. 2014. *Walter Lippmann: Public Economist*. Cambridge, MA: Harvard University Press.
Gopnik, Alison. 2009. *The Philosophical Baby: What Children's Minds Tell Us about Truth, Love and the Meaning of Life*. New York: Picador.
———. 2016. *The Gardener and the Carpenter: What the New Science of Child Development Tells Us about the Relationship Between Parents and Children*. New York: Picador.
Gopnik, Alison, and A. N. Meltzoff. 1997. *Words, Thoughts, And Theories*. Cambridge, MA: MIT Press.
Gottschall, Jonathan. 2012. *The Storytelling Animal: How Stories Make Us Human*. New York: Mariner Books.
Gould, Stephen Jay. 1981. *The Mismeasure of Man*. New York: W. W. Norton.
"Grad Inflation." 2019, Jan 5. *The Economist*. Retrieved from www.economist.com
Graeber, David. 2015. *The Utopia of Rules: On Technology, Stupidity, and the Secret Joys of Bureaucracy*. Brooklyn, NY: Melville House.
———. 2018. *Bullshit Jobs. A Theory*. New York: Simon & Schuster.
Graff, Gerald. 1992. *Beyond the Culture Wars: How Teaching the Conflicts Can Revitalize American Education*. W. W. Norton & Company.
Grant, Gerald. 1988. *The World We Created at Hamilton High*. Cambridge, MA: Harvard University Press.
Gray, John. 1989. *Liberalisms: Essays in Political Philosophy*. London: Routledge.
———. 1995. *Enlightenment's Wake*. London: Routledge.

———. 2018. *Seven Types of Atheism*. New York: Farrar, Straus and Giroux.
Green, Elizabeth. 2015. *Building a Better Teacher: How Teaching Works (and How to Teach it to Everyone)*. New York: W. W. Norton & Company.
Grossmann, Matt, and David A. Hopkins. 2016. *Asymmetric Politics: Ideological Republicans and Group Interest Democrats*. Oxford: Oxford University Press.
Grove, Andrew S. 2015. *High Output Management*. New York: Vintage Books.
Grubb, W. Norton and Associates. 1999. *Honored but Invisible: An Inside Look at Teaching in Community Colleges*. New York: Routledge.
Grubb, W. Norton, and Marvin Lazerson. 1988. *Broken Promises: How Americans Fail Their Children*. Chicago: The University of Chicago Press.
———. 2004. *The Education Gospel: The Economic Power of Schooling*. Cambridge, MA: Harvard University Press.
Gutmann, Amy. 1987. *Democratic Education*. Princeton: Princeton University Press.
Hacker, Andrew, and Claudia Dreifus. 2010. *Higher Education? How Colleges Are Wasting Our Money and Failing Our Kids—and What We Can Do About It*. New York: St. Martin's Griffin.
Hagel III, John, John Seely Brown, and Lang Davison. 2010. *The Power of Pull: How Small Moves, Smartly Made, Can Set Big Things in Motion*. New York: Basic Books.
Halpert, Julie. 2012. "Do We Still Segregate Students?" *Pacific Standard*, 24–27.
Hammersley, Martyn, and Paul Atkinson. 1995. *Ethnography: Principles in Practice*. 2nd ed. London: Routledge.
Handy, Charles. 1993. *Understanding Organizations*. 4th ed. New York: Penguin Books.
Harris, Judith Rich. 1999. *The Nurture Assumption: Why Children Turn Out the Way They Do*. New York: Touchstone.
Harvey, David. 2005. *A Brief History of Neoliberalism*. Oxford: Oxford University Press.
Havelock, Eric A. 1963. *Preface to Plato*. Cambridge, MA: Harvard University Press.
Heath, Chip, and Dan Heath. 2007. *Made to Stick: Why Some Ideas Survive and Others Die*. New York: Random House.
———. (2010). *Switch: How to Change Things When Change Is Hard*. New York: Broadway Books.
Hebdige, Dick. 1979. *Subculture, The Meaning of Style*. London: Routledge.
Heckman, James J. 2013. *Giving Kids a Fair Chance*. Cambridge, MA: MIT Press.
Heckman, James J., Jora Stixrud, and Sergio Urzua. 2006. "The Effects of Cognitive and Noncognitive Abilities on Labor Market Outcomes and Social Behavior." *Journal of Labor Economics* 24 (3): 411–482.
Henig, Jeffrey R. 1994. *Rethinking School Choice: Limits of the Market Metaphor*. Princeton: Princeton University Press, 1995.
———. 2008. *Spin Cycle: How Research Gets Used in Policy Debates: The Case of Charter Schools*. Russell Sage Foundation.
Hersh, Richard, and John Merrow eds. 2005a. "Introduction." In Richard Hersh and John Merrow, eds., *Declining by Degrees: Higher Education at Risk*, 1–9. New York: PalgraveMacmillan.

———. 2005b. *Declining by Degrees: Higher Education at Risk.* New York: PalgraveMacmillan.

Hibbing, John R., Kevin B. Smith, and John R. Alford. 2014. *Predisposed: Liberals, Conservatives, and the Biology of Political Differences.* London: Routledge.

Himmelstein, David U., Terry Campbell, and Steffie Woolhandler. 2020, Jan 21. "Health Care Administrative Costs in the United States and Canada, 2017." *Annals of Internal Medicine* 172 (2): 134–142.

Hirsch, Fred. 1976. *Social Limits to Growth.* Cambridge, MA: Harvard University Press.

Hirsch Jr., E. D. 1988. *Cultural Literacy: What Every American Needs to Know.* New York: Vintage Books.

Hobbins, Daniel. 2009. *Authorship and Publicity Before Print: Jean Gerson and the Transformation of Late Medieval Learning.* Philadelphia: University of Pennsylvania Press.

Hobsbawm, Eric, and Terence Ranger, eds. 1983. *The Invention of Tradition.* Cambridge, UK: Cambridge University Press.

Hochschild, Jennifer L., and Nathan Scovronick. 2003. *The American Dream and the Public Schools.* Oxford: Oxford University Press.

Holmes, Stephen. 1995. *Passions and Constraint: On the Theory of Liberal Democracy.* University of Chicago Press.

Horsman, Reginald. 1981. *Race and Manifest Destiny: The Origins of American Racial Anglo-Saxonism.* Cambridge, MA: Harvard University Press.

Hughes, Jonathan R. T. 1982. "Douglass North as a Teacher." In Roger L. Ransom, Richard Sutch, and Gary M. Walton, eds., *Explorations in the New Economic History: Essays in Honor of Douglass C.* New York: Academic Press.

Hunt, Morton. 1993. *The Story of Psychology.* New York: Doubleday.

Hunter, James Davison. 1991. *Culture Wars: The Struggle to Define America.* New York: Basic Books

———. 2000. *The Death of Character: Moral Education in an Age Without Good or Evil.* New York: Basic Books.

Hunter, James Davison, and Paul Nedelisky. 2018. *Science and the Good: The Tragic Quest for the Foundations of Morality.* New Haven: Yale University Press.

Hutt, Ethan L., and Jack Schneider. 2018. "A Thin Line Between Love and Hate: Educational Measurement in the United States." In C. A. Lopez and M. Lawn, eds., *Assessment Cultures: Historical Perspectives.* New York: Peter Lang.

Illich, Ivan, 1970. *Deschooling Society.* New York: Harper and Row.

Isaacs, William. 1999. *Dialogue and the Art of Thinking Together: A Pioneering Approach to Communicating in Business and in Life.* New York: Currency.

Jackson, C. Kirabo. 2016. "What Do Test Scores Miss? The Importance of Teacher Effects on Non–Test Score Outcomes." National Bureau of Economic Research, Working Paper 22226. Retrieved from www.nber.org/papers/w22226

Jacoby, Russell, and Naomi Glauberman, eds. 1995. *The Bell Curve Debate: History, Documents, Opinions.* New York: Times Books.

Jacques, Martin. 2012. *When China Rules the World: The End of the Western World and the Birth of a New Global Order.* New York: Penguin.

Johnson, Valen E. 2003. *Grade Inflation: A Crisis in College Education.* New York: Springer.

Kaestle, Carl F. 1983. *Pillars of the Republic: Common Schools and American Society, 1780-1860.* New York: Hill and Wang.

Kalogrides, Demetra, and Susanna Loeb. 2013. "Different Teachers, Different Peers: The Magnitude of Student Sorting Within Schools." *Educational Researcher* 42 (6): 304–316.

Kaplan, Robert S., and David P. Norton. 1996. *The Balanced Scorecard: Translating Strategy into Action.* Boston, MA: Harvard Business School Press.

Kaufman, Scott Barry, and Carolyn Gregoire. 2016. *Wired to Create: Unraveling the Mysteries of the Creative Mind.* New York: TarcherPerigee.

Keeling, Richard, and Richard Hersh. 2012. *We're Losing Our Minds: Rethinking American Higher Education.* New York: Palgrave Macmillan.

Kellerman, Barbara. 2008. *How Followers are Creating Change and Changing Leaders.* Boston, MA: Harvard School Press.

———. 2012. *The End of Leadership.* New York: Harper Business.

———. 2015. *Hard Times: Leadership in America.* Stanford University Press.

Kelly, Matthew Gardner. 2020, June/July. "The Curious Case of the Missing Tail: Trends Among the Top 1% of School Districts in the United States, 2000–2015." *Educational Researcher* 49 (5): 312–20.

Kelley, Robert Earl. 1992. *The Power of Followership: How to Create Leaders People Want to Follow, and Followers Who Lead Themselves.* New York: Doubleday.

Kelly, Sean, ed. 2012a. "Understanding Teacher Effects: Market Versus Process Models of Educational Improvement." In Sean Kelly, ed., *Assessing Teacher Quality: Understanding Teacher Effects on Instruction and Achievement,* 7–32. New York: Teachers College Press.

———. 2012b. *Assessing Teacher Quality: Understanding Teacher Effects on Instruction and Achievement.* New York: Teachers College Press.

Keltner, Dacher. 2016. *The Power Paradox: How We Gain and Lose Influence.* New York: Penguin.

Kempf, Arlo. 2016. *The Pedagogy of Standardized Testing: The Radical Impacts of Educational Standardization in the US and Canada.* New York: Palgrave Macmillan.

Kennedy, Mary M. 2019, March. "How We Learn About Teacher Learning." *Review of Research in Education: Changing Teaching Practice in P–20 Educational Settings* 43 (1): 138–162.

Kezar, Adrianna, Tom DePaola, and Daniel T. Scott. 2019. *The Gig Academy: Mapping Labor in the Neoliberal University.* Baltimore: Johns Hopkins University Press.

Khurana, Rakesh. 2002. *Searching for a Corporate Savior: The Irrational Quest for Charismatic CEOs.* Princeton: Princeton University Press.

Kimbrough W. M. 2020, Feb 23. "It's Time to Stop Calculating Graduation Rates." *The Chronicle of Higher Education.* Retrieved from www.chronicle.com

King, Adelaide Wilcox. 2007, Jan. "Disentangling Interfirm and Intrafirm Causal Ambiguity: A Conceptual Model of Causal Ambiguity and Sustainable Competitive Advantage." *Academy of Management Review* 32 (1): 156–178.

King, Stephen. 2000. *On Writing: A Memoir of the Craft*. Simon and Schuster.

Kirp, David. 2019. *The College Dropout Scandal*. Oxford: Oxford University Press.

Kliebard, Herbert M. 1999. *Schooled to Work. Vocationalism and the American Curriculum, 1876–1946*. New York: Teachers College Press.

———. 2004. *The Struggle for the American Curriculum, 1893–1958*. New York: RoutlegeFalmer.

Kloppenberg, James T. 1998. *The Virtues of Liberalism*. Oxford University Press.

Kohn, Alfie. 1992. *No Contest: The Case Against Competition*. Revised Edition. Boston: Houghton Mifflin Company.

Konner, Melvin. 2010. *The Evolution of Childhood: Relationships, Emotion, Mind*. Cambridge, MA: Harvard University Press.

Konstantopoulos, Spyros. 2012. "Teacher Effects: Past, Present, and Future." In Sean Kelly, ed., *Assessing Teacher Quality: Understanding Teacher Effects on Instruction and Achievement*. 7–32. New York: Teachers College Press.

Koretz, Daniel. 2017. *The Testing Charade: Pretending to Make Schools Better*. Chicago: The University of Chicago Press.

Kozol, Jonathan. 1991. *Savage Inequalities: Children in America's Schools*. New York: Harper Perennial.

Kuh, George D. 2001. "Assessing What Really Matters to Student Learning Inside the National Survey of Student Engagement." *Change: The Magazine of Higher Learning* 33 (3): 10–17.

Kuper, Adam. 1999. *Culture: The Anthropologists' Account*. Cambridge, MA: Harvard University Press.

Labaree, David. 1984. "Setting the Standard: Alternative Policies for Student Promotion." *Harvard Educational Review*, 54 (1): 67–88.

———. 1992. "Power, Knowledge, and the Rationalization of Teaching: A Genealogy of the Movement to Professionalize Teaching." *Harvard Educational Review*, 62 (2): 123–154.

———. 1997a. *How to Succeed in School Without Really Learning: The Credentials Race in American Education*. New Haven, CT: Yale University Press.

———. 1997b. "Public Goods, Private Goods: The American Struggle Over Educational Goals." *American Educational Research Journal* 34 (1): 39–81.

———. 2000, May/June. "On the Nature of Teaching and Teacher Education." *Journal of Teacher Education*, 51 (3): 228–233.

———. 2004. *The Trouble with Ed Schools*. New Haven, CT: Yale University Press.

———. 2005, Feb. "Progressivism, Schools and Schools of Education: An American Romance." *Paedagogica Historica*, 41 (1–2): 275–288.

———. 2010. *Someone Has to Fail: The Zero-Sum Game of Public Schooling*. Cambridge, MA: Harvard University Press.

———. 2011. "The Lure of Statistics for Educational Researchers." *Educational Theory*, 61 (6): 621–632.

———. 2012. "School Syndrome: Understanding the USA's Magical Belief that Schooling Can Somehow Improve Society, Promote Access, and Preserve Advantage." *Journal of Curriculum Studies* 44 (2): 143–163.

———. 2017. *A Perfect Mess: The Unlikely Ascendancy of American Higher Education*. Chicago: University of Chicago Press.

Lefstein, Adam, Dana Vedder-Weiss, and Aliza Segal. 2020. "Relocating Research on Teacher Learning: Toward Pedagogically Productive Talk." *Educational Researcher* 49 (5): 360–368.

Lerner, Gerda. 1986. *The Creation of Patriarchy*. Oxford: Oxford University Press.

———. 1993. *The Creation of Feminist Consciousness: From the Middle Ages to Eighteen-Seventy*. Oxford: Oxford University Press.

Levitsky, Steven, and Daniel Ziblatt. 2018. *How Democracies Die*. New York: Crown.

Levitt, Steven D., and Stephen J. Dubner. 2009. *Freakonomics: A Rogue Economist Explores the Hidden Side of Everything*. New York: Harper Perennial.

Lewis, Sarah. 2014. *The Rise: Creativity, the Gift of Failure, and the Search for Mastery*. New York: Simon and Schuster.

Lortie Dan C. 2002. *Schoolteacher: A Sociological Study*, 2nd ed. Chicago: University of Chicago Press.

Lowi, Theodore. 1969. *The End of Liberalism: Ideology, Policy, and the Crises of Public Authority*. New York: W. W. Norton.

Lucas, Christopher J. 1994. *American Higher Education: A History*. New York: St. Martin's Griffin.

Lucas, Samuel Roundfield. 1999. *Tracking Inequality: Stratification and Mobility in American High Schools*. New York: Teachers College Press.

Lupia, Arthur, and Mathew D. McCubbins. 2000. "The Institutional Foundations of Political Competence: How Citizens Learn What They Need to Know." In Arthur Lupia, Mathew Daniel McCubbins, and Samuel L. Popkin eds., *Elements of Reason: Cognition, Choice, and the Bounds of Rationality*. 47–66. Cambridge, UK: Cambridge University Press.

MacCulloch, Diarmaid. 2004. *The Reformation: A History*. New York: Penguin.

MacIntyre, Alasdair. 1981. *After Virtue*. Notre Dame: The University of Notre Dame Press.

MacPhail, Theresa. 2019, Jan 27. "Are You Assigning Too Much Reading? Or Just Too Much Boring Reading?" *The Chronicle of Higher Education*. Retrieved from www.chronicle.com

Markovits, Daniel. 2019. *The Meritocracy Trap: How America's Foundational Myth Feeds Inequality, Dismantles the Middle Class, and Devours the Elite*. New York: Penguin.

Marsh, Herbert W., and Michael J. Dunkin. 1992. "Students' Evaluations of University Teaching: A Multidimensional Perspective." *Higher Education: Handbook of Theory and Research* 8: 142–233.

Matthews, Anne. 1998. *Bright College Years: Inside the American College Today*. Chicago: University of Chicago Press.

McGonigal, Kelly. 2015. *The Upside of Stress: Why Stress is Good for You, and How to Get Good at It*. New York: Avery.

McGrath, Dennis, and Martin B. Spear. 1991. *The Academic Crisis of the Community College*. Albany, NY: State University of New York.

McMahon, Darrin. 2013. *Divine Fury: A History of Genius*. New York: Basic Books.

McNeil, Linda M. 1986. *Contradictions of Control: School Structure and School Knowledge*. New York: Routledge.

———. 2000. *Contradictions of Reform: Educational Costs of Standardized Testing*. New York: Routledge.

McPherson, Peter, and David E. Shulenburger. 2005. *Improving Student Learning in Higher Education Through Better Accountability and Assessment*. Washington, DC: National Association of State Universities and Land Grant Colleges.

McShane, Steven, and Mary Ann Von Glinow. 2018. *Organizational Behavior*. 8th ed. New York: McGraw-Hill.

Mead, George Herbert. 1965. *On Social Psychology: Selected Papers*. Chicago: The University of Chicago Press. Originally published 1934.

Melguizo, Tatiana, and Federick Ngo. 2020. "Mis/Alignment Between High School and Community College Standards." *Educational Researcher* 49 (2): 130–133.

Mercier, Hugo, and Dan Sperber. 2017. *The Enigma of Reason*. Cambridge, MA: Harvard University Press.

Meyer, John W., Brian Rowan, and M. W. Meyer. 1978. "The Structure of Educational Organizations." In M. W. Meyer, ed., *Schools and Society: A Sociological Approach to Education*. San Francisco, CA: Jossey-Bass.

Milner, Murray. 1994. *Status and Sacredness: A General Theory of Status Relations and an Analysis of Indian Culture*. Oxford: Oxford University Press.

———. 2006. *Freaks, Geeks, and Cool Kids: American Teenagers, Schools, and the Culture of Consumption*. New York: Routledge.

Milton, John. 2006. "John Milton." In Stephen Greenblatt and Meyer Howard, eds., *The Norton Anthology of English Literature: The Major Authors*, 8th ed. New York: W. W. Norton.

Milton, Ohmer, Howard R. Pollio, and James A. Eison. 1986. *Making Sense of College Grades*. San Francisco, CA: Jossey-Bass.

Mischel, Walter. 2014. *The Marshmallow Test: Why Self-Control is the Engine of Success*. New York: Little, Brown and Company.

Mitchell, Corey. 2017, Dec 19. "A Cheating Scandal Rocked Atlanta's Schools. Ten Years Later, Efforts to Help Affected Students Fall Short." *Education Week*. Retrieved from www.edweek.org

Mitchell, Kevin J. 2018. *Innate: How the Wiring of Our Brains Shapes Who We Are*. Princeton: Princeton University Press, 2020.

Molinsky, Andy. 2016, July 29. "If You're Not Outside Your Comfort Zone, You Won't Learn Anything." *Harvard Business Review*. Retrieved from www.hbr.org

Mote, Frederick W. 1971. *Intellectual Foundations of China*. New York: Knopf.

Mukherjee, Siddhartha. 2016. *The Gene: An Intimate History*. New York: Scribner.

Mullen, Ann L., Kimberly A. Goyette, and Joseph A. Soares. 2003. "Who Goes to Graduate School? Social and Academic Correlates of Educational Continuation After College." *Sociology of Education* 7 (6): 143–169.

Muller, Jerry Z. 2018. *The Tyranny of Metrics*. Princeton, NJ: Princeton University Press.

Murphy Heather. 2019, May 20. "Why High-Class People Get Away with Incompetence." *The New York Times*. Retrieved from www.nytimes.com

Murphy, Michelle. 2017. *The Economization of Life*. Durham, NC: Duke University Press.

Nayar, Vineet. 2010. *Employees First, Customers Second: Turning Conventional Management Upside Down*. Boston, MA: Harvard Business Review.

Nettles, Michael, and John Cole. 2001. "A Study in Tension: State Assessment and Public Colleges." *The States and Public Higher Education Policy: Affordability, Access, and Accountability*. 198–218. Baltimore: The Johns Hopkins University Press.

Nichols, Sharon L., and David C. Berliner. 2005. "The Inevitable Corruption of Indicators and Educators Through High-Stakes Testing." East Lansing, MI: Great Lakes Center for Education Research and Practice.

———. 2007. *Collateral Damage: How High-Stakes Testing Corrupts America's Schools*. Cambridge, MA: Harvard Education Press.

Nichols, Tom. 2017. *The Death of Expertise: The Campaign Against Established Knowledge and Why it Matters*. Oxford: Oxford University Press.

Nocera, Joe. 2020, Jan 16. "How Boeing Lost Its Way." *Bloomberg*. Retrieved from www.bloomberg.com

North, Douglass C. 1990. *Institutions, Institutional Change and Economic Performance*. Cambridge, UK: Cambridge University Press.

Nussbaum, Martha C. 1997. *Cultivating Humanity: A Classical Defense of Reform in Liberal Education*. Cambridge, MA: Harvard University Press.

Oakes, Jeannie. 1985. *Keeping Track: How Schools Structure Inequality*. New Haven, CT: Yale University Press.

Oettingen, Gabriele. 2014. *Rethinking Positive Thinking: Inside the New Science of Motivation*. New York: Portfolio/Penguin.

Olson, Methew. H., and B. R. Hergenhaun. 2009. *An Introduction to Theories of Learning*, 8th ed. Upper Saddle River, NJ: Pearson-Prentice Hall.

Ortner, Sherry B. 2006. *Anthropology and Social Theory: Culture, Power, and the Acting Subject*. Durham, NC: Duke University Press.

Panda, Satchin. 2020. *The Circadian Code: Lose Weight, Supercharge Your Energy, and Transform Your Health from Morning to Midnight*. New York: Rodale Books.

Pascarella, Ernest T., and Patrick T. Terenzini. 2005. *How College Affects Students: A Third Decade of Research. Volume 2*. San Francisco: Jossey-Bass.

Pattison, Evangeleen, Eric Grodsky, and Chandra Muller. 2013. "Is the Sky Falling? Grade Inflation and The Signaling Power of Grades." *Educational Researcher* 42 (5): 259–265.

Payne, Charles M. 2008. *So Much Reform, So Little Change: The Persistence of Failure in Urban Schools*. Cambridge, MA: Harvard Education Press.

Perin, Dolores, and Jodi Patrick Holschuh. 2019. "Teaching Academically Underprepared Postsecondary Students." *Review of Research in Education: Changing Teaching Practice in P-20 Educational Settings* 43 (1): 363–393.

Perkins, David N. 1985. "Post-Primary Education Has Little Impact on Informal Reasoning." *Journal of Educational Psychology,* 77 (5): 562.

Peter, Laurence J., and Raymond Hull. 2009. *The Peter Principle: Why Things Always Go Wrong.* New York: Harper Business.

Peurach, Donald J., David K. Cohen, Maxwell M. Yurkofsky, and James P. Spillane. 2019. "From Mass Schooling to Education Systems: Changing Patterns in the Organization and Management of Instruction." *Review of Research in Education: Changing Teaching Practice in P-20 Educational Settings,* 43(1): 32–67.

Pfeffer J. 1992. *Managing with Power: Politics and Influence in Organizations.* New York: Harper Business.

———. 2010. *Power: Why Some People Have It—and Other Don't.* New York: Harper Business.

———. 2015. *Leadership BS: Fixing Workplaces and Careers one Truth at a Time.* New York: Harper Business.

Pianta, Robert C., and Arya Ansari. 2018. "Does Attendance in Private Schools Predict Student Outcomes at Age 15? Evidence from a Longitudinal Study." *Educational Researcher* 47 (7): 419–434.

Pink, Daniel. H. 2009. *Drive: The Surprising Truth About What Motivates Us.* New York: Riverhead books.

Pinker, Steven. 1997. *How the Mind Works.* New York: W. W. Norton.

———. 2002. *The Blank Slate: The Modern Denial of Human Nature.* New York: Penguin.

———. 2011. *The Better Angels of our Nature: Why Violence Has Declined.* New York: Penguin.

Polanyi, Michael. 1962. *Personal Knowledge: Towards a Post-Critical Philosophy.* Chicago: University of Chicago Press.

———. 1967. *The Tacit Dimension.* New York: Doubleday.

Pollan, Michael. 2008. *In Defense of Food: An Eater's Manifesto.* New York: Penguin.

"Populations of One: Personalized Medicine." 2020, March 14. *Technology Quarterly: Medicine Gets Personal. The Economist.* 3–4.

Putnam, Robert D. 2015. *Our Kids: The American Dream in Crisis.* New York: Simon and Schuster.

Ransom, Roger L., Richard Sutch, and G. Walton, Eds. 1982. *Explorations in the New Economic History: Essays in Honor of Douglass C. North.* New York: Academic Press.

Ravitch, Diane. 2000. *Left Behind: A Century of Battles Over School Reform.* New York: Touchstone.

———. 2010. *The Death and Life of the Great American School System: How Testing and Choice are Undermining Education.* New York: Basic Books.

Reese, William J. 1995. *The Origins of the American High School.* New Haven: Yale University Press.

———. 2013. *Testing Wars in the Public Schools: A Forgotten History.* Cambridge, MA: Harvard University Press.

Reich, Justin, and José A. Ruipérez-Valiente. 2019, Jan 11. "The MOOC Pivot: What Happened to Disruptive Transformation of Education?" *Science,* 363 (6423): 130–31.

Remmers, Hermann H., F. D. Martin, and Donald N. Elliott. 1949. "Are Students' Ratings of Instructors Related to Their Grades?" *Purdue University Studies in Higher Education* 6 (6): 17–26.

Rendon, Jim. 2015. *Upside: The New Science of Post-Traumatic Growth.* New York: Touchstone.

Richardson, Ken. 1999. *The Making of Intelligence.* London: Weidenfeld and Nicolson.

Richerson, Peter J., and Robert Boyd. 2005. *Not by Genes Alone: How Culture Transformed Human Evolution.* Chicago: University of Chicago Press.

Ridley, Matt. 2003. *Nature Via Nurture: Genes, Experience, And What Makes Us Human.* New York: Harper Collins.

Robinson, Ken. 2001. *Out of Our Minds: Learning to Be Creative.* Chichester, UK: Capstone.

Rogers, David. 1969. *110 Livingston Street: Politics and Bureaucracy in The New York City School System.* New York: Vintage.

Rogoff, Barbara. 1969. *Apprenticeship in Thinking: Cognitive Development in Social Context.* Oxford: Oxford University Press.

———. 2003. *The Cultural Nature of Human Development.* Oxford University Press.

Roksa, Josipa, Teniell L. Trolian, Ernest T. Pascarella, Cindy A. Kilgo, Charles Blaich, and Kathleen S. Wise. 2017, March. "Racial Inequality in Critical Thinking Skills: The Role of Academic and Diversity Experiences." *Research in Higher Education* 58 (2): 119–140.

Rosenbaum, James E. 2001. *Beyond College for All: Career Paths for the Forgotten Half.* New York: Russell Sage Foundations.

Rosenbaum, James E., Regina Deil-Amen, and Ann E. Person. 2006. *After Admission: From College Access to College Success.* New York: Russell Sage Foundations.

Rosenberg, Shawn W. 1988. *Reason, Ideology and Politics.* Princeton: Princeton University Press.

Rosovsky, Henry, and Matthew Hartley. 2002. *Evaluation and the Academy: Are We Doing the Right Thing. Grade Inflation and Letters of Recommendation.* The American Academy of Arts and Sciences. Cambridge, MA: Author.

Rossi, Peter H. 1987. "The Iron Law of Evaluation and Other Metallic Rules." In Miller Judith L. and Michael Lewis, eds., *Research in Social Problems and Public Policy* 3–20, 4. Greenwich, CT: JAI Press.

Rumbaugh, Duane M., and David A. Washburn. 2008. *Intelligence of Apes and Other Rational Beings.* New Haven, CN: Yale University

Rush, Benjamin. 1806. *Essays, Literary, Moral and Philosophical,* 2nd ed. Philadelphia: Thomas and William Bradford.

Ryan, Alan. 1995. *John Dewey and the High Tide of American Liberalism.* New York: W. W. Norton.

Ryan, Richard M., and Jerome Stiller. 1991. "The Social Contexts of Internalization: Parent and Teacher Influences on Autonomy, Motivation and Learning." *Advances in Motivation and Achievement* 7: 115–149.

Ryrie, Alec. 2017. *Protestants: The Faith that Made the Modern World*. New York: Viking.

Sacks, Oliver. 2015. *On the Move: A Life*. New York: Vintage Books.

———. 2017. *The River of Consciousness*. New York: Vintage Books.

Sandel, Michael J. 2012. 1996. *Democracy's Discontent: America in Search of a Public Philosophy*. Cambridge, MA: Harvard University Press.

———. 2012. *What Money Can't Buy: The Moral Limits of Markets*. New York: Farrar, Straus and Giroux.

Santoro, Doris A. 2018. *Demoralized: Why Teachers Leave the Profession They Love and How They Can Stay*. Cambridge, MA: Harvard University Press.

Sapolsky, Robert M. 2004. *Why Zebras Don't Get Ulcers*, 3rd ed. New York: St. Martin's Griffin.

———. 2017. *Behave: The Biology of Humans at Our Best and Worst*. New York: Penguin.

Sass, Tim, Jane Hannaway, Zeyu Xu, David N. Figlio, and Li Feng. 2012. "Value Added of Teachers in High-Poverty Schools and Lower Poverty Schools." *Journal of Urban Economics* 72 (2): 104–122.

du Sautoy, Marcus. 2016. *What We Cannot Know: Explorations at the Edge of Knowledge*. London: 4th Estate.

Scheidel, Walter. 2017. *The Great Leveler: Violence and the History of Inequality from the Stone Age to the Twenty-First Century*. Princeton, NJ: Princeton University Press.

Schneider, Jack. 2014. *From the Ivory Tower to the Schoolhouse: How Scholarship Becomes Common Knowledge in Education*. Cambridge, MA: Harvard Education Press.

———. 2017. *Beyond Test Scores: A Better Way to Measure School Quality*. Cambridge, MA: Harvard Education Press.

Schneider, Jack, and Ethan Hutt. 2013. "Making the Grade: A History of the A–F Marking Scheme." *Journal of Curriculum Studies*. Retrieved from http://dx.doi.org/10.1080/00220272.2013.790480

Schon, Donald A. 1983. *The Reflective Practitioner: How Professionals Think in Action*. New York: Basic Books.

Schultz, Theodore W. 1961. Investment in Human Capital. *The American Economic Review* 5 (11): 1–17.

Schumpeter, Joseph A. 1950. *Capitalism, Socialism, and Democracy*, 3rd ed. New York: Harper Perennial.

Schwartz-Chrismer, Sara, Shannon T. Hodge, and Debby Saintil, eds. 2006. "Assessing NCLB: Perspectives and Prescriptions." *Harvard Educational Review* 76 (4).

Scott, W. Richard. 1992. *Organizations: Rational, Natural, and Open Systems*, 3rd ed. Englewood Cliffs, NJ: Prentice Hall.

Searle, John R. 1995. *The Construction of Social Reality*. New York: Free Press.

Seifert, Tricia A., Benjamin Gillig, Jana M. Hanson, Ernest T. Pascarella, and Charles F. Blaich. 2014. "The Conditional Nature of High Impact/Good Practices on Student Learning Outcomes." *The Journal of Higher Education* 85 (4): 531–564.

Selznick, Philip. 1984. *Leadership Administration: A Sociological Interpretation*. Berkeley, CA: The University of California Press. Originally published in 1957.

Sen, Amartya. 2006. *Identity and Violence: The Illusion of Destiny.* New York: W. W. Norton.

Senge, Peter M. 2006. *The Fifth Discipline: The Art and Practice of the Learning Organization*, 2nd ed. New York: Currency. Originally Published 1990.

Seth, Michael J. 2002. *Education Fever: Society, Politics, and the Pursuit of Schooling in South Korea.* Honolulu, HA: University of Hawai'i Press.

Sigmund, Karl. 2017. *Exact Thinking in Demented Times: The Vienna Circle and the Epic Quest for the Foundations of Science*. New York: Basic Books.

Sizer, Theodore R. 1992. *Horace's Compromise: The Dilemma of the American High School*. Boston: Houghton Mifflin.

Smeyers, Paul, and Nicholas Burbules. 2006. "Education as Initiation into Practices." *Educational Theory* 56 (4): 440–42.

Smith, B. Othanel. 1969. *Teachers for the Real World*. Washington, DC: American Association of Colleges for Teacher Education.

Smith, Kevin B. 2003. *The Ideology of Education: The Commonwealth, the Market, and America's Schools*. Albany, NY: SUNY Press.

Snedden, David. 1920. *Vocational Education*. New York: Macmillan.

Song, Zurui, and Katherine Baicker. 2019. "Effect of a Workplace Wellness Program on Employee Health and Economic Outcomes: A Randomized Clinical Trial." *JAMA* 321 (15): 1491–1501.

Spence, Michael A. 1974. *Market Signaling: Informational Transfer in Hiring and Related Screening Processes*. Cambridge: Harvard University Press.

Sperber, Murray. 2000. *Beer and Circus: How Big-Time College Sports is Crippling Undergraduate Education.* New York: Henry Holt and Company.

Spindler, Michael. 2002. *Veblen and Modern America: Revolutionary Iconoclast*. London: Pluto Press.

St. John, Edward P., and Michael D. Parsons, eds. 2004. *Public Funding of Higher Education: Changing Contexts and New Rationales*. Baltimore: Johns Hopkins University Press.

St. John, Edward P., Kimberly A. Kline, and Eric H. Asker. 2001. "The Call for Public Accountability: Rethinking the Linkages to Student Outcomes." In *the States and Public Higher Education Policy: Affordability, Access, and Accountability*, ed. Donald E. Heller, 219–242. Baltimore: Johns Hopkins University Press.

"Staff and Nonsense." 2019, May 11. *Economist*, 55.

Stanovich, Keith E. 2009. *What Intelligence Tests Miss: The Psychology of Rational Thought*. New Haven: Yale University Press.

Stark, Philip B., and Freishtat, Richard. 2014, Sept 26. *An Evaluation of Course Evaluations*. University of California, Berkeley. Retrieved from www.stat.berkeley.edu/~stark/Preprints/teachEval14.pdf

Starr, Douglas. 2020, Jan 2. "This Italian Scientists Has Become a Celebrity by Fighting Vaccine Skeptics." *Science*. Retrieved from www.sciencemag.org

Starr, Paul. 2017. *The Social Transformation of American Medicine:* Updated Edition. New York: Basic Books.

Steinberg, Lawrence D. 1996. *Beyond the Classroom: Why School Reform Has Failed and What Parents Need to Do.* New York: Simon and Schuster.

———. 2014. *Age of Opportunity: Lessons from the New Science of Adolescence.* New York: Mariner Books.

Sternberg, Robert J. 1988. *The Triarchic Mind: A New Theory of Human Intelligence.* New York: Viking.

Stewart, Matthew. 2009. *The Management Myth: Debunking Modern Business Philosophy.* New York: W. W. Norton.

Stone, Deborah. 2002. *Policy Paradox: The Art of Political Decision-Making,* revised edition. New York: W. W. Norton.

Stray, Christopher. 2005. "From Oral to Written Examinations: Cambridge, Oxford and Dublin, 1700–1914." *History of Universities* 20 (2): 76–130.

Strong, Edward K. 1922. *Introductory Psychology for Teachers*, Revised Edition. Baltimore, MD: Warwick and York.

Sunstein, Cass R. 1997. *Free Markets and Social Justice*. Oxford: Oxford University Press.

Swartz, David. 1997. *Culture and Power: The Sociology of Pierre Bourdieu*. Chicago: University of Chicago Press.

Taleb, Nassim Nichola. 2012. *Antifragile: Things that Gain from Disorder*. New York: Random House.

Tett, Gillian. 2015. *The Silo Effect: The Peril of Expertise and the Promise of Breaking Down Barriers.* New York: Simon and Schuster.

"The Curse of Efficiency." 2019, July 27. *Economist,* 55.

"The Eyes Have It." 2019, Sep 14. *Economist*, 60.

"The Second Half of the Internet: A Global Timepass Economy." 2019, June 8. *The Economist*, 23–26.

Thelin, John R. 2004. *A History of American Higher Education.* Baltimore, MD: Johns Hopkins University Press.

Tocci, Charles, Ann Marie Ryan, and Terry D. Pigott. 2019. "Changing Teaching Practice in P–20 Educational Settings: Introduction to the Volume." *Review of Research in Education: Changing Teaching Practice in P–20 Educational Settings* 43 (1): 7–13

Tomasello Michael. 1999. *The Cultural Origins of Human Cognition*. Cambridge, MA: Harvard University Press.

———. 2009. *Why We Cooperate*. Cambridge, MA: MIT Press.

———. 2014. *A Natural History of Human Thinking*. Cambridge, MA: Harvard University Press.

———. 2016. *A Natural History of Human Morality*. Cambridge, MA: Harvard University Press.

Tversky, Barbara. 2019. *Mind in Motion: How Action Shapes Thought*. New York: Basic Books.

Twenge, Jean Marie. 2017. *iGen: Why Today's Super-Connected Kids Are Growing Up Less Rebellious, More Tolerant, Less Happy—and Completely Unprepared for Adulthood*. New York: Altria Books.
Tyack, David B. 1974. *The One Best System: A History of American Urban Education*. Cambridge, MA: Harvard University Press.
Tyack, David, B., and Elisabeth Hansot. 1982. *Managers of Virtue: Public School Leadership in America, 1820–1980*. New York: Basic Books.
Tyack, David, B., and Larry Cuban. 1995. *Tinkering Toward Utopia: A Century of Public-School Reform*. Cambridge, MA: Harvard University Press.
Tyler, Ralph W. 1949. *Basic Principles of Curriculum and Instruction*. Chicago: University of Chicago Press.
Vygotsky, Lev S. 1978. *Mind in Society: The Development of Higher Psychological Processes*. Cambridge, MA: Harvard University Press.
Waddington, Conrad Hai. 1957. *The Strategy of the Genes*. London: Allen and Unwin.
Wagner, Tony, Robert Kegan, Lisa Laskow Lahey, Richard W. Lemons, Jude Garnier, Deborah Helsing, Annie Howell, and Harriette Thurber Rasmussen. 2006. *Change Leadership: A Practical Guide to Transforming Our Schools*. San Francisco, CA: Jossey-Bass.
Waller, Willard. 1932. *The Sociology of Teaching*. New York: J. Wiley and Sons.
Walton, Mary. 1986. *The Deming Management Method*. New York: Perigee Books.
Wang, Yand, Benjamin F. Jones, and Dashun Wang. 2019. "Early-Career Setback and Future Career Impact." *Nature Communications* 10 (4331). https://doi.org/10.1038/s41467-019-12189-3
Washburn Jennifer. 2005. *University, Inc.: The Corporate Corruption of American Higher Education*. New York: Basic Books.
Weaver, Constance. 2007. "Teaching Grammar in Context." In *Teaching Developmental Writing: Background Readings*, 3rd ed., 153–162 Edited by Susan Naomi Bernstein. Boston: Bedford/St. Martin's.
Weick, Karl E. 1976. "Educational Organizations as Loosely Coupled Systems." *Administrative Science Quarterly* 21 (1): 1–19.
Wenger, Etienne. 1998. *Communities of Practice: Learning, Meaning, and Identity*. Cambridge, UK: Cambridge University Press.
Wertsch, James V. 1991. *Voices of the Mind: A Sociocultural Approach to Mediated Action*. Cambridge, MA: Harvard University Press.
Westover, Tara. 2018. *Educated: A Memoir*. New York: Random House.
"When Rank Leads to Rancour." 2020, February 29. *Economist*, 52.
Whittington, Keith. E. 2018. *Speak Freely: Why Universities Must Defend Free Speech*. Princeton: Princeton University Press.
Wildavsky, Aaron. 1979. *Speaking Truth to Power: The Art and Craft of Policy Analysis*. Boston: Little, Brown and Company.
Wilde, Oscar. 1989. A Few Maxims for the Instruction of the Over-Educated. In *Oscar Wilde: The Major Works*. Oxford, UK: Oxford University Press. Originally published 1894.
Wilson, David Sloan. 2002. *Darwin's Cathedral: Evolution, Religion, and the Nature of Society*. Chicago: University of Chicago Press.

Wilson, E. O. 2017. *The Origins of Creativity*. New York: Liveright.
Winiecki, Jan. 1996. "Why Economic Reforms Fail in the Soviet System: A Property Rights-Based Approach." In *Empirical Studies in Institutional Change*, ed. Lee J. Alston, Thrainn Eggertsson, and Douglass C. North, 63–91. Cambridge, UK: Cambridge University Press.
Wise, Arthur E. 1979. *Legislated Learning: The Bureaucratization of the American Classroom*. Berkeley, CA: University of California Press.
Wolf, Alison. 2002. *Does Education Matter? Myths About Education and Economic Growth*. London: Penguin.
Wolfe, Tom. 2004. *I Am Charlotte Simmons*. New York: Picador.
Wood, David, Jerome Bruner, and Gail Ross. 1976. "The Role of Tutoring in Problem Solving." *Journal of Child Psychology and Psychiatry* 17 (2): 89–100.
Woodruff, David J., and Robert L. Ziomek. 2004. "Differential Grading Standards Among High Schools." *ACT Research Report Series, 2004-2*. Iowa City, IA: ACT.
Wrangham, Richard, and Dale Peterson. 1996. *Demonic Males: Apes and the Origins of Human Violence*. New York: Mariner.
Yin, Yian, Yang Wang, James A. Evans, and Dashun Wang. 2019. "Quantifying Dynamics of Failure Across Science, Startups, and Security." *Nature* 575 (7781): 190–194.

Preview of This Book's Companion Volume

The Myths of Measurement and Meritocracy: Why Accountability Metrics in Higher Education are Unfair and Increase Inequality

In the rush to create accountability metrics, few asked how this process should be done so as to foster the educational purpose of schooling. In particular, for institutions of higher education, few administrators or researches have asked, what does student success look like? And how should colleges and universities measure student success so as to reinforce institutional goals?

For the most part, the accountability metrics that were established for colleges and universities all boiled down to money, in one way or another. The ends of higher education were defined primarily in terms of human capital and labor market earnings. Most people have come to believe that students learn important knowledge and skills in college. They further believe that these products are then used by students to barter for a wage in the labor market.

Thus, in creating accountability metrics, college administrators have been primarily focused on measuring knowledge or skills, and then correlating these products to labor market earnings. In this effort, student evaluation surveys have become the foundational assessment for almost all colleges and universities (Johnson 2003, 140; Schneider 2017, 152).

College administrators now believe that student surveys accurately measure both teaching quality and student learning. Administrators also believe that teachers *produce* student learning. This learning then produces learning products, which in turn produce economic benefits for the student and society.

In some institutions, and for certain kinds of teachers, like adjunct instructors in community colleges and nonselective universities, student surveys have become the only method of assessment for employment purposes. Student evaluation surveys have become high-stakes instruments. They now largely determined if a teacher is hired, fired, or promoted.

While nearly all educational administrators, and many teachers as well, seem to believe that student surveys offer insight into student learning and instructor teaching (Schneider 2017, 152), researchers have overwhelmingly found that these student surveys do not measure either teaching or learning directly, or very effectively. Why? Part of the problem is that student evaluation surveys are improperly designed, calibrated, administered, and interpreted.

So, the question then becomes, if these accountability measurements aren't valid, then how can they be fair assessment tools to evaluate either teachers or students? And further, if these instruments are not effective or fair, then what is the effect of hiring, promoting, and firing teachers based on flawed and unfair assessment tools?

The evidence is discouraging. As many researchers have documented over the past several decades, (Nichols 2017; Keeling and Hersh 2012; Rosovsky and Hartley 2002; Chen 2013), many institutions of higher education have been conducting fraud, or "academic malpractice" (Nichols 2017, 89, 87). Students don't want to learn so many teachers are lying to students by giving them superficial knowledge and inflated grades. This leads many students to believe that "they're actually smarter than they are," which ends up harming them in many ways when they leave school to navigate the labor market (Nichols 2017, 89, 87; see also Sperber 2000, xiv; Koretz 2017, ch 5).

There is also another discouraging unintended consequence with accountability metrics in higher education. It has to do with the unexamined assumption that students actually learn useful knowledge and skills in college, and that these products actually drive labor market earnings. What if this assumption is false?

Index

accountability agencies, 24–31
accountability measurements: as conventional wisdom, 12; as destructive force, xxi–xxii; ineffectiveness of, 135–38; myths of, investigating, xix–xxv; questioning validity of, 116–18; skepticism of, xvii–xviii. *See also specific topics*
accountability movement: accountability agencies for establishing school standards in, 24–31; discovery of human capital in, 31–35; economic efficiency as motivator of, 13–16; measurement and control of inputs and outputs of schooling in, 16–20; morality of I.Q. and bell curve distribution in, 20–24; paradox, 109; public schooling loss of faith in, 35–42; purpose of, xv
accountability yardsticks, 16, 131
accreditation agencies, 28–29
Adams, Henry, 89
administrative coup d'état, 119–26
adolescents: inability to change behavior of, 82; motivation lacking for, 104; peers influence on, 105–7
Alexander, Lamar, 36
aristocracy of talent, 10
athletic achievement, 49

authentic learning: benefits of engaging in, 70–71; knowledge and skill from, 69–70; regarding control, 73; salience as requirement of, 68
autodidacts, 90, 92, 93

Bacon, Francis, 3
Bagehot, Walter, 4
Bagley, William C., 13–14, 15
Bakhtin, Mikhail, 71–72
bankruptcy, 126, 128
behavioral psychology, 17
bell curve distribution: creation of, 18–19; morality of, 20–24
Best, Joel, 120–21
best practices concept, 112–14
Boeing, 128
Bridges, David, 65
Burioni, Roberto, xvii
Bush, George W., 55
businesses: employee performance reviews, 133–34; human resources of, 110; ideals as foundation of, 109; school management compared to managing, xxiii–xxiv; schools as, 11–12, 15

California Ideal, 29–30
Campbell, Donald T., 53

Campbell's Law, 53
Canada, 128–29
Caplan, Bryan, 34–35
captains of erudition, 119–20
CEOs: ineffectiveness of, 123; salaries of, 124
charter schools, 126
cheating: grade inflation as form of, 55–58; on standardized tests, 53, 54–55
Chernobyl, 111
China, 44, 45
Christensen, Clayton M., 137
churches: as sacred institutions, 1; schooling managed by, 3
Classroom Management (Bagley), 14
coaches: athletic achievement influence from, 49; control of learning process regarding, 79–80
collaborative learning, 73
college. *See* higher education
comfort zone, 77–78
command-and-control model, 123
community colleges, 29–30
competition: origin of word, 70; from ranking, 58–59
conditioning: from culture, 62–63; psychologists on, 17
conformity, 4
consumers: myth about, 137; students as, xxi, 11
control: administrative coup d'état of education for, 118–25; authentic learning regarding, 73; command-and-control model of, 122; learning in relation to, 79–80; myth of, 119; paradox regarding teachers and, 140; of schooling inputs and outputs, 16–20; of teachers, 15
corruption of schooling, 52–59
coup d'état of education, 118–25
Cremin, Lawrence A., 4
cultural tools, 63
culture: complexity of, 66; conditioning from, 62–63; enculturation and, 1; freedom restricted by, 63–64; games of, 65–66; genes in relation to, 99; importance of values in, 65; oral, 44; organizational, 125; peer, 105–7; practice of education for creating, 67–68; traditions as scripts of, 64
culture wars, 4

Darwinian scenario, 54
Deacon, Terrence W., xvi
Deci, Edward L., 140
degree inflation, 27
democracy preservation, 147–48
deschooling, 131–34
developmental randomness, 98–99
Dewey, John, 90
d'Holbach, Baron, 3–4
diplomas: as magic piece of paper, 67; over-reliance on, 55
discovery: of human capital, 31–35; insights on, xvi
DNA: human biology determined by, 62; natural selection programming, 95–96
Drucker, Peter F., 13, 40–41, 121–22

economic efficiency: accountability as, 13–16; as neoliberal political agenda, xv; of standardized tests, 18
economic entities, 9
economics: focus on, 5; free market, 8, 9–10; transformation of, 5–6
economy: debate on public and private sectors of, 125–29; GNP of, 8, 135, 136; human capital of, 11, 31–35; public awareness of, 8
education: administrative coup d'état of, 118–25; belief in transformative power of, xviii; creation of culture through practice of, 67–68; goal of genuine, 72; health, 82–83; heart and soul of, 142; high impact practices, 86; liberal arts tradition of, 147–48; middle-men eliminated from, 142–45; neoliberal gospel of, 5–12;

reinvention of, 138–42; schooling compared to, 61, 66–67, 131; as social practice, 61–72; student as catalyst of, 93; subjectivity of, 61–62; value of, dissolving faith in, xv–xvi. *See also* higher education
educational credentials, 33–35
educational institutions, 111, 112–16
educational reform: failure of, 141; higher education as focus of, 37–38; ineffectiveness of, xix–xxi; key to, 140; misunderstanding surrounding, 40–41; need for clarity on, xvi; political agendas of, xv; reassessment of, 131–34; resistance to, 31–32; roadblocks to effective, 111–12; skepticism of, xvii–xviii
Education and Freedom (Rickover), 35
efficiency: curse of, 109, 110–12; economic, xv, 13–16, 18; paradox regarding failure and, 109
embodied cognition, 75
emotional support, 76
employee performance reviews, 133–34
emulation learning, 72
enculturation, 1
Erasmus, Desiderius, 3

failure: of educational reform, 141; learning from, 76–77, 78; meaningful, 77, 144; paradox regarding efficiency and, 109; probability of, 82; in teaching and learning, 112–16; of untutored learning, 94
Flynn effect, 101–2
freedom: culture restricting, 63–64; genes regarding, 101; individual agency and, 63; knowledge in relation to, 148
free market economics, 8, 9–10
Friedman, Milton, 13
funding: expansion of assistance with, 25–26; inequality in, 30–31;

performance-based, 12, 40; responsibility for, 24–25

Gallup, George, 39
General Electric, 128
genes/genetics: culture in relation, 99; definition of, 62; regarding destiny, 100; developmental randomness and, 98–99; regarding freedom, 101; heritability, 96–98; human biology determined by, 62; I.Q. in relation to, 103; natural selection programming, 95–96; social and physical environment in relation to, 32, 96–98, 99–100; student achievement in relation to, 102–3; variations in, 96
GI Bill, 25, 28
GNP. *See* Gross National Product
Goodhart's Law, 53
The Good Society (Lippmann), 9
grade inflation: college graduate lingering impacts of, 57–58; example of, 55; lack of resistance to, 56–57; negative impacts of, 55–56
grades/grading: artificial scarcity produced by, 58; bell curve distribution and, 18–19; confusion around, 20; as farce, 49; meaninglessness of, 48; origins of, 45–46; over-reliance on, 55; problems with goals of, 46; questions on purpose of, 48; report cards for, 46; student learning, knowledge, and skill non-correlation to, 47; subjectivity of, 48, 51–52; validity and reliability issues with, 47, 48, 51; variability of, 51–52
Graeber, David, 127
Gross National Product (GNP), 8, 135, 136

habit: creatures of, 63; of learning, 69
habitus, 100
Handy, Charles, 109, 110, 139

Harris Poll, 39
Harvey, David, 9–10
health care industry study, 128–29
health education, 82–83
heritability: gene, 96–98; of I.Q., 101, 103
higher education: accreditation agencies in, 28–29; college dropout scandal, 124; College Entrance Examination Board, 28; community colleges of, 29–30; educational reform focus on, 37–38; expansion of access to, 25–26; grade inflation impacting graduates of, 57–58; medical schools of, 26–28; privilege in relation to access in, 29–31; responsibility for cost of, 24–25; unpreparedness for, 36–37
The Higher Learning in America (Veblen), 119
high-impact practices, 86
human ability, 93–104
human biology: developmental randomness and, 98–99; genes and DNA determining, 62; imitation coded in, 71; natural selection programming, 95; student achievement influenced by, 50
human brain: learning environment alternatives for, 90; mental simulation and, 75; plasticity of, 32, 100
human capital: discovery of, 31–35; schools for producing, 11
human nature: theory, 94–95; understanding complexity of, 62–63
human resources, 110
human society, 64–65

ideals, 109
Illich, Ivan, 131
imitative learning, 71, 72–73
individual agency, 63
The Innovator's Dilemma (Christensen), 137

instructed learning, 73
intelligence: over morality, 17; privilege in relation to, 21–24; psychologists studying, 20–21; social and physical environment influencing development of, 32
intelligence quotient (I.Q.): development of, 102; genes in relation to, 103; heritability of, 101, 103; morality of, 20–24; as political tool, 24; standardized tests in relation to, 20–21
internet, 94
Introduction to the Use of Standardized Tests (Meyer), 19
I.Q. *See* intelligence quotient
Ireland, 103
iron law of liberalism, 128

job security, 119

Kirp, David, 125
knowledge: from authentic learning, 69–70; freedom in relation to, 148; grades non-correlation to, 47; information compared to, 69; as purpose of schooling, 33–35; seeking out, 93; tacit, 74–75
Korea, 45

language, 71–72
laws of learning, 17, 90
leadership myth, 122–23
learning: authentic, 68, 69–71, 73; collaborative, 73; control in relation to, 79–80; defining meaning of, 139; emulation, 72; from failure, 76–77, 78; failure to address teaching and, 112–16; genetic variations influencing, 96; goals, 74; habit of, 69; imitative, 71, 72–73; instinct, 72; instructed, 73; laws of, 17, 90; to learn, 138–42, 147–48; mental simulation for, 75; myths about, 91; observational, 71;

outside of comfort zone, 77–78;
outside of schools, 89–90, 91–92;
from personal experiences, 67–68;
personal mastery from, 69–70;
persuasion as requirement for,
73; plan for, 137–38; schooling
compared to, 90–91; social, 73, 74;
from stress, 77; students performing,
72–81; by teachers, 80–81; types
of, 72–73; untutored, 94. *See also*
student learning
liberal arts tradition, 147–48
liberalism: introduction to, 6; iron law
of, 127; periods of, 7–11. *See also*
neoliberalism
Lippmann, Walter, 9
literacy, 44

MacIntyre, Alasdair, 65
market society, 6
Massive Open Online Courses
(MOOCs), 94
mastery: learning for personal, 69–70;
of skills, 76
McLuhan, Marshall, xvi
meaningful failures, 77, 144
medical schools, 26–28
mental simulation, 75
Meyer, Max, 18–19
middle-men, 142–45
Milton, John, 3
MOOCs. *See* Massive Open
Online Courses
moral hazards, 53, 54
morality: intelligence over, 17; of I.Q.
and bell curve distribution, 20–24; of
teachers, 78–79

*The Myths of Measurement and
Meritocracy*, 34

National Commission on Excellence in
Education, 36
National Defense of Education Act
(1958), 35

National Governors Association, 37–38
natural selection, 95–96
nature and nurture, 93–104
neoliberalism: defining, 9–10; gospel of
education, 5–12; political agendas of,
xv; progressivism compared to, 9
No Child Left Behind law, 55
North, Douglas C., 88–89
nurture and nature, 85–108

observational learning, 71
office folklore, 120–21
oral cultures, 44
organizational accountability: as
neoliberal political agenda, xv;
schemes, xix
organizational culture, 125

paradox: regarding efficiency and
failure, 109; regarding teachers and
control, 140
parents: participation needed of, 138;
peer influence over, 105–7; student
achievement influenced by, 50, 87;
student achievement measured by,
46; teaching in relation to, 88
peer culture, 105–7
performance: reviews, 133–34;
test of, 126
performance-based funding, 12, 40
personal experiences: development
through, 104; education as learning
from, 67–68; student achievement
influenced by, 50
personal mastery, 69–70
Peter, Laurence J., 125
Peter principle, 125
physical environment. *See* social and
physical environments
Pinker, Steven, 94–95
policy makers: on bell curve
distribution, 20; as educational
reform issue, 111–12
private schools, 31
private *vs.* public debate, 125–29

privilege: California Ideal and, 29–30; higher education access in relation to, 29–31; intelligence in relation to, 21–24; race and, 21–22; schooling for preservation of, 67
progressivism: economic efficiency and, 13–16; neoliberalism compared to, 9; period of, 7–8
Prussia, 44, 45–46
psychologists: belief in educational product of student learning, 18; on bell curve distribution, 18–19; on conditioning, 17; on I.Q., 20–21; on meaningful failures, 77, 144; on stress, 77
public debates, 45
public schooling: command-and-control model applied to, 122; criticism of, 13; economic transformation of, 5–6; era of mass, 25; loss of faith in, 35–42; planning establishment of, 148
public vs. private debate. *See* private vs. public debate
punishment system, 52–53, 54

race, 21–22
ranking: common sense on, 52; competition from, 58–59; negative impacts of, 49, 117–18
report cards, 46
research: foundation of, xxv; hope for, xviii; inspiration and methodology, xvi–xvii; purpose of, xix, xxv
research universities, 115–16
Review of Research in Education, xxv
reward system, 52–53, 54
Rickover, Hyman, 35
ritualization, 68–69
role models, 78–79
rowing team metaphor, 120–21
Rush, Benjamin, 148

Sacks, Oliver, 51, 90
Sandel, Michael J., 6

Scholastic Aptitude Test (SAT), 23, 28
school administrators: belief in educational product of student learning, 18; on bell curve distribution, 20; cheating by, 53, 54–55; as corporate managers, 11–12; coup d'état of education, 118–25; as educational reform issue, 111–12; ignorance of, 116; management expertise for, 14; training program issues, 113–14
schooling: availability expansion of, 5; capitalistic system of, 15; churches managing, 3; contradictions in, 29; corruption of, 52–59; definition of, 67; disenchantment with, 26; dysfunctional bureaucracy of, 112; education compared to, 61, 66–67, 131; historic critics of, 2–4; learning compared to, 90–91; measurement and control of inputs and outputs of, 16–20; negative impacts of, 90–91; ritualization of, 68–69; student knowledge and skill development as purpose of, 33–35; student learning redefined as end-product of, 17–18; tradition of, 67. *See also* public schooling
schooling rule, 2
schools: accountability agencies for establishing standards in, 24–31; as businesses, 11–12, 15; business management compared to managing, xxiii–xxiv; charter, 126; as culture war epicenters, 4; deschooling, 131–34; as educational institutions, questioning, 111, 112–16; as factories, 119; focus needed for, 138; historic purpose of, 43; human capital produced in, 11; learning outside of, 89–90, 91–92; origins of student assessment in, 43–46; private, 31; root of dysfunction in, 115–16; as sacred institutions, 1–2; student achievement influence

from, 49; types of problems identified with, 36
Senge, Peter M., 69–70
sense-making, 71–72
Sizer, Theodore R., 141
skills: from authentic learning, 69–70; grades non-correlation to, 47; purposeful practice for mastery of, 76; as purpose of schooling, 33–35; reading and writing, 36–37; soft, 104
SMART goals. *See* Specific, Measurable, Actionable, Relevant, and Timely goals
Snedden, David, 23
social and physical environments: conditioning from, 62–63; freedom restricted by, 63–64; genes in relation to, 32, 96–98, 99–100; student achievement impacted by, 50, 87; student learning and intelligence development in relation to, 32
social learning, 73, 74
social practice: defining, 65; education as, 61–72
social status, 34–35
socio-economic status, 103
Socrates, 2–3
soft skills, 104
Soviet Union, 110–11, 112
Specific, Measurable, Actionable, Relevant, and Timely (SMART) goals, 74
Spellings Commission on the Future of Higher Education, 38
Sperber, Murray, 57
standardized tests: artificial scarcity produced by, 58; bell curve distribution and, 18–19; as big business, 19–20; cheating on, 53, 54–55; China inventing, 44, 45; corruption from, 53; critics of, 19; economic efficiency of, 18; I.Q. in relation to, 20–21; limitations of, xxiii; SAT, 23, 28

standards: accountability agencies for establishing school, 24–31; of excellence, 65; grade inflation and lowering of, 55–58; search for holy grail of common, 47
Steinberg, Laurence D., 106–7
stress, 77
Strong, Edward Kellogg, 19
student achievement: falsification of, 53; genes in relation to, 102–3; human biology and personal experiences as most important to, 50; out-of-school factors important to, 48–49; parents influencing, 50, 87; parents measurement of, 46; peers shaping, 106–7; predictors of, 86–87; problems with, 86; social and physical environment impacting, 50, 87; teachers and schools influence on, 49; value-added statistical analysis and, 50–51; variables impacting, 48–52
student assessment origins, 43–46
student evaluation surveys, 116
student knowledge. *See* knowledge
student learning: assumptions on teachers role in, xxi; grades non-correlation to, 47; invisibility of, 41; misunderstanding of connection between teaching and, 40–41, 89–93, 107–8, 142–45; problem of measuring, xv; reconceptualizing, 33; redefining end-product of schooling as, 17–18; responsibility for, 83, 85–86; scaffolding for, 74, 85; social and physical environment influencing development of, 32; teaching behaviors in relation to, 85–86
students: as apprentices, traditionally, 43; as consumers, xxi, 11; as education catalysts, 93; as focus, 140; as heart and soul of education, 142; as human capital, 11, 31–35; learning performed by, 72–81; mental simulation by, 75; motivation

loss for, 68; participation needed of, 138; purposeful practice by, 76; as raw material, 119; sense-making by, 71–72; sortation and tracking of, 22–24, 33; teachers learning from, 80–81

student skill. *See* skills

subjectivity: of education, 61–62; of employee performance reviews, 133–34; of grading, 48, 51–52

surgery origin metaphor, 121–22

symbolic tokens, 2

tacit knowledge, 74–75

tax dollars, 13

teachers: blaming of, 141–42; cheating by, 53, 54–55; control and restriction of, 15; control of learning process regarding, 79–80; as craftsmen, 43; difficulty measuring ability of, 88–89; disdain for, 114; as educational reform issue, 111–12; emotional support and feedback from, 76; as experts, traditionally, 43; fear of being fired, 118; as focus, 138, 140; grade inflation by, 55–58; grading variability among, 51–52; as heart and soul of education, 142; job security lacking for, 118; learning by, 80–81; as manual laborers, 119; morality of, 78–79; need for effective, 93–94; paradox regarding control and, 140; practice properly demonstrated by, 71, 74–75; as prophets, 1; purging of good quality, 115; purpose and duties of, 73–81; as role models, 78–79; standardized tests criticized by, 19; student achievement influence from, 49; student learning assumptions regarding role of, xxi; student learning scaffolding provided by, 74, 85; training program issues, 113–14

teaching: behaviors, 85–86; difficulty of, 87–88; failure to address learning and, 112–16; invisibility of, 41; misunderstanding of connection between student learning and, 40–41, 89–93, 107–8, 142–45; mystery of, 89; parenting in relation to, 88; resentment of good, 83; unpredictability and complications of, 81–84

technocratic measurement strategy, xix

test-based accountability, xix–xx. *See also* standardized tests

test of performance, 126

Thiry, Paul-Henri, 3–4

Tomasello, Michael, 72–73

tradition: conformity to, 4; as cultural scripts, 64; liberal arts, 147–48; metaphor on power and authority, 121–22; of schooling, 67; truth in relation to, 1

training programs, 113–14

Trump, Donald, 148

truth, 1

uniqueness, 64, 103

untutored learning, 94

vaccines, xvii

value-added statistical analysis, 50–51

values: as standards of excellence, 65; teachers exemplifying, 78–79

Veblen, Thorstein, 119–21

Waller, Willard, 61–62

welfare states, 8

Westover, Tara, 91–92, 93

Wildavsky, Aaron, 39

World Wide Web, 94

About the Author

J. M. Beach is a scholar, teacher, entrepreneur, investor, and a poet. He is the founder and director of 21st Century Literacy, a nonprofit organization focused on literacy education and teacher training. The organization offers a free Web textbook and other educational materials. Beach is available for workshops, teacher training seminars, and consulting. For more information, visit www.21centurylit.org.

Beach has advanced degrees in the fields of English, history, philosophy, and education and is finishing degrees in business administration and marketing. He was a lecturer in higher education for more than twenty years in the U.S., South Korea, and China. Beach is a member of the American Educational Research Association and the American Association for the Advancement of Science. His scholarly research focuses on several distinct, but interrelated subjects: the philosophy of knowledge, the science of culture and society, the history and philosophy of education, and literature.

Beach has two new books coming out this year: *Can We Measure What Matters Most? Why Educational Accountability Metrics Lower Student Learning and Demoralize Teachers* and *The Myths of Measurement and Meritocracy: Why Accountability Metrics in Higher Education Are Unfair and Increase Inequality*. Some of Beach's previous books include *How Do You Know? The Epistemological Foundations of 21st Century Literacy* (2018), *Gateway to Opportunity? A History of the Community College in the United States* (2011), *Children Dying Inside: Education in South Korea* (2011), and *Studies in Poetry: The Visionary* (2004).

For more information, visit the author's website at www.jmbeach.com.

www.ingramcontent.com/pod-product-compliance
Lightning Source LLC
Chambersburg PA
CBHW020737230426
43665CB00009B/464